Pastoral Theology and Care

# Pastoral Theology and Care

Critical Trajectories in Theory and Practice

*Edited by Nancy J. Ramsay*

This edition first published 2018
© 2018 John Wiley & Sons Ltd

The right of Nancy J. Ramsay to be identified as the author of the editorial material in this work has been asserted in accordance with law.

*Registered Office(s)*
John Wiley & Sons Ltd, The Atrium, Southern Gate, Chichester, West Sussex, PO19 8SQ, UK

*Editorial Office*
9600 Garsington Road, Oxford, OX4 2DQ, UK

For details of our global editorial offices, customer services, and more information about Wiley products visit us at www.wiley.com.

Wiley also publishes its books in a variety of electronic formats and by print-on-demand. Some content that appears in standard print versions of this book may not be available in other formats.

*Library of Congress Cataloging-in-Publication Data*

Names: Ramsay, Nancy J. (Nancy Jean), 1949– editor.
Title: Pastoral theology and care : critical trajectories in theory and practice / edited by Nancy Ramsay.
Description: First edition. | Chichester, UK ; Hoboken, NJ : John Wiley & Sons, 2018. | Includes bibliographical references and index. |
Identifiers: LCCN 2017037355 (print) | LCCN 2017044590 (ebook) | ISBN 9781119292548 (pdf) | ISBN 9781119292593 (epub) | ISBN 9781119292524 (cloth) | ISBN 9781119292562 (pbk.)
Subjects: LCSH: Pastoral theology. | Pastoral care.
Classification: LCC BV4011.3 (ebook) | LCC BV4011.3 .P368 2018 (print) | DDC 253–dc23
LC record available at https://lccn.loc.gov/2017037355

Cover Image: © reklamlar/Gettyimages
Cover Design: Wiley

Set in 10/12pt Warnock by SPi Global, Pondicherry, India
Printed and bound in Malaysia by Vivar Printing Sdn Bhd

10  9  8  7  6  5  4  3  2  1

For
Peggy Ann Brainerd Way
1931–2016

and

Emma Justes
1941–2017

Trailblazing women whose intelligence, courage, commitment, and passion
shaped the foundations of contemporary
pastoral theology and care in the United States.
They spoke "truth to power" with piercing honesty.
They understood justice is the context in which love flourishes.

# Contents

# List of Contributors

*Kathleen J. Greider*
Research Professor
Claremont School of Theology

*David A. Hogue*
Professor of Pastoral Theology
and Counseling
Garrett-Evangelical Theological
Seminary

*Emmanuel Y. Amugi Lartey*
L. Bevel Jones, III Professor
of Pastoral Theology,
Care and Counseling
Chandler School of Theology,
Emory University

*Mary Clark Moschella*
Roger J. Squire Professor
of Pastoral Care and Counseling
Yale University Divinity School

*Nancy J. Ramsay*
Professor of Pastoral Theology
and Pastoral Care
Brite Divinity School

*Bruce Rogers-Vaughn*
Associate Professor of the Practice
of Pastoral Theology and Counseling
The Divinity School,
Vanderbilt University

*Phillis Isabella Sheppard*
Associate Professor of Religion,
Psychology, and Culture
The Divinity School and
Graduate Department of Religion,
Vanderbilt University

# Introduction

*Nancy J. Ramsay*

The chapters in this volume invite students, pastors, and faculty to engage seven critical trajectories emerging in the literature of pastoral theology in the United States and internationally among pastoral and practical theologians. While these seven trajectories do not exhaust important points of activity in the field, they do represent especially promising resources for theory and practice. These trajectories include: qualitative research and ethnography, implications arising from advances in neuroscience, care across pluralities and intersections in religion and spiritualities, the influence of neoliberal economics in experiences of socio-economic vulnerabilities, postcolonial theory and its implications, the intersections of race and religion in caring for black women, and the usefulness of intersectional methodologies for pastoral practice. The contributors are closely identified with the trajectories they trace and extend. Each chapter richly illustrates the implications for practices of care relationally and in public contexts engaging structures and systems. The essays include not only a review of recent literature giving shape to each trajectory, but also the author's constructive proposals for further advancing the trajectory's horizons. Particularly helpful is an opportunity in each chapter to identify how scholars in various international contexts are also exploring these themes.

Mary Clark Moschella helped to introduce qualitative research and ethnographic methods to the field of pastoral theology. In her essay, we find explorations of several diverse "streams" in this trajectory allowing students a comparative review of the creativity across the trajectory as a whole, as well as Dr. Moschella's new constructive proposals drawing on narrative theory and therapy to advance the usefulness of ethnographic practices to confront and redress the oppressive effects of hegemonic factors such as racism and ethnocentrism embedded in the narratives of individuals and of communities.

While neuroscience is not technically a new area of research among pastoral theologians, recent advances in neuroscience have lately sparked a wider

*Pastoral Theology and Care: Critical Trajectories in Theory and Practice,*
First Edition. Edited by Nancy J. Ramsay.
© 2018 John Wiley & Sons Ltd. Published 2018 by John Wiley & Sons Ltd.

engagement. David Hogue brings a depth of reflection and engagement with neuroscience to his review of this trajectory. He also offers constructive theological and theoretical explorations of the implications for practices of care with individuals and in public life, such as new insights in neuroscience for resisting the hegemonic force of privilege and domination that, once learned, shape neurological connections.

Bruce Rogers-Vaughn brings new perspectives to bear that demonstrate how rarely pastoral theologians have engaged issues of class and economic inequality as important factors in practices of care for individuals and families and in public contexts. He rightly points to the limitations this has created in literature and resources. He illustrates how neoliberal economic policies have become cultural in scope as a radical individualism in the United States and beyond. This neoliberalization of our culture is implicated in epidemic levels of addiction, suicide, and depression, as well as the stress of economic precarity in the "second Gilded Age" in the United States.

Emmanuel Lartey is a primary voice in the trajectory shaped by the use of postcolonial critical theories that disclose the defacing and subjugating effects of colonial oppression. Here Lartey not only traces the emergence of this trajectory but pays close attention to three key themes explored in its literature: voice, epistemology, and praxis. He demonstrates how engaging postcolonial insights offers reciprocal benefits for those whose heritage is shaped by coloniality. In particular, drawing especially on experiences and practices of care in African cultures, Lartey argues that recentering care around spirituality extends its efficacy in building community and transforming cultures.

Kathleen Greider is a primary voice in shaping pastoral theology's trajectory of resources for responding with understanding and skill in an increasingly spiritually plural and interreligious culture in the United States and beyond. She develops a richly illustrated journey with Israelis and Palestinians who have suffered the death of family members in decades of religiously fueled violence, and who nonetheless seek to communicate with care and respect across the intersections of a culture marred by violence. Greider helps us learn about care across distances that arise in such religious and spiritual plurality. She explores the priority of receiving otherness for practices of care in spiritual and religious plurality.

Phillis Sheppard is a central contributor to current womanist theory and care. Here she explores the trajectory of intersectional approaches in womanist literature and offers new proposals for the particular intersections of race, gender, sexuality, and religion. In particular, she brings constructive contributions to the particular intersection of black women's lived religion and sexuality that is more plural and complex than it often appears in pastoral theology and womanist literature. She also provides new proposals for intersectional attention to a womanist psychology of religion currently undertheorized in pastoral theology.

My own work especially attends to pastoral theological engagement in public life. This essay introduces the metatheory of intersectionality, first voiced by

African American women as well as other women whose historic and current experience reflect the oppressive effects of coloniality. Intersectional methodologies name and resist situations of social inequality. This chapter illustrates the close alignment of intersectional commitments with those of public pastoral theology. It illustrates the methodological usefulness of intersectional approaches for assisting pastoral and practical theologians to name and engage abuses of power in relational, communal, and public contexts.

# 1

# Practice Matters

New Directions in Ethnography and Qualitative Research

*Mary Clark Moschella*

*I trace my own nascent interest in ethnography and pastoral care back to 1993, when I attended the famous* Re-imagining *conference sponsored by the Ecumenical Decade Committee for Churches in Solidarity with Women, held in Minneapolis, Minnesota. There I participated in my first anti-racism workshop, where personal experiences of racism were poignantly described and blatant instances of racism in the media were dissected. I remember feeling overwhelmed by emotion and asking the leaders of the workshop what I could do, as a white woman, to make a difference. The leaders gave me a surprising answer: learn more about your own ethnicity. Ever the literalist, I took this on in graduate school, where I conducted an ethnographic study of Italian Catholic devotional practices in Mary, Star of the Sea parish in San Pedro, California (Moschella, 2008a). Through immersion in one Italian American community, a picture of the people's lives, faith, and practices began to appear. Through studying the history of immigration, I saw how the process of Italian immigrants becoming American in the early to mid-20th century was clearly linked to a process of "becoming white." My research helped me understand how discrimination and racism have persisted in the US and how these forces can be challenged or supported by religious practices. This research experience also convinced me that pastoral care itself must be reimagined if it is to be a truly liberating endeavor.*

For me, engaging in an ethnographic study was a transformative experience, and one that set the stage for my work in developing a methodology for pastoral ethnography (Moschella, 2008b). I soon discovered that I was not alone in reaching toward this new approach and that I was participating in a growing trajectory of scholarship employing qualitative research as a means toward pastoral (or practical) theological ends. In this chapter, I will offer a brief

*Pastoral Theology and Care: Critical Trajectories in Theory and Practice,*
First Edition. Edited by Nancy J. Ramsay.
© 2018 John Wiley & Sons Ltd. Published 2018 by John Wiley & Sons Ltd.

history of this trajectory in the field of pastoral theology, with some attention to the wider discipline of practical theology as well. I will then describe a number of recent, exemplary studies within this trajectory, grouping them into three streams of work, and noting how the issues animating the broader field of qualitative research have echoes and analogues in pastoral research. The three streams include: ethnographic and qualitative research that illuminates and invigorates pastoral practices; the work of the Ecclesiology and Ethnography Network of scholars that focuses on the intersection between theology and ecclesial practices; and narrative qualitative studies. These three streams are not exhaustive; neither are they entirely discrete, as will become evident. Many of the exemplary studies I reference demonstrate the overlapping concerns, methods, and goals in each category. Nevertheless, this broad classification helps illumine the contours of pastoral scholars' current questions, goals, and contributions. Following this exploration of the literature, I will make a case for the importance of qualitative research in pastoral theology and care, arguing that *practice matters*, and that exploring actual practice is in fact central to the field's stated identity of "constructive theology growing out of the exercise of caring relationships" (Mission Statement, *Journal of Pastoral Theology*). In the last section, I will address future directions in this research trajectory, articulating my particular interest in the development of the third research stream, narrative qualitative research, and its burgeoning creative, therapeutic, and prophetic capacities.

## Development of the Research Trajectory

The qualitative research trajectory in pastoral theology and care participates in a broader "turn to culture" in theological and religious studies that can be seen in the work of historians, ethicists, systematic theologians, and biblical scholars.[1] Timothy Snyder offers an apt description of this pronounced shift:

> The turn to culture in academic theology has recovered its incarnational, or embodied, nature, which has at times been obscured by the abstract and universalizing tendencies of theological reflection in the post-Enlightenment era. Most of all, it reintroduced a creative tension between the particular and the universal in theological reflection. (Snyder, 2014)

Don Browning helped set the stage for pastoral and practical theologians to participate in this turn to culture with his emphasis on social and cultural description (Browning, 1991). Robert Schreiter's work (1985) on local theologies embraces an inter-connected view of theology and culture. Elaine Graham

(1996) illuminates the transformational and revelatory dimensions of practice, highlighting the "creative tension" of which Snyder speaks, and arguing for an interpretive rather than prescriptive role for pastoral and practical theologians.

John Patton's description of the communal contextual paradigm of care, along with his image of the pastoral caregiver as a "mini-ethnographer" (Patton, 2005, p. 43) encourages pastors and scholars alike to pay careful attention to the lives of persons and communities in order to be able to practice genuinely helpful pastoral care. At the same time, multiple contributions of scholars of color, feminists, womanists, and others from under-represented or marginalized social groups have challenged the pastoral field to recognize the dominant cultural paradigms embedded in the literature that do not adequately represent their lived religious experiences. Their focus on the cultural contexts of care, now routine in introductory pastoral theology and care courses, spurred the need for new methodologies in pastoral research.

The field of congregational studies provided impetus and resources for the pastoral trajectory in qualitative research by emphasizing the study of congregations in their complex social and geographic ecologies (Ammerman et al., 1998; Eiesland, 2000). Participatory action research, with its emphasis on community-based research for the purpose of social change, is a related approach that practical theologians have taken up with vigor (Cameron et al., 2010; Conde-Frazier, 2012). My work on ethnography as a pastoral practice brings ethnographic principles and methods to the practice of pastoral care (Moschella, 2008b). To date, numerous scholars from pastoral and practical theology as well as other theological fields have been engaging in qualitative research studies linked to theological reflection (Scharen and Vigen, 2011).

Similarly, the teaching of ethnography and qualitative research in theological schools has been expanding dramatically. Once the sole purview of sociology of religion, such courses are now taught by pastoral, practical, and systematic theologians, ethicists, field education supervisors, clinical pastoral educators, and others. Susan Willhauck (2016), in research funded by Wabash, found that qualitative research methods are being taught in more than 50 theological schools in the US and Canada alone.

I argue that the disciplined study of religious practices is one way of keeping pastoral scholars and practitioners accountable to the people in the ecclesial, social, and political worlds we address. In pastoral theology, in particular, we need to be informed about the particular practices and experiences of a wide array of culturally and religiously diverse persons, congregations, and communities. Rather than prescribing overly general theories of care, we need the wisdom that can only come from close exploration of lived theology and practice. The qualitative research trajectory helps us reclaim the central importance of listening, of attending to people in their socio-cultural particularity, and allowing ourselves to learn *from* the people who share their stories with us.

## The Field of Qualitative Research

This trajectory in pastoral theological research has required us to adapt the methodological resources of the broader field of qualitative research. In their Introduction to *The Discipline and Practice of Qualitative Research*, Norman Denzin and Yvonna Lincoln (2011) review the various research paradigms animating that field. Rehearsing the history of debates among proponents of quantitative, positivist, constructivist, and critical theory paradigms, the authors show how forms of resistance to qualitative research still loom over the field. While many quantitative researchers regard qualitative studies as "unreliable, impressionistic, and not objective" (Denzin and Lincoln, 2011, p. 9), qualitative researchers assert the value of studying "the world of lived experience, for this is where individual belief and action intersect with culture" (Denzin and Lincoln, 2011, p. 2). These tensions linger, contributing to a range of interpretive paradigms within qualitative research, ranging from positivist/postpositivist, constructivist, feminist, ethnic, Marxist, cultural studies, to queer theory (Denzin and Lincoln, 2011, p. 13). Each of these approaches has distinct criteria for evaluation, theories of analysis, and types of narration. Denzin and Lincoln stress that the politics of interpretation must always be kept in view. They write:

> The interpretive practice of making sense of one's findings is both artistic and political. Multiple criteria for evaluating qualitative research now exist, and those we emphasize stress the situated, relational, and textual structures of the ethnographic experience. There is no single interpretive truth. (Denzin and Lincoln, 2011, p. 15)

Denzin and Lincoln's postmodern perspective, though still contested, finds echoes in much of the current work in pastoral and practical theology.

Such multiple interpretive paradigms can be seen in the three streams of ethnography and qualitative research that I describe below. These streams include: research in pastoral ethnography and qualitative research designed to illuminate and invigorate pastoral practices; the work of the Ecclesiology and Ethnography Network, with its focus on theology; and qualitative studies that emphasize the development of alternative, justice-oriented narratives. In each stream there are slightly different embedded values concerning not only the subject(s) of the research, but also the methods of evaluation, analysis, and narration. Norwegian practical theologian Tone Stangeland Kaufman, describing the "conundrum" of theologically motivated qualitative research, calls such embedded values, "theory-laden practices with inherent normative dimensions" (2016, p. 146). It is also important for pastoral theologians to recognize the political dimensions of interpretation.

# Pastoral Ethnography and Qualitative Research

The first broad stream of pastoral work with this trajectory employs qualitative research in order to elucidate and invigorate pastoral practices. The term "pastoral ethnography" implies the intention that the research process itself is conducted in such a way as to honor the voices of the participants, embody ethical regard in research relationships, and facilitate the participants' increasing agency in their collective theology and practice (Moschella, 2008b). This work is often conducted by religious insiders (including but not limited to Christians) who acknowledge that they incorporate their theological values and questions into the research process. Studies of this sort plumb the wisdom and limitations of particular and/or local religious practices, which may inspire analogical insights for scholars and practitioners in diverse settings. This stream of work has been nurtured by the Study Group on Religious Practices and Pastoral Research at the Society for Pastoral Theology's annual meetings since 2004. An early edited volume highlights the contributions of a number of these scholars (Maynard et al., 2010). Also included in this category are qualitative studies that are not ethnographic in nature, but utilize qualitative methods and purposes of inquiry. The Association for Practical Theology, the International Academy of Practical Theology, the Congregational Studies Project Team, and the Religious Education Association have also nurtured scholars' use of qualitative research methods.[2]

A fine example of pastoral ethnography can be found in Leanna K. Fuller's (2016) study, *When Christ's Body is Broken: Anxiety, Identity, and Conflict in Congregations*. Here Fuller utilizes ethnographic methods to compare the experiences of conflict in two mostly white, mainline Protestant congregations. Through qualitative interviews and participant observation (the author had been on the staff of one of the churches when a conflict that split the church occurred), Fuller studies how the conflicts erupted, identifying the practices that helped each congregation manage the conflict and those practices that hurt and/or contributed to breakdown and alienation in each case. By comparing data from the two congregations' experiences, and using psychodynamic, social psychological, and theological lenses to analyze her findings, Fuller gleans a layered understanding of these conflicts. This then enables her to offer broader practical, constructive proposals that are grounded in experience. *How* a congregation deals with conflict, Fuller points out, is as important as the substance of the conflict. Students, pastors, and other religious leaders can imagine points of intersection and insight for their diverse congregations and groups. Fuller makes transparent her pastoral theological commitment to offer a religious response to human suffering (Miller-McLemore, 1998, p. 179; Fuller, 2016, p. 191), thereby enabling readers to evaluate the significance of her conclusions and recommendations more readily.

As noted above, pastoral and practical theologians are also employing qualitative methods (other than ethnography) to study a topic, a practice, or the experiences of a cohort of persons in similar situations. Such topics include: the faith lives of adolescent girls (Parker, 2007; Mercer, 2008), war (Graham, 2011), forced displacement (Holton, 2016), and so on. In *A Womanist Theology against Intimate and Cultural Violence*, Stephanie Crumpton (2014) offers a pastoral theology based on a qualitative study involving extensive individual and group interviews with six African American women who experienced childhood sexual abuse and/or intimate violence as adults. Through her analysis of these interviews, Crumpton identifies the extensive spiritual harm done to the women by their abusers and by a wider society that is quick to stereotype, blame, disbelieve, or disregard black women. Describing insights articulated by the women themselves, Crumpton constructs "working images of Womanist/Care" (p. 125) to inform congregational responses to such violence. She goes on to add a chapter on clinical considerations for pastoral counseling, utilizing self-psychological theory in her analysis. The author's explicit reference to her theology and womanist values exemplifies an interpretive paradigm that acknowledges the political commitments operative in all research and, rather than pretending to be neutral or disinterested, makes those commitments transparent. This paradigm is also evident in Phillis Sheppard's essay in this volume.

An important larger-scale study by pastoral theologian Brett Hoover (2014) demonstrates the benefits of doing ethnography in combination with extensive sociological research, both qualitative and quantitative. In *The Shared Parish: Latinos, Anglos, and the Future of U.S. Catholicism*, Hoover describes how recent demographics have led to the phenomenon of "the shared parish" in Catholic churches in the US. Different from assimilationist American parishes or ethnic parishes, this phenomenon involves two or more cultural groups inhabiting the same church, "living in the tension between cultural difference and human connectedness" (Hoover, 2014, p. 222). Hoover's in-depth ethnography gives readers a close-up view of how this phenomenon plays out in one such parish. By linking this ethnography to wider currents in Catholic parish life in the US, the author increases the credibility and relevance of his findings. At the conclusion of his study, Hoover offers a well-grounded theological vision of community that honors cultural distinctiveness. Hoover's work is rigorously interdisciplinary; significantly, he participates in the scholarly guilds of both theologians and social scientists.

These three exemplary studies suggest a range of recent work in this stream within the larger trajectory of qualitative research in pastoral and practical theology. In each case, the author is in some sense an insider, emic, exploring worlds of religious experience through face-to-face contact with research participants or partners. In these studies, we can see echoes of the constructivist, feminist and womanist, and ethnic interpretive paradigms found in the broader field of qualitative studies. Fuller's study illumines the nature of conflict and pastoral responses in two mostly white US Protestant churches, providing much transferable wisdom for religious leaders. Crumpton's study lifts up the particularity of African American women's experiences of both intimate and cultural violence and shows how each kind of violence compounds the other. Hoover employed a postmodern research paradigm in his ethnography, where he participated as a bilingual Catholic priest, in order to understand how Latino and Euro-Americans develop and manage intercultural practices in a shared parish. In these studies, the authors explore religious practice through research relationships in which they share their questions and their goals openly with their research partners. Their accounts demonstrate their convictions that the practices of the church really do matter on the ground, in the lives of people.

## Ecclesiology and Ethnography

The second stream of work within the broad trajectory of qualitative research in practical and pastoral theology is associated with the Ecclesiology and Ethnography Network. Founded by Pete Ward and Christian Scharen in 2007, this trans-Atlantic network of scholars hosts a series of conferences taking place in Durham, UK, and other parts of Europe, a book series and a journal (Ward, 2012; *Ecclesial Practices*), as well as a thriving pre-conference study group held at the annual meeting of the American Academy of Religion. This body of work explores the intersection of Christian theology— particularly ecclesiology— with the study of local and particular faith practices. This work has been described, variously, as "constructive theological ethnography," "ecclesial practices," or "fieldwork in theology." Contributors to this conversation include but are not limited to: Pete Ward, John Swinton, Mary McClintock Fulkerson, Christian Scharen, Luke Bretherton, Tone Stangeland Kaufman, Jonas Ideström, Natalie Wigg-Stevenson, and Eileen Campbell-Reed. Establishing a starting point in Christian theology as the basis for qualitative research typifies some, but not all, of these authors' approaches, which vary widely. These scholars are engaging in rigorous reflection upon theology, method, and practice, taking up questions of normativity, reflexivity, and representation. Some broadly define this area as "research in service of the church."[3]

The issue of normativity appears prominently in the influential book, *Practical Theology and Qualitative Research*, written by Scottish practical theologians John Swinton and Harriett Mowat (2015). They argue that the veracity of Christian theology precedes and ultimately overrides the knowledge gained from social scientific study. This represents one end of a continuum of views that scholars in the network hold. These authors resolve the tension between practical theology and empirical knowledge by prioritizing

Christian (Barthian) theology over other kinds of truth. Problems with this approach include the relative devaluation of human experience and an apparent disregard for the diversity and complexity of Christian theologies (Kaufman, 2016). Here we can hear echoes of the tensions in the larger field of qualitative research, where norms for interpretation are contested. Epistemological debates over which kinds of knowledge count in the academy and in the church are also at play.

Christian Scharen (2015) in *Fieldwork in Theology* begins with different theological warrants for engaging in the study of lived practices of faith: "the task of understanding [the complexity of this beautiful and broken world] requires a careful, disciplined craft for the inquiry—a craft I call fieldwork in theology—if one seeks both to claim knowledge of divine action and to discern an appropriate human response" (p. 5). He then turns to the social science of Pierre Bourdieu, arguing against many critics that for Bourdieu, "every act of research is simultaneously scholarship and a social commitment to make a better world" (p. 29). For Scharen, the aim of fieldwork is to analyze and clarify the church's work in the world; it is to find with Merleau-Ponty, "an entryway into a grounded, fleshly, incarnational approach to being in the world" (p. 29), so that concrete social realities can be identified and the church can be engaged in "moral solidarity with those in need" (p. 89). His work suggests a fuller role for qualitative research in practical and pastoral theology. Though normativity is still implied or "interwoven" in Scharen's approach, as Tone Stangeland Kaufman's helpful essay (2016) might suggest, there is more authority granted to the "grounded, fleshly, incarnational approach to being in the world" (Scharen, p. 29). For Scharen, the relationship between theology and human response (or practice) is more symmetrical in terms of what counts for valid understanding.

Perhaps the foremost example of an ethnographic study that explicitly engages reflexivity is *Places of Redemption: Theology for a Worldly Church* (McClintock Fulkerson, 2007). This is the study of Good Samaritan United Methodist Church, an intentionally racially integrated congregation in Durham, North Carolina. This congregation also made an explicit commitment to welcoming members of a group home who had significant physical and intellectual dis/abilities. The church sought to provide, in McClintock Fulkerson's phrase, "a place for all to appear" (p. 231). She offers a thick description of the worship services and other religious practices of the congregation. Employing reflexivity, McClintock Fulkerson describes her discomfort as a participant observer in this place. She acknowledges feeling ill-at-ease when she, a white southern woman, comes to worship one day and notices that three-quarters of the congregation has dark skin. She also admits to finding herself at a loss for words and not knowing how to hold her body when meeting and trying to interact with a disabled man in a wheelchair. She analyzes her own bodily felt discomfort and asserts that accounts of social oppression ought to be linked with "the experiential field upon which the visceral register plays"

(p. 20). Her analysis of the intersection of culture, race, and power dynamics in this setting is further grounded in a study of the history of Durham and the wider United Methodist Church. Her interpretation accounts for the ways in which the local church's embodied practices of worship and hospitality both meet and fail to meet its theological goals.

This study is especially valuable for pastoral theologians who value embodied experience and seek to overcome social oppression. This kind of visceral reflection helps draw back the curtain from what the author calls "obliviousness" to race and dis/ability. It reveals the incorporated character of white privilege and able-bodied privilege, and how these "can co-exist with belief in equality and (Christian) inclusiveness" (McClintock Fulkerson 2007, p. 20). Taking both beliefs and enacted practices seriously, McClintock Fulkerson's study lifts up *"the primacy of the situation* for theological reflection" (p. 235). She notes that theology alone cannot tell us what is necessary for "redemptive alteration" (p. 254); needed are creative attempts to work with the available bits and pieces of inherited tradition to interrupt dominant groups' obliviousness. Grace, too, takes place in the context of a (this)-worldly church.

A third example of research associated with the Ecclesiology and Ethnography Network is pastoral theologian Eileen Campbell-Reed's (2016) noteworthy study, *Anatomy of a Schism*, which, while not strictly speaking an ethnography, employs qualitative methods of study and highlights the issue of representation. Campbell-Reed relies upon her extensive interviews with five Baptist clergywomen to forge a new interpretation of the schism of the Southern Baptist Convention (1979–2000). Through a close reading of the five clergywomen's stories, Campbell-Reed narrates the struggle within the Southern Baptist Convention between theological Biblicists and Autonomists, highlighting the gendered, psychological, and theological dimensions of the schism. Her layered interpretation describes the history of the Southern Baptist Convention and its contested views of gender complementarity. The author articulates the psychological dimensions of "splitting," understood as both an intra-psychic experience and the historical event of the schism, and draws out implications for theology and evolving meanings of ministry. Similar to McClintock Fulkerson, Campbell-Reed concludes with an emphasis on the creativity needed to go forward in faithful living, which involves challenging the "dehumanization of the disempowered" (Campbell-Reed, 2016, p. 145).

The feminist commitments of the author are evident in her choice of participants and her focus on their stories as a lens through which to view the larger historical struggle. In presenting clergywomen as complex historical actors and not just the subject of Southern Baptist debates over the ordination of women, Campbell-Reed breaks through the taken-for-granted knowledge of much previous scholarship. In retelling religious history from the point of view of those whose voices have been marginalized, the study participates in the narrative stream in qualitative research as well.

The Ecclesiology and Ethnography Network continues to generate much exciting scholarship, demonstrating a range of positions on issues of normativity, reflexivity, and representation. Natalie Wigg-Stevenson, who calls her work "ethnographic theology," helps push forward the question of how "ethnographic methods can help us foster the already organic relationship between everyday and academic theologies" (Wigg-Stevenson, 2014, p. 11). Pastoral and practical theologians, always working at integration of theory and practice, have much to learn from this conversation.

## Narrative Approaches to Qualitative Research

The third stream of work within the ethnography and qualitative research trajectory is the one that I find the most compelling and simultaneously the most difficult to describe. I am calling it narrative qualitative research because it foregrounds the development of personal and social narratives as sites of transformation. This work draws upon insights of the field of narrative therapy (White and Epston, 1990) and the recognition that hegemonic cultural narratives can control and distort our human stories and lives. In order to redress the political power of such destructive cultural stories, researchers are deliberately using ethnographic and qualitative study to lift up alternative stories, stories that are life-giving and oriented toward relational justice (Graham, 1992). This stream of work also embraces the position of Denzin and Lincoln that "the interpretive practice of making sense of one's findings is both artistic and political" (2011, p. 15). The prophetic, therapeutic, and artistic dimensions of these studies are what make them so compelling to me.

One example is Kathleen Greider's (2007) landmark volume, *Much Madness is Divinest Sense*, which takes an exploratory approach to understanding psychiatric illness in a way that goes beyond positivist explanations. Not a field study, this investigation analyzes the published memoirs of 18 religiously diverse "soul-sufferers" (Greider's term for those who suffer from psychiatric illness). From their memoirs she draws rich descriptions of issues of identity, suffering, care, and healing. Greider asserts that we must take into consideration the ways in which "the sickness of society sometimes causes or complicates the sickness of persons" (p. 93). While Greider does not explicitly draw upon narrative theory in this text, I classify it here because the text does the work of narrative practice in that it deconstructs both popular and medical explanations of madness, explores what insiders have to say, and "thickens" the cultural story by describing the daunting social conditions that contribute to or exacerbate the suffering of persons with psychiatric conditions and their families. By focusing on the spiritual wisdom found in the memoirists' accounts, Greider honors the hard-won wisdom and God-given "divinest sense" that the poet Emily Dickinson (1890), herself a soul-sufferer, named. The artistic dimension of interpretation is also on view in this study, both in its reference to poetry and in the very use of memoirs as the basis for study. The beauty and power of the personal accounts conveys the authority of insiders to tell their own stories and transports the reader into a more experience-near understanding of the gifts and challenges in soul-sufferers' experiences.

A salient new contribution to the narrative research stream is *We Are Not All Victims*, by Pamela Couture (2016). Based on ethnographic research in Kamina, Democratic Republic of Congo, from 2003 to 2014, this book tells an alternative story of the peacemaking activities of the people of Kamina and their religious leaders. Couture's account is based on the recorded (and in some cases, translated) testimonies of 78 persons who publicly bore witness to the Luba struggle, along with numerous qualitative interviews and prolonged periods of participant observation. Remarking on the tendency of Western authors to interpret Congolese life only in terms of violence, intrigue, victims, and perpetrators, Couture writes:

> In contrast, the alternative story shows the Luba as agents of their own peacebuilding, using both indigenous and Christian religion as warrants for peace, and engaging in these activities inland, where people live ordinary lives and rise to extraordinary courage when the times call for it. (Couture, 2016, p. 4)

Couture deliberately prioritizes the multiple and rich stories that the people tell her about their lives, their experiences of the conflict, and their efforts to build peace. Her narrative offers a striking contrast to extant histories and journalism related to the area.

Couture's methodology relies explicitly upon two narrative therapy concepts: the importance of social witness and recognition; and the therapeutic value of contributing to a cause that is larger than oneself (Combs and Freedman, 1996; Couture, 2016). Couture positioned herself first as a ghost writer attempting to tell the people's story faithfully, from their point of view. Later, after years of research, getting to know the people, and working with them on drafts of the book, she came to see her role rather as "their spirit-writer: my spirit, *mutyima muyampe*, literally, my thinking heart, accompanies their *muya*, literally, their soul, in these words" (Couture, 2016, p. 18). Couture now recognizes that this is a collaborative story that expresses her own voice and "thinking heart" as well as the voices and souls of the people who have opened their lives to her.

Couture's research might thus be considered a form of narrative pastoral care in that it anticipates the impact of the research upon the people and the readers for whom it is written. Narrative theory emphasizes people's authority over their own stories, and the therapeutic value of sharing such richly developed stories with other persons and groups.

A choice that Couture has made along these lines is to house her digital interviews and other primary source material in the Drew University archives so that future scholars can have access to them. In particular, she wants the interviews to be available to Congolese scholars so that they can reinterpret them from the original languages.[4]

Work in the narrative stream also overlaps with the intercultural and postcolonial trajectory in pastoral theology. Melinda McGarrah Sharp points out the likelihood of "misunderstanding stories" taking place when people attempt to communicate across cultural boundaries, due to the legacy of colonialism that has tacitly influenced even well-meaning institutions such as Christian missions and the Peace Corps (McGarrah Sharp, 2014, p. 3). This presents a conundrum for qualitative researchers, who—like many of the above authors—must contend with the challenge of writing stories in ways that accurately and fairly represent their research partners, without idealization or condescension. Other tensions for researchers attempting to coauthor stories include tensions between voice and silence, and questions of who can speak in a given situation. As McGarrah Sharp points out, while on the one hand there is the danger of speaking for others, on the other there is the danger of remaining silent, if that means ignoring pressing social concerns in local or global communities (2014, p. 127). Further reflections on postcolonial pastoral theology can be found in Emmanuel Lartey's essay in this volume (Chapter 4).

## Why Practice Matters

Having reviewed these three overlapping approaches within the trajectory of qualitative research, I turn now to making a case as to why the study of religious practice matters for students and scholars of pastoral theology and care. Given that the field foregrounds human experience as a starting place for theological reflection, it makes sense to continue to study religious practices *in situ*, attending to the lived experiences of diverse persons and groups in their historical and socio-cultural contexts, as well as to explore their first-person published accounts. In the same way in which many pastoral theologians in the past (and some in the present) have found that staying active in a pastoral counseling practice keeps their teaching about pastoral counseling honest, pastoral theologians now need to continue to read and engage in qualitative studies in order to stay honest and informed about the social and political dimensions of lived religion. In order to teach and practice pastoral care that helps more than it hurts, we need ethnographic and qualitative research studies that illumine the embodied experience of persons and groups in their cultural complexity and evaluate the impact of religious practices. Pastoral ethnography and qualitative research force us to see social realities to which we might otherwise be oblivious, and in this way help the field promote more intelligent, sensitive, and life-giving forms of care.

For these reasons I argue that practice matters. By this I mean that individuals and organizations, such as churches, synagogues, mosques, counseling centers, chaplaincy departments, and so on, proclaim certain theological values not only through what they say, but also through what they (we) do, and importantly, through what we do regularly, habitually, and ritually, wittingly or unwittingly. For example, Mary McClintock Fulkerson's (2007) study, noted above, demonstrates how the long history of segregated worship in the US exerts an impact upon well-meaning worshippers (including researchers) even as they try to form a truly integrated congregation. Here is a congregation intentionally interrupting the most segregated hour of the week in America, 11:00 a.m. on Sunday morning, as Martin Luther King, Jr. once put it. Yet when McClintock Fulkerson gives us a glimpse into the worship life of this congregation, and a reflexive glimpse into her awareness of her anxieties as she feels them in her body in this situation, it becomes clear how much practice matters. In particular, it becomes clear that patterns of practice that have been long ingrained into embodied persons at worship do not easily give way to change. We see what Paul Connerton means when he says that the past is "sedimented in the body" (1989, p. 72). Liturgy, preaching style and substance, dress, and language all function to signify identity in particular ways. It is in the nitty-gritty interactions between and among pastors and people that the resilience of social power arrangements of privilege become visible. If pastoral and practical theologians cannot "see" what goes on in living human faith communities, we cannot hope to challenge the structures that hold white privilege and other forms of injustice in place.

Ethnographic and qualitative studies, when they are done well, lay bare the social realities that pastoral practitioners are up against when trying to work for healing, justice, and transformation. Through engaged qualitative study, we discover the "theologies-in-practice" (Graham et al., 2005, pp. 170–199) that are enacted by persons and/or groups, as well as researchers. While such discoveries may be alarming—they may challenge previously held notions of the loving quality of group life, for example, when we see that social hierarchies prevail in that same group—it is important that we recognize the gaps between spoken theology and lived practice, and engage with faith communities in authentic theological reflection upon them. In this way we can help to create the conditions for new, more just, and faithful living.

## The Meaning of Practice

Ideas of what constitutes a religious or pastoral practice are highly contested in theological circles. Ted Smith (2012) highlights theoretical differences posed in the work of Alasdair MacIntyre and Pierre Bourdieu (as well as others) that have influenced the conversation. Smith notes that in MacIntyre's moral philosophy, the importance of an authoritative tradition of excellence in "activities like medicine, agriculture, prayer, and the care of souls" is emphasized (Smith, 2012, p. 247). MacIntyre's influence is evident in the focus on normativity in the work of some of the scholars engaged in the Ecclesiology and Ethnography Network conversation described above. John Swinton and Harriett Mowat, for example, state that the task of practical theology "is to work towards the unification of the Church's theological understandings and her practices in the world, and in so doing, ensure that her public performances of the faith are true to the nature of the Triune God" (Swinton and Mowat, 2016, p. 25). Here we see a primary concern with defining Christian practices in terms of their coherence with a particular theological understanding of the nature of God.

Bourdieu's social theory offers a broader definition of practice, one that relies less on the authority of a religious tradition and more on embodied, cultural knowledge. Some of the authors we have cited above, such as Mary McClintock Fulkerson and Christian Scharen, rely more on Bourdieu's understanding of practice, especially in the way that it helps elucidate and account for the "material relations of race, class, gender, and citizenship" (Smith, 2012, p. 249). Similarly, I have embraced a broader definition of practice for the work of pastoral ethnography, influenced by Bourdieu (1977, 1984), Paul Connerton (1989), and others: "Just about any activity, if it is performed regularly and with a shared understanding of religious intent or meaning, can be considered a religious practice. ... Nothing can be deemed too secular to study, because the secular and the sacred, like the intellect and the spirit, and like theology and practice, dwell in us together" (Moschella, 2008b, p. 51).

Though I do not think it is possible to separate entirely religious practices from secular ones, some scholars seek to do just that, imagining emphatic differences between the church and the world. A chief example of this approach can be found in *Resident Aliens* (Hauerwas and Willimon, 1989), as noted by Scharen (2015, pp. 7–11). Besides the obvious problem of a lack of humility in asserting such clear lines of demarcation between the church and the world, this approach cannot account for the complexity of religious experience inside congregations or outside of them, nor within Christians or other religious or spiritual practitioners. Nancy Ammerman's (2014) sociological study, *Sacred Stories, Spiritual Tribes*, for example, finds a range of theologies and spiritual practices within the membership of American religious congregations and in other groups, such as neo-pagans and non-affiliates. When participants are encouraged to offer their own definitions of spiritual practice, a wide array of activities and committed actions is named, including Bible study and worship attendance for some, as well as praying, serving others, or walking outside in nature. Yet none of these practices is limited to those who hold to classic Christian doctrines. Nor are religious beliefs the key factor in church membership or participation. Studying religious practices with a broader lens provides insight into the variety and messiness of lived experience. The church and the world are part of each other, just as human faith and doubt are also entangled within Christians and other humans.

Tom Beaudoin (2016), in his essay, "Why Does Practice Matter Theologically?" argues that practical theology has been too confident in its Christian center, too narrow in its focus on Christian practice (p. 12). In this, he raises awareness of the ways in which Christian-centrism can limit practical theologians' capacity to see clearly (a topic Kathleen Greider addresses in her essay in this volume, Chapter 5). Beaudoin writes, "What counts as Christian practice is always generated out of local inherited available materials, conscious and personally/culturally unconscious" (Beaudoin, 2016, p. 27). It is incumbent upon practical and pastoral theologians to recognize the historicity of practice, that is, the way in which all religious practices have been invented, borrowed, translated, improvised, and cobbled together, rather than handed down by the divine in some pristine or unchanging form. Theology, too, arises out of human-made traditions, scriptures, and activities, and is therefore also a product of culture, not something that stands outside of it (Tanner, 1997). As Beaudoin notes, it is no simple or easy adjustment for practical (or pastoral) theologians to even consider moving Christianity out of the center of its discourse—this is why he calls it a conundrum (Beaudoin, 2016, p. 12). Indeed, it is difficult to research and write and practice pastoral or spiritual care in ways that express one's own theological tradition and values, while at the same time upholding the utmost respect for alterity (Doehring, 2015, pp. 1–4). Qualitative research can assist us with this conundrum. It can help us recognize both the limitations of our theologies-in-practice (e.g. short-sightedness, self-interest, lack of awareness of the impact of privilege and power arrangements), as well as our potential to alter our practices and enlarge our worldviews (e.g. by respectful listening to and engagement with those who differ religiously, unmasking white privilege, working for structural change). When we see what is really happening on the ground, we see how faith practices are both loving and flawed, both life-giving and life-limiting. By engaging respectfully and even reverently in research relationships (Campbell-Reed and Scharen, 2013), we open ourselves to be moved by peoples' stories and to share in the vulnerability of relationships (McGarrah Sharp, 2013, pp. 105–132). Qualitative study of religious practices can increase mutual understanding and help keep us humble in the face of religious difference.

I endorse a broad concept of religious practice, one that can hold together McIntyre's emphasis on intentional pursuit of greater excellence within a religious tradition with Bourdieu's emphasis on the materiality and social distinctions inherent in and produced by practice. Pamela Couture's study, described above, helps to illustrate what such an approach makes possible. In Kamina in the Democratic Republic of Congo, she finds that both Christianity and the local Luba indigenous traditions helped to support practices of peacemaking. She notes that "motivated by spirituality, the local people themselves have created a complex, organic model of peacebuilding, including capacity building, conflict transformation, and development" (Couture, 2016, p. 22). Her close, shared experiences of practice promoted a deeper understanding of both religious influences.

For pastoral theologians, religious practices matter in that they reveal the messy and complex ways in which human beings enact their religious values and strive to flourish. The qualitative study of practice matters in that it grounds theological reflection in lived experience, revealing both its beauty and inspiration, as well as its ongoing need for transformation in the face of injustice, violence, poverty, or peril. Practice matters in that it is what we do in the name of the holy and what we offer to those seeking care.

## Moving Forward: Narrative Means to Pastoral Theological Ends

As we look ahead, I am particularly captivated by the potential of narrative qualitative research projects to enhance the liberative and empowering goals of pastoral theology and care. Narrative theory brings intentionality and values to the fore: whose stories will be lifted up? Whose words, whose language, whose loyalties, and whose royalties are at stake? We write for the academy, of course. Or do we/can we write for the wellbeing of the world, and of the diverse communities of persons who share their stories with us?

In the past 30 years, numerous pastoral theologians have described the value of stories and story-telling in pastoral care practices. The work of Charles Gerkin, Andrew Lester, Edward Wimberly, Anne Streaty Wimberly, Christie Cozad Neuger, Herbert Anderson and Edward Foley, Carrie Doehring, Duane Bidwell, and Karen Scheib, among others, has advanced forms of pastoral care that emphasize the telling and hearing of stories, both human and divine. Ruard Ganzevoort (2012) notes that "In a sense, theological reflection on religious practices has … always been a reflection on the convergences, confluences, and conflicts between the myriads of stories" (p. 214). Pastoral care, in particular, involves assisting care-seekers in gathering up the threads of meaning in their lives, and weaving them into authentic and life-giving stories. While listening to individuals has long been a key pastoral practice, the field has now gained a greater appreciation for the pastoral task of co-creating communal and collective stories as well.

Narrative approaches to qualitative research involve at least three significant dimensions that support these pastoral goals. The first is an emphasis on empowering marginalized persons and groups, through creating space for them to tell their stories and an audience to hear them (Ganzevoort, 2012, p. 214). I will call this dimension, "stories seldom heard." The second dimension I want to note is the use of narrative approaches to deconstruct harmful hegemonic narratives and coauthor thicker, more life-giving stories. The third dimension concerns the artistic and poetic possibilities inherent in researching and writing narrative accounts of religious practice.

## Stories Seldom Heard

If pastoral theologians are trying to advance a postcolonial or decolonial agenda, as Emmanuel Lartey, Melinda McGarrah Sharp, and Nancy J. Ramsay (in her essay in this volume, Chapter 7) suggest, the principals of narrative theory can help us honor the rich and complex stories that colonized and subjugated peoples have to tell. Ethnographies and qualitative research projects that focus on the lives of people who are marginalized due to race, gender, geography, dis/abilities, homelessness, poverty, sexual orientation, ethnicity, and so on, are helping to "change the subject," as Mary McClintock Fulkerson (1994) might put it. Qualitative research that foregrounds the faith stories and religious practices of persons and groups who are marginalized, oppressed, or stigmatized changes the pastoral conversation.

Of course, there are tensions and risks associated with such research, as has already been noted above. The subject of research matters, as does the subjectivity of the persons involved in the study. The burden of representation is considerable and complex. Phillis Sheppard points out, for example, that practices of reflexivity alone do not necessarily overcome the risk of reifying racism when raced bodies are portrayed in practical theology (Sheppard, 2016). I assert that researchers need to work collaboratively in order to challenge each other's biases and blind spots. Even so, there is no guarantee that researchers will do no unwitting harm.

Nevertheless, I maintain that qualitative research is needed to lift up of the voices of those whose stories are seldom heard. Sarah Farmer, for example, studies experiences of hope among incarcerated and formerly incarcerated women (Farmer, 2016). Such work helps to break down the boundaries between insiders and outsiders, those who are imprisoned and those who are free, in a context of mass incarceration marked by racial discrimination (Alexander, 2010). To be sure, special ethical hurdles must be met in research with such vulnerable populations; it is critical that protocols for informed consent and other measures for the safety of research partners are observed. At the same time, it is an ethical lapse to fail to consider the stories of those whose freedoms are severely curtailed, both while they are incarcerated and when they return to living in the outside world.

Additional studies with immigrant communities and other-documented persons in the US, now experiencing greater political scrutiny and pressure, are also needed. Conde-Frazier (2011) offers an example that lifts up the needs of children in immigrant families. Jan Holton's work on forced displacement helpfully foregrounds the experiences of refugees, veterans, and homeless persons (Holton, 2016). In the current regressive political climate, it becomes all the more important to attend to the conditions of the most vulnerable, and to create venues in which their stories can be richly told and brought into greater public awareness. These efforts support the liberative and prophetic functions of pastoral theology and care.

## Stories and Strength

Barbara Wingard and Jane Lester (2001), two narrative therapy leaders from indigenous communities in Australia, sum up a key goal of collective narrative therapy in the title of their book, *Telling Our Stories in Ways that Make Us Stronger*. Qualitative research that combines the insights of narrative therapy with the study of religious practices (broadly defined) has the potential to make pastoral theology stronger. Though pastoral theologians have talked about communal contextual models of care for many years now, we have not fully theorized or realized them in pastoral care and counseling practices (McClure, 2010). Collective narrative therapies work with people to develop thicker, richer stories about themselves—stories that take social and historical contexts into account, and stories that honor suppressed knowledges that support people's agency, intentionality, faith, and moral integrity.

As we have seen, ethnographic and qualitative research projects can probe the dominant cultural myths operating within people's lives. Narrative therapy, relying on critical theory, involves conversations that map the historicity of problems that constrict and constrain human stories. One of the strengths of ethnographic and qualitative research is that it often involves studying and articulating the history of social conditions that contribute to current practices. In narrative therapy, one goal is to map out the history of problems through questions that probe their origins, periods of waxing and waning, and the social situations that support or diminish them. When the social and historical dimensions of a problem become clearer to a person or group, the internal grip of the problem is eased, and the capacity to redress it is increased (Moschella, 2016, p. 256).

In the vignette at the start of this chapter, I offered my story of the way in which studying the religious practices of a group of Italian American immigrants opened a window into the history of immigration, discrimination, and racism for me. As the leaders of the anti-racism workshop I attended may have anticipated, coming to terms with the history of Italian immigration and the cultural construction of ethnicity helped me appreciate the history of diverse racial groups and the cultural construction of race as well. I came to understand both the painful history of discrimination that Italians and other immigrants from southern Europe experienced and the ways in which these immigrants and their descendants, particularly after World War II when the "melting pot" ideology took hold, could gain status and economic advantages as they started to be perceived as white. I could also see the clear difference in the experiences of darker-skinned peoples, whose racial and ethnic markers did not "melt," and who have been targeted for ongoing discrimination and violence since the days of slavery. As historian Mathew Frye Jacobson (1999) points out, there are three large areas in which the effects of historical and ongoing racism in the US are clearly documented (housing, education, and jobs). While this understanding does not make the evil of racism less vexing, it does make the situation clearer, and it helps make me less oblivious.

Similarly, the narrative practice of mapping helps to make personal and social problems visible as historically situated, rather than as the taken-for-granted, natural realities that they may at first appear to be. In narrative qualitative research, mapping the history of local religious practices can help persons and groups tell their stories in ways that strengthen their historical understanding, theological values, and ethical clarity. Thus, collective, narrative accounts can make people as well as pastoral theology stronger.

## Artistic and Poetic Dimension

A third important dimension of narrative approaches to qualitative research and writing has to do with art, creativity, and poetics. In narrative therapy, rich story-telling is not a precise science: it relies on the give-and-take of relationships and the wisdom of words that are spoken and "rescued" by the hearer. Similarly, the process of writing ethnographies and qualitative research accounts involves the creative activity of composing. Consideration of the intended audience is one aspect of this imaginative work. In addition, however rigorous the process of analysis may be, researchers do not simply "write up" their findings in a mechanical way. Writing ethnographic narratives involves both rigorous rational thinking and a more receptive kind of reflection. Immersion in the many stories, language(s), and rituals of religious life may cause images to bubble up in the researcher's mind (Moschella, 2008b, p. 191). The use of writing conventions such as metaphor is key to the imaginative work of communicating complicated understandings in a clear and concise way. Janet Soskice writes, "A strong metaphor compels new possibilities of vision" (1985, p. 58).

Heather Walton (2016), a proponent of poetics in practical theology, emphasizes the capacity of artistic methodologies to: "promote deep forms of empathetic engagement with the other and OTHER," and to "render the familiar strange provoking epiphanies, re-enchantment, sacralisation, and return of soul" (Walton, 2016, p. 9). Narrative approaches to research, in part because of their artistic dimensions, draw out similar capacities.

Pamela Couture's work (2016), cited above, employs the genre of creative non-fiction. In this, she draws inspiration from practical theologians' reflections on poetics and spiritual life writing, noting the work of Heather Walton (2015). Couture's commitment to telling true stories is explicit, as is her conviction that the truth of the people's stories she heard is best expressed in a creative and compelling narrative.[5] She takes license in recreating dialogue and in abbreviating some stories for the sake of poetics and narrative coherence (Couture, 2016, p. 18). In choosing this approach, Couture articulates her values and narrative purposes: she seeks to honor the people who have entrusted her with their stories, not only by allowing them to review the drafts and influence her interpretations, but also by writing their stories in an engaging literary form that she hopes will serve the people's goal of getting their story out to a broad readership.

Walton notes that the poetic dimensions of practical theology are controversial, perhaps suggesting an echo of the debates within the social sciences noted above over the relative merits of quantitative and qualitative study. Given that both pastoral and practical theologians have been anxious to secure their place in the academy, and given the academic trend toward supporting evidence-based knowledge, such controversy is understandable. If we get caught up in our metaphors and moments of encounter, might we stray away from empirical knowledge and undermine the field's quest "to see and think clearly in order to make a difference in the world" (Walton, 2012, p. 174)? Yet, Walton points to Terry Veling's claim that "aesthetic reasoning" is needed "to safeguard a practical theological ecclesiology from becoming so spellbound with a critical analytic method that it ultimately has a very positivistic approach toward human actions" (Veling, 2005, pp. 195–203, cited in Walton, 2012, p. 174).

Narrative qualitative research, in all of its prophetic, therapeutic, and artistic dimensions, can enhance our work in pastoral theology and care. Studies written in this vein help us imagine more attentive forms of care, care that transforms the stories and structures that haunt and limit human persons beloved of God. Such sensitive and compelling accounts have the potential to open up new understanding and increase the likelihood that religious and spiritual practices of care will be a source of blessing, wonder, and hope.

## Conclusion

In this chapter, I have described an evolving trajectory of ethnographic and qualitative research in the field of pastoral theology and argued for the continuing relevance of such practice-oriented research. While examining only a fraction of the vast array of critical studies employing qualitative methods and modes of interpretation, I have highlighted some recent and exemplary studies within three research streams. Moving forward, I hope to see pastoral theologians, religious leaders, chaplains, and other practitioners continue to do ethnography and qualitative research in these various ways, so that our theories, theologies, and practices can be informed by rigorous research and theological reflection upon particular, multiple, and varied religious experiences and practices. In particular, I advocate for the prophetic, therapeutic, and poetic possibilities of narrative qualitative research.

# Notes

1  In the study of religion, see David D. Hall, Ed. *Lived Religion in America: Toward a History of Practice* (Princeton, NJ: Princeton University Press, 1997); and Robert Orsi, *Between Heaven and Earth: The Religious Worlds People Make and the Scholars Who Study Them* (Princeton, NJ: Princeton University Press, 2005). In systematic theology, see Kathryn Tanner, *Theories of Culture: A New Agenda for Theology* (Minneapolis, MN: Fortress, 1997). In biblical studies, see, for example, Erin Runions, *The Babylon Complex: Theopolitical Fantasies of War, Sex, and Sovereignty* (New York: Fordham University Press, 2014).

2  This research stream is related to the fields of congregational studies and participatory action research, though space does not allow me to fully take up these approaches here. See Elaine Graham, "Is Practical Theology a form of 'Action Research'?" in *International Journal of Practical Theology*, Vol. 17, Issue 1, August 2013, 148–178. Also see the multimedia journal, *Practical Matters: A Journal of Religious Practices and Practical Theology* (Emory University), an academic space that fosters conversations about and between religious practices, practical theology, and qualitative research.

3  I am indebted to Eileen Campbell-Reed and Pete Ward for help with this section.

4  This transparency is a good scholarly practice, in that readers who have access to the data can more fully evaluate the author's conclusions. In presentations of her work, Couture has also raised money to support an educational foundation for Congolese students. She emphasizes the importance of "giving back" benefits to her research partners (e-mail conversation with the author, December 30, 2016).

5  This dimension of the writing is reminiscent of Karen McCarthy Brown's landmark volume, *Mama Lola: A Haitian Vodou Priestess in Brooklyn* (Berkeley, CA: University of California Press, 1991). Brown broke with conventions in anthropology and the study of religion by interspersing historical chapters with fictional chapters that she composed out of the many bits and pieces of stories that she had heard and recorded during her field study.

# References

Alexander, Michelle. 2010. *The New Jim Crow: Mass Incarceration in the Age of Colorblindness*. New York: The New Press.

Ammerman, Nancy T., Jackson W. Carroll, Carl S. Dudley, and William McKinney. 1998. *Studying Congregations: A New Handbook*. Nashville, TN: Abingdon Press.

Ammerman, Nancy T. 2014. *Sacred Stories, Spiritual Tribes: Finding Religion in Everyday Life*. New York: Oxford University Press.

Beaudoin, Tom. 2016. "Why Does Practice Matter Theologically?" In *Conundrums in Practical Theology*, edited by Joyce Ann Mercer and Bonnie J. Miller-McLemore, pp. 8–32. Leiden: Brill.

Bourdieu, Pierre. 1984. *Distinction: A Social Critique of the Judgement of Taste.* Oxford: Routledge Kegan & Paul.

Bourdieu, Pierre. 1977. *Outline of a Theory of Practice.* Cambridge: Cambridge University Press.

Browning, Don S. 1991. *A Fundamental Practical Theology: Descriptive and Strategic Proposals.* Minneapolis, MN: Augsburg Fortress.

Cameron, Helen, Deborah Bhatti, Catherine Duce, James Sweeney, and Clare Watkins. 2010. *Talking About God in Practice: Theological Action Research and Practical Theology.* London: SCM Press.

Campbell-Reed, Eileen R. 2016. *Anatomy of a Schism: How Clergywomen's Narratives Reinterpret the Fracturing of the Southern Baptist Convention.* Knoxville, TN: University of Tennessee Press.

Campbell-Reed, Eileen R. and Christian Scharen. 2013. "Ethnography on Holy Ground: How Qualitative Interviewing Is Theological Work." *International Journal of Practical Theology.* Volume 17, Issue 2, 232–259. DOI:https://doi.org/10.1515/ijpt-2013-0015.

Combs, Gene and Jill Freedman. 1996. *Narrative Therapy: The Social Construction of Preferred Realities.* New York: W.W. Norton.

Conde-Frazier, Elizabeth. 2011. *Listening to the Children: Conversations with Immigrant Families.* Valley Forge, PA: Judson Press.

Conde-Frazier, Elizabeth. 2012. "Participant Action Research." In *The Wiley-Blackwell Companion to Practical Theology*, edited by Bonnie J. Miller-McLemore, pp. 234–243. Oxford: Wiley-Blackwell.

Connerton, Paul. 1989. *How Societies Remember.* Cambridge: Cambridge University Press.

Couture, Pamela. 2016. *We Are Not All Victims: Local Religious Peacebuilding in the Democratic Republic of Congo.* Zürich: Lit Verlag.

Crumpton, Stephanie M. 2014. *A Womanist Theology against Intimate and Cultural Violence.* New York: Palgrave Macmillan.

Denzin, Norman K. and Yvonna S. Lincoln. 2011. *The SAGE Handbook of Qualitative Research*, 4th edn. Thousand Oaks, CA: SAGE Publications.

Doehring, Carrie. 2015. *The Practice of Pastoral Care: A Postmodern Approach*, rev. and expanded ed. Louisville, KY: Westminster John Knox.

Eiesland, Nancy L. 2000. *A Particular Place: Urban Restructuring and Religious Ecology in a Southern Exurb.* Piscataway, NJ: Rutgers University Press.

Farmer, Sarah F. 2016. "Hope in Confinement: Moving Toward a Pedagogy of Restorative Hope." PhD diss., Emory University.

Fuller, Leanna K. 2016. *When Christ's Body is Broken: Anxiety, Identity, and Conflict in Congregations.* Eugene, OR: Pickwick.

Ganzevoort, R. Ruart. 2012. "Narrative Approaches." In *The Wiley-Blackwell Companion to Practical Theology*, edited by Bonnie J. Miller-McLemore, pp. 214–223. Oxford: Wiley-Blackwell.

Graham, Elaine L. 1996. *Transforming Practice: Pastoral Theology in an Age of Uncertainty*. London: Mowbray.

Graham, Elaine, Heather Walton, and Francis Ward. 2005. *Theological Reflection: Methods*. London: SCM Press.

Graham, Larry Kent. 1992. *Care of Persons, Care of Worlds: A Psychosystems Approach to Pastoral Care and Counseling*. Nashville, TN: Abingdon.

Graham, Larry Kent. 2011. "Narratives of Families, Faith, and Nation: Insights from Research." *Journal of Pastoral Theology*. Volume 2, Issue 2, 1–18. DOI:http://dx.doi.org/10.1179/jpt.2011.21.2.005.

Greider, Kathleen. 2007. *Much Madness is Divinest Sense: Wisdom in Memoirs of Soul-Suffering*. Cleveland, OH: Pilgrim.

Hauerwas, Stanley and William Willimon. 1989. *Resident Aliens: Life in the Christian Colony*. Nashville, TN: Abingdon.

Holton, M. Jan. 2016. *Longing for Home: Forced Displacement and Postures of Hospitality*. New Haven, CT: Yale University Press.

Hoover, Brett C. 2014. *The Shared Parish: Latinos, Anglos, and the Future of U.S. Catholicism*. New York: New York University Press.

Jacobson, Matthew Frye. 1999. *Whiteness of a Different Color: European Immigration and the Alchemy of Race*. Cambridge, MA: Harvard University Press.

Kaufman, Tone Stangeland. 2016. "From the Outside, Within, or In Between? Normativity at Work in Empirical Practical Theological Research." In *Conundrums in Practical Theology*, edited by Joyce Ann Mercer and Bonnie J. Miller-McLemore, pp. 134–162. Leiden: Brill.

Maynard, Jane F., Leonard Hummel, and Mary Clark Moschella, Eds. 2010. *Pastoral Bearings: Lived Religion and Pastoral Theology*. Lanham, MD: Lexington Books.

McClintock Fulkerson, Mary. 1994. *Changing the Subject: Women's Discourses and Feminist Theology*. Minneapolis, MN: Fortress.

McClintock Fulkerson, Mary. 2007. *Places of Redemption: Theology for a Worldly Church*. New York: Oxford University Press.

McClure, Barbara J. 2010. *Moving Beyond Individualism in Pastoral Care and Counseling: Reflections on Theory, Theology, and Practice*. Eugene, OR: Cascade.

McGarrah Sharp, Melinda. 2014. *Misunderstanding Stories: Toward a Postcolonial Pastoral Theology*. Eugene, OR: Pickwick.

Mercer, Joyce Ann. 2008. *Girltalk, Godtalk: Why Faith Matters to Teenage Girls—and Their Parents*. San Francisco, CA: Jossey-Bass.

Miller-McLemore, Bonnie J. 1998. "The Subject and Practice of Pastoral Theology as a Practical Theological Discipline: Pushing Past the Nagging Identity Crisis to the Poetics of Resistance." In *Liberating Faith Practices: Feminist Practical*

*Theologies in Contexts*, edited by Denise M. Ackermann and Riet Bons-Storm, pp. 175–198. Leuven: Peeters.

Moschella, Mary Clark. 2008a. *Living Devotions: Reflections on Immigration, Identity, and Religious Imagination*. Eugene, OR: Pickwick.

Moschella, Mary Clark. 2008b. *Ethnography as a Pastoral Practice: An Introduction*. Cleveland, OH: Pilgrim.

Moschella, Mary Clark. 2016. *Caring for Joy: Narrative, Theology, and Practice*. Leiden: Brill.

Parker, Evelyn. 2007. *The Sacred Stories of Adolescent Girls: Hard Stories of Race, Class, and Gender*. Cleveland, OH: Pilgrim.

Patton, John. 2005. *Pastoral Care in Context: An Introduction to Pastoral Care*. Louisville, KY: Westminster John Knox.

Scharen, Christian. 2015. *Fieldwork in Theology: Exploring the Social Context of God's Work in the World*. Grand Rapids, MI: Baker Academic.

Scharen, Christian and Aana Marie Vigen, Eds. 2011. *Ethnography as Christian Theology and Ethics*. New York: Continuum.

Sheppard, Phillis Isabella. 2016. "Raced Bodies: Portraying Bodies, Reifying Racism." In *Conundrums in Practical Theology*, edited by Joyce Ann Mercer and Bonnie J. Miller-McLemore, pp. 219–249. Leiden: Brill.

Schreiter, Robert J. 1985. *Constructing Local Theologies*. Maryknoll, NY: Orbis.

Smith, Ted A. 2012. "Theories of Practice." In *The Wiley-Blackwell Companion to Practical Theology*, edited by Bonnie J. Miller-McLemore, pp. 244–254. Oxford: Wiley-Blackwell.

Snyder, Timothy K. 2014. "Theological Ethnography: Embodied." *The Other Journal*. Volume 23, Issue 5. https://theotherjournal.com/article-author/timothy-k-snyder/.

Soskice, Janet Martin. 1985. *Metaphor and Religious Language*. Oxford: Clarendon.

Swinton, John and Harriett Mowat. 2015. *Practical Theology and Qualitative Research*, 2nd edn. London: SCM Press.

Tanner, Kathryn. 1997. *Theories of Culture: A New Agenda for Theology*. Minneapolis, MN: Fortress.

Veling, Terry. 2005. *Practical Theology: "On Earth as in Heaven."* Maryknoll, NY: Orbis.

Walton, Heather. 2012. "Poetics," In *The Wiley-Blackwell Companion to Practical Theology*, edited by Bonnie J. Miller-McLemore, pp. 173–182. Oxford: Wiley-Blackwell.

Walton, Heather. 2015. *Not Eden: Spiritual Writing for this World*. London: SCM Press.

Walton, Heather. 2016. "Being Spiritual in Social Research: Some Recent Debates in Practical Theology," unpublished, used with author's permission.

Ward, Pete, Ed. 2012. *Perspectives on Ecclesiology and Ethnography*. Grand Rapids, MI: William B. Eerdmanns.

White, Michael and David Epston. 2009. *Narrative Means to Therapeutic Ends.* New York: W.W. Norton.

Wigg-Stevenson, Natalie. 2014. *Ethnographic Theology: An Inquiry into the Production of Theological Knowledge.* New York: Palgrave Macmillan.

Willhauck, Susan. 2016. "Teaching Qualitative Research in Theological Education to Enhance Leadership for Change in the Church," unpublished report on Wabash research.

Wingard, Barbara and Jane Lester. 2001. *Telling Our Stories in Ways that Make Us Stronger.* Adelaide: Dulwich Centre Publications.

## For Further Study

Higgs, Joy, Angie Titchen, Debbie Horsfall, and Donna Bridges. 2011. *Creative Spaces for Qualitative Researching: Living Research.* Rotterdam: Sense Publishers.

## 2

## How the Brain Matters

*David A. Hogue*

## Introduction and Literature Review

Recent decades have seen an enormous rise in neuroscientific discoveries around the world. Every day new reports of brain research appear in newspapers, social media, and in workshops for artists, attorneys, financial forecasters, musicians, and for the "spiritual but not religious." Few, if any, domains of human experience are untouched today by the brain sciences, as colorful pictures of scans adorn articles proclaiming "this is your brain on..." And in order to gain readers' attention in an information-saturated society, these headlines tout such promises as new cures for Alzheimer's, making someone fall in love with you, reading other people's minds, improving our memories, and finding new treatments for drug and behavioral addictions.

To be sure, there is much promise even in the incremental improvements that are already being made in the slowing of dementias including Alzheimer's, mobility for the physically impaired, and tracing the development and treatment of addictions. And if history is any clue, the best is yet to come. Yet the very complexity of the science and the variety of claims make understanding and interpreting these fascinating discoveries complicated. There is a strong temptation either to reject the science out of hand (as too difficult to understand or irrelevant) or to place unwarranted trust in the claims made by some scientists and their press agents.

The reach of the neurosciences into our understanding of human nature is just beginning, but the promise and peril of such a development are yet to be realized. Nobel prize-winning neuroscientist Eric Kandel, for instance, notes that in the 20th century "the most valuable insights into the human mind ... id not come from the disciplines traditionally concerned with mind – from philosophy, psychology, or psychoanalysis." Instead they have emerged from "a new science of mind, a science that uses the power of molecular biology to examine the great remaining mysteries of life" (Kandel, 2006, p. xii).

*Pastoral Theology and Care: Critical Trajectories in Theory and Practice*, First Edition. Edited by Nancy J. Ramsay.
© 2018 John Wiley & Sons Ltd. Published 2018 by John Wiley & Sons Ltd.

As important for religious leaders is the increasing familiarity that congregants, counselees, and the broader public have with the brain and its functioning, and the profound questions such discoveries raise for those who turn to us for care, guidance, wisdom, and interpretation of the deeper implications of our religious faith.

Knowledge of the brain is vital to effective ministry today, primarily because the emerging research is deepening and reshaping our understanding of human beings—how we think and feel, how we relate to each other, how we make sense of our world, how we suffer, and how we heal. Many professions beyond traditional medical and research specialties now require competence in the neurosciences. Clinical psychology has long required knowledge of the brain, and other counseling professions, including addictions and rehabilitation counseling, are following suit. Teachers, social workers, attorneys, economists, art and music therapists, speech and language therapists, and audiologists are increasingly calling for the inclusion of neuroscientific principles for responsible and ethical professional practice.

## Review of Literature

Pastoral theologians and practitioners, as well as scholars in other theological disciplines, need the careful work of dedicated scholars in neuroscience and in pastoral theology if they are to mine responsibly the resources of this complex, growing field of research. The neurosciences are not simple to comprehend, much less to evaluate in terms of their implications for ministry. Those seeking input directly from neuroscientists will profit from reading the work of Mario Beauregard and Denyse O'Leary (2007), Andrew Newberg and Mark Waldman (2009), and Patrick McNamara (2009), who have written in accessible ways about prayer, meditation, and charismatic experiences, suggesting that our brains are not only changed by religious practices but require them. Malcolm Jeeves of St. Andrew University and Warren Brown of Fuller Theological Seminary (Jeeves and Brown, 2009; Jeeves, 2013), as well as scholars at Biola University have offered Evangelical perspectives on the interdisciplinary dialogue and document the embodied nature of our faith, often looking specifically at the ways religious practices reshape brain functions.

And several pastoral theologians have immersed themselves in this work, primarily in the US. The pioneer in this integration was the late James Ashbrook during the last two decades of the last century (Ashbrook, 1995; Ashbrook and Albright, 1997). Focusing primarily on pastoral counseling, Ashbrook also participated in the international science and religion dialogue, highlighting theological and clinical implications of the burgeoning science. As his later colleague, my work has sought to make these sciences understandable to practitioners and theologians, focusing initially on memory and imagination (Hogue, 2003) and then turning to explorations of empathy, race, and human relationality (Hogue, 2010, 2015, 2017). More recently a new generation of scholars is developing a critical literature in the field. Kirk Bingaman (2014) has written on neuroplasticity, contemplative prayer, and meditation, and is editing a new series with Lexington Books. Jason Whitehead has contributed a volume on fear (2015), and William Roozeboom recently published work exploring the body–brain connection in self-care (2016).

But more specifically, how can the neurosciences help us deepen our practices of pastoral care? Can this research inform our understanding of human suffering and healing? Do current neuroscientific discoveries confirm or challenge our long-held beliefs about human nature and about the imago dei? Particular forms of human suffering such as dementias (including Alzheimer's disease), trauma, head injury, and stroke are obvious areas in which neurological information can be helpful. Here, however, we will develop a more general approach to incorporating neuroscientific principles as we consider the story of Daniel, a composite vignette of an older man who might belong to a congregation any of us leads or attends. (His social location, it should be noted, is similar to the author's as a white, middle class, straight male of a similar age.) We will then explore several threads in recent research that shed important light on both the suffering and the healing that Daniel's story illustrate, particularly the ways the human brain functions in remembering (and forgetting), in emotion, and in religious practices. We will briefly consider ways the neurosciences can contribute to our understanding of the systemic sin that leads to violence against vulnerable persons marginalized by social structures. Daniel's healing and recovery would be inadequate and incomplete without acknowledging the larger social issues in which Daniel has participated. These insights can also inform those who hope to provide spiritual and pastoral care to persons they encounter. We will suggest some theological implications and ponder future directions at the chapter's conclusion.

## Daniel's Story

Daniel, a 65-year-old white male, is a recently divorced middle-management executive with a bank. Six months ago he suddenly experienced his heart racing, dizziness, and shortness of breath in the middle of a work day. Afraid he was having a heart attack, he went to the emergency room of a nearby hospital. Medical staff found no signs of heart disease or other causes for his symptoms and concluded that Daniel had experienced an unexplained anxiety attack. He was relieved that his heart was okay, but angry that they could find no reason for the frightening event; he refused a Xanax prescription. Preoccupied by a special project at work, he soon forgot about the event until a few weeks later when the same symptoms reappeared. This time he closed his office door, lay down on a couch, closed his eyes, and tried to tell himself that he could manage this, that he wasn't crazy. After 20 minutes of unsuccessful self-talk, he stood up, picked up his coat, and alerted staff that he had to take care of something at home. Arriving home, he changed clothes and fixed himself a drink. Eventually his heart rate returned to normal and he assured himself he was okay. When a third episode occurred one week later, he had gone to his own physician, who confirmed that he was physically healthy and that his symptoms were likely due to unidentified stresses. Again he refused medication, but did agree to see a pastoral counselor.

Daniel described growing up and attending high school in a midsize Midwestern city in the 1960s. Racial tensions had been mounting in the school district as African American families purchased homes and current residents engaged in "white flight." Daniel and his family attended a neighborhood main-line Protestant church, which had formerly consisted of affluent white members and was now attempting to come to terms with their "changing" neighborhood. Unable to integrate their worship services and membership, several clergy nonetheless preached tolerance and welcome, though they stopped short of participating in marches and civil rights protests downtown. Daniel's school was integrating with little disruption or violence, but white and black students had little to do with each other outside of class. After graduating from high school, he attended a private college that counted a few students of color among its student body. His parents were eventually the last white family in the neighborhood to sell their house and move to a suburb. Daniel intended to major in pre-med, but eventually found the science courses too demanding and followed his father into the banking profession.

Daniel met his wife in college and they married at the end of their senior year. He located a job with his current company and has been there ever since. The couple has two daughters, both of whom finished college and married shortly thereafter; they have five grandchildren. Five years ago Daniel's wife told him she had fallen in love with another attorney at her firm and was leaving. He was caught off guard; he spoke a couple of times with his pastor about his shock and pain, but concluded he needed to be strong and get through this. He has tried dating a few times, but nothing "clicked." Other than church, which he attends weekly, he has few social contacts. Most evenings he returns to his condo in the city, has dinner and a few drinks, watches TV and goes to bed. Twice a week he works out at a local gym.

Daniel's investment firm instituted cultural and gender sensitivity training earlier this year following several incidents of workplace harassment that had led to the departure of several key employees and charges of institutional discriminatory practices with lawsuits still pending. Daniel was not directly involved in any of the alleged incidents, though one of his colleagues was charged and later exonerated. The company stepped up recruitment efforts to build a more diverse employee base. Daniel willingly attended the training sessions, considering himself tolerant and anything but prejudiced. He had worked closely with several black colleagues on important projects and currently had a woman supervisor.

Daniel and his counselor spent their first session exploring his panic attacks as well as the impact of his unexpected divorce. They noted together his social isolation and the ongoing stress of his work. In a second session, Daniel talked about his family of origin and relationship with his parents and older sister. She was a natural student, and following her in many of the same classes, he was often compared unfavorably. Nonetheless, he completed public school and a college degree with honors. Daniel was not sure about the need for all this history review, but was intrigued by the connections he and the counselor were making between his family, his school, and his work.

Later Daniel and his counselor returned to the immediate stresses of work. While the business was recovering well from the 2008 recession, the strain of losing and adding employees was taking an emotional toll on him and many of his co-workers. Eventually discussion turned to the company's cultural awareness program. One recent exercise called for Daniel and a black colleague to tell each other a story from their high school years. His younger partner had lived in a housing project where gang violence was rampant. He described constant feelings of fear as he made the long walk to school and of shootings near his school grounds. When it was Daniel's turn to speak, he began confidently speaking of the "easy" integration of his own high school. When asked about any black friends, Daniel became uneasy, recalling how little memory he had of contact with students of color. He quickly reassured his colleague that the school had managed the transitions well, and that they all "just seemed to get along." The first panic attack came that afternoon.

The counselor invited Daniel to recall that work encounter in more detail and wondered about any earlier memories of events that might have seemed similar. Unable initially to identify any connection with his anxiety, before long a troubling episode from his junior year in high school flooded into memory. He was on lunch break returning from a nearby fast food restaurant. A group of white students were gathered outside the school building and, as Daniel approached, he saw that they had surrounded a young black student and were threatening him. The boy was trembling and clearly feared for his safety, glancing all around for help. Daniel later learned that the boy had been hospitalized from blows to the head and kicks to his body, and threats of retaliation had come from the boy's family and friends. Daniel recalled feeling horrified for him, but was unable to move to help. He was also terrified for his own safety and feared being attacked if he were to intervene or even alerted anyone else to what had happened. He slipped in a side door of the school and into his first afternoon class. He remembered trembling and finding it impossible to concentrate, but he "pulled himself together" for the rest of the day and proceeded to forget the incident.

Recalling the incident nearly 50 years later Daniel could recall the terrified face of his black classmate and his impulse to rush in and protect him. He also felt physically frightened and paralyzed, as he later imagined he must have felt at the time; eventually feelings of shame washed over him as he realized his inability to help and that he had abandoned the scene; he had even attempted to abandon the memory of the event. The image of himself as one who "doesn't see color" began to crumble, and the picture of "easy integration" of his high school years shattered. He began to reconstruct years in which conflict was avoided primarily by mutual ignorance and neglect, never really developing close enough relationships with persons of color to engage differences and discover similarities.

Several more sessions with his pastoral counselor provided the opportunity to revisit similar stories. Daniel began to confront his feelings of impotence and avoidance, but also to recognize the powerful systemic and cultural shifts that were underway at the time and that undoubtedly made responding in different ways difficult. He began to recognize that his very real experiences of panic, both on behalf of his classmate and himself, had been "forgotten," disconnected from the stories that now resurfaced. Daniel became aware of the ways his earlier painful experiences had made him fearful of intimate relationships and of taking risks when he encountered injustice. He explored the ways his lack of intimacy might have contributed to difficulties in his marriage and his current social isolation. He wanted people to get along and so avoided raising difficult issues for fear of estranging others or subtly jeopardizing his own emotional self.

Daniel wasn't sure that change was possible, or whether he would ever be able to free himself from the guilt, shame, and powerlessness evoked by these earlier stories. He wanted empirical evidence. His therapist recalled his college interest in medicine and knew that he read widely in the popular and financial presses. They talked about neuroscientific descriptions of the brain's emotional systems, particularly the fear system, and about the ways brains change with regular practice. They reviewed how his use of alcohol had often served as a sedative for his underlying anxiety, and the ways in which overuse could actually "hijack" brain systems that would otherwise press him to invest in close relationships. They talked about memory, and about how memories can change even when the actual events cannot. They spoke about the deep connections between physical health, including diet and exercise, and emotional and spiritual health. He noticed that the emotional changes he was experiencing matched the science they were discussing, and over time, he became more certain that his emotional changes were "real" and not manufactured or imagined. Hope took a different shape now, as he acknowledged that changes could continue well beyond his sessions with the counselor; that engaging in closer relationships with friends and families could also "change his brain" to live more fully in the time that he had.

As Daniel's personal story came into focus he confessed his own fear and self-deception as well as their consequences for himself. But vivid memories of the face of his terrified black classmate returned and he realized how little he understood about that young man's life or experience as a student of color in an era of civil unrest. He had begun to understand how those social and biological forces had shaped him, but how had they shaped the stories and threatened the lives of the victims of racism? Some connection with his former classmate still haunted him, and he was startled to realize how little he knew, how little he understood. This was a critical point in Daniel's counseling; his concerns slowly turned toward others and transcended his own; his worries about himself became part of a larger picture as the sufferings of others were revealed.

These changes came slowly. Daniel first "tested the waters" with his daughters and grandchildren, and later began spending lunch hours at work with colleagues. As importantly, he paid closer attention to his own responses during sensitivity training sessions at work and slowly began spending one weekend a month with a church group that had partnered with an inner-city African American church to counter violence. He found an old high school yearbook for the name of his classmate and searched for him on social media, but couldn't locate him. He would always wonder. At times these approaches produced anxiety, but again, over time, his emotional resilience emerged.

## Remembering and Forgetting

Daniel's story highlights how central our memories are to both our suffering and our healing. His story was, in many ways, familiar in its outline: growing up in an intact middle class family, competing with an older sibling, college, marriage, family, and career. A surprising divorce disrupted the life he had imagined, and the cultural volatility of his high school years locates his story within a particular time and place. Daniel may not have paid much attention to his own life story before, but in recalling life events in the presence of an interested and attentive listener, both plot and specific details emerge in a narrative that uncovers deeper meanings and places his current struggles within a broader context.

Much evidence has accumulated to confirm that we human beings require stories to know who we are and how we can navigate our world. All cultures make use of them. Studies have demonstrated that the human brain needs stories and creates them to explain the world when none is available. Psychologists Michael Gazzaniga and Joseph LeDoux studied so-called "split-brain" patients after the primary nerve bundle that connects the two hemispheres of the brain, the corpus callosum, was severed in order to lessen the effects of intractable epileptic seizures. Since the two hemispheres could not "talk" to each other, the patients occasionally engaged in puzzling behavior, such as pairing two unconnected objects during testing. When asked why they had just behaved in that way, patients routinely quickly offered stories to explain what they had just done, even though the psychologists knew the confusion was a result of the recent surgery. Gazzaniga dubbed the impulse of the human brain to seek explanations the "left brain interpreter." (For a fuller description, see Hogue, 2003, pp. 84–87.)

Interestingly, contemporary neuroscience and other studies have discovered that our memories are more malleable than we had once imagined, exposing memory's strength as well its vulnerability. Such realizations can be disconcerting given the conviction with which we recall our most vivid memories; we trust them and live our lives under their direction. And these "mishaps" are even more alarming to trial lawyers, journalists, and historians, who rely on the accuracy of recall to make important decisions and influence public beliefs and policies. But memory's apparent weakness, or as Harvard psychologist Daniel Schacter describes it, memory's "fragile power" (1997), ironically also offers hope to pastoral leaders and counselors in engaging congregants and clients in deeper exploration of their sometimes troubled early histories. How we understand ourselves and the worlds we live in relies on the foundation of our memories. Without recalling his past, Daniel has no future, and he cannot even know who he is in the present. Without memory, we have no sense of self or community; some would even say we have no soul (Ashbrook and Albright, 1997, p. 173).

But caregivers and receivers often resign themselves to the fixed nature of the past; they can't change what has already happened to them, or undo something they had done years before. We experience our memories as fixed units—stored in their own "files" awaiting our need for them in the future. Yet the brain stores and retrieves memories in much more complicated ways. Rather than recording each event in one location, each time we experience an event in our lives our brains break down that experience into its various components: what we see, what we hear, what we smell or touch, and what we feel. Each component then is stored in the brain region most responsible for that sense. Visual images are stored in the occipital regions of the brain, sound and language in the temporal lobes on each side of the brain, the movements we were making or imagining are recorded in the motor cortex, and our emotional responses register primarily in the deep recesses of the limbic system. In other words, our memories are not stored in one location to be pulled off the shelf in one piece. Each time we remember an event each component of the experience must be reassembled to produce the rich, full, vivid experiences we recall.

And while our memories, particularly those of unusual or personally relevant events, tend to be accurate in general outline, each time we recall events, we are recreating the memory. Each time we do, we imbue it with the meaning it has for us at the moment of recall, including the feelings that color the recalled event. Our brains then store the event as we recalled it rather than in the shape in which we originally experienced it, much like the overwrite feature on a computer. In all likelihood these changes of narrative are recorded in shifted neural connections, enabled by the brain's ability to change.

At its simplest level, our memories consist of patterns of connections made between brain cells known as neurons (Kandel, 2006). For decades scientists have known that neurons conduct business by communicating with other neurons through neurochemical processes that transfer electrical charges from one neuron to the next. The father of neuropsychology Donald Hebb developed the theory that is now famously summarized as "neurons that fire together wire together" (Hebb, 1949). That is, each time a neuron fires and a second responds, the likelihood that they will fire together increases. So memories are formed by rich patterns of connections between neurons, and change, including healing, means changing those patterns.

But pastoral care involves dimensions of memory far beyond their cellular foundation, and memory is much more than a single capacity. Psychologists have documented as many as 256 types of memory, but our interest here is in three main types: episodic or autobiographical memories, procedural memories, and semantic memory. *Autobiographical memories* include explicit personal incidents or stories, such as Daniel's school years, meeting and marrying his wife, the jolt of his divorce, and his anxious response to the cultural exercise; they are records of events in which he participated and they give his life meaning and shape. *Procedural memories* encompass the skills and habits developed over time—how we ride bicycles, play the piano, or make the sign of the cross. As they are learned, procedural memories generally become automatic and enable us to carry out tasks without the level of attention required when we first learn them. We'll consider procedural memories more specifically when we consider religious rituals. A third type, *semantic memory*, includes knowledge of facts about ourselves and the world; semantic memories do not require that we associate them with a particular event, such as when we learned them. Each of these memory systems appears to rely on different brain circuits. Daniel certainly relied on all three types of memory to manage his life and work, but our first interest here is in autobiographical memory—the events that he recalls as well as those he has forgotten.

Memory is selective; the human brain is simply not capable of recording every detail of every event in our lives, nor is it able to recall every event. Instead, our brains record only details of importance to us when we are experiencing the event. And this "decision" can happen either consciously (those details we attend to) or unconsciously and automatically. Some decades ago neurosurgeon Wilder Penfield mapped the brain during surgeries which required that his patients be awake. Probing particular areas of the brain appeared to elicit memories of very distant events, often from childhood, which included vivid details the patients never recalled before. He concluded that our brains remember every event we have experienced, complete with details. More recent research has reversed that conviction (at least in part because many of these stories changed over time and there was often no way to confirm them—they appear to have been stories constructed to explain random memory traces). It is clear now that we do, in fact, forget. Sometimes the memory loss is permanent, but other times those memories can eventually be recalled. The beating of Daniel's classmate was likely both traumatic and too far from the image he had of himself as a responsible and compassionate human being. Such episodes may be lost because we consciously choose not to think of them or remember them, or they may disappear apparently of their own accord.

If forgetting shapes the stories we author about our lives, recalling or learning of missing events reshapes them. Daniel's recall of that beating, imperfect as it may have been, reframed the story of his life. Reclaiming that event as part of his own story, Daniel rethinks his past and its impact on his current life; along with the shame of having failed to intervene on his classmate's behalf, he was able at the same time to recognize his own powerlessness and fear, as well as the particular systemic cultural demands of that time in history. Eventually he may have been able both to judge his failure and accept a degree of grace and forgiveness as he and his counselor explored the very real physical and emotional constraints he was under at the time. His image of himself and his world changed: he was not the tolerant, accepting person he had always imagined. But at last his panic attacks made new sense to him and new future possibilities opened.

The implications of these findings are critical to the ways we provide care for others. Remembering that each time a sufferer tells the story of a loss, an abuse, or a joy, he or she reconstructs the memory of the earlier event in the present; the past is made new again and open to new telling. The broad outlines of what happened may not appear to change, but the added detail, the altered perspective that comes from sharing the story in the presence of a new listener, the subtle shift in emotional tone that unfolds today, provide ample opportunity for new insight, new perspective, indeed for a new story. In their retelling, stories become open, shifting our relationships to the past and imagining a more hopeful future. We cannot change what happened, but our stories about them can change. And in that transformation, we change. (For a fuller description, see Neuger, 2001.)

## Thinking and Feeling

Daniel sought help for his unexplained panic attacks. He reported many important events in his life, but at first he spoke very little about the emotional responses these stories triggered. He considered himself a logical man, but he gradually recognized that rational thought could only take him so far: he wasn't able to "talk himself out of how he felt." He also discovered that he had a very limited vocabulary when he talked about the emotional dimensions of his life. In fact, much of the neuroscience research adopted by helping professions in the past focused on articulating and correcting conscious thoughts. Such an emphasis reflects psychotherapeutic emphases on cognitive and behavioral approaches to treatment. But more recently the role of feeling has re-emerged as a central dimension of human experience in many disciplines, including pastoral care and counseling.

Feelings, emotions, or affects may be both conscious and unconscious, depending on the definitions put forth by particular scholars (see, e.g., Damasio,

1994, 1999 and Panksepp, 2012). Humans share these emotional processes with most other species, and feelings often function more powerfully than do the logical processes on which human beings pride themselves. Recent research highlights the emotional drives that propel human relationships—the loves, fears, desires, and hates that emerge before we find reasons for them or even names for them. Biblical writers recognized how hidden our motives can be and commonly attributed human desires to the heart. "The heart is devious above all else; it is perverse—who can understand it? I the Lord test the mind and search the heart, to give to all according to their ways, according to the fruit of their doings" (Jeremiah 17:9–10).

One important source of insight into the relationship between reason and emotion comes from studies of children before they develop the capacity for language. During the critical first 18 months of life infants and toddlers begin to integrate emotional processes with rational assessments. This capacity is deeply rooted in strong attachments to parents and other caregivers, and dramatically affects the ways the maturing child's brain structures itself (Schore, 1994, 2012; Siegel, 2015). (Much of the interaction between adults and infants relies on touch, sight, and tone rather than on language.) The brains of children who are "securely attached," that is, they have strong emotional ties to a sensitive, responsive caregiver, demonstrated marked brain differences from children who receive less nurturing, or especially neglectful or abusive, relationships. Securely attached children demonstrate stronger neural connections between the prefrontal cortex (a structure that enables judgment and reason, located behind the eyes) and the emotional limbic system below the brain's outer cortex. Effective parenting actually shapes brains that form deeper connections between thought and feeling. Psychologists refer to this process as "affect regulation," though the process involves more richly the child's maturing capacities for self-understanding, direction, and relational connections later in life.

These processes underscore the deeply relational dimensions of being human, embedded in a matrix of others, a living human web. We do not develop as whole human beings outside of our relationships, nor do we cease needing them as we grow older. We are shaped in the inner recesses of our brains and bodies by the relationships we inhabit, for better and for ill, through-out life. Christian theologians will recognize in this claim echoes of our under-standings of God whose inter-relational nature is represented in the Trinity; the imago dei proclaims along with John Donne that none of us "is an island … entire unto itself." We are, in fact, pieces "of the continent, A part of the main." Attempts to live unto ourselves are vulnerable to a withering isolation, empti-ness, and the potential for damage to others. Since Westerners live in a culture that valorizes self-sufficiency, personal success, and mastery, effective pastoral care reclaims the church's imperative to resist the "principalities and powers of this world" that blind us to the needs of the "last and the least," and instead open room for vulnerability and care for the other.

Neuroscientific research adds to many voices insisting that the horizons of pastoral care and counseling extend far beyond the parish or counseling office. Revelations about the "social brain" have implications well beyond intimate relationships with family and close friends, with parishioners and clients. Children's brains are profoundly shaped by family and community with consequences that last a lifetime. Poverty, violence, and the absence of parents through mass incarceration lead to well-documented damage to children's lives and futures. Contemporary pastoral care echoes and extends John Wesley's famous claim that "the world is my parish" so that Daniel's wellbeing is neither his nor his counselor's only concern: the unknown lives of those like his classmate matter as fully.

Daniel's family had been a "normal" family; he would have called his life happy, though he didn't recall particular warmth from his parents or sister. His parents were encouraging; at times though he feared that he disappointed them, especially in comparison to his sister's achievements. As his work continued with his counselor, in contrast, he felt understood in ways he never had before. As his sense of trust grew, he allowed long-ignored feelings to emerge, to find words for them and eventually to act on them in ways that moved toward more honesty and vulnerability in his relationships with others. In part, these changes were due to the attentive caring of the counselor, which re-activated emotional responses from the past and provided a safe relationship in which to welcome and process them. Pastoral counseling relationships do not generally carry the emotional intensity of parent–infant interactions. But persons seeking pastoral care and counseling are often in emotionally fraught experiences, struggling to hold thought and feeling together, desperate to make sense of life's crises. Attentive relationships of care, embodied in deep neurological changes, offer possibilities for wholeness of self through connection with others. Reclaiming the prominence of emotion in human experience compels us to find and construct social settings and practices that embrace our emotional lives as central to human flourishing. For reason has not been eliminated—it is only being dethroned.

## Empathy

Daniel's pastoral counselor attended carefully to his language and the outline of his autobiographical memories. She noted gaps and occasional contradictions within the story and maintained a respectful curiosity as he struggled to put the pieces together. Her ability to engage him in this process of self-discovery required the capacity to enter that story with him, listening with careful empathy.

The neurosciences have demonstrated that our brains are "built" to empathize, that understanding the experiences of others involves natural practices of the healthy human brain. Even young infants are capable of "catching" the emotional distress of other children in a process known as emotional contagion. As children grow in trustworthy relationships with caregivers they gradually develop the capacity to understand their own emotional responses and detect and respond to the emotional states of others. Experiences of abuse, loss, or neglect, on the other hand, can inhibit or distort a child's developing brain's natural ability to comprehend the experience of another with little distortion.

Daniel's story highlights a contribution of the brain sciences to our understanding of the relationship between social location (gender, race, and class) and personal experience. His story, both in childhood and adulthood, reflects a traditionally middle class Caucasian context. The context of his classmates of color in a "changing neighborhood" may have been less financially secure and likely much more marginalized within broader cultural frames. Socio-economic status has long been associated with poorer health, less access to health care, and higher mortality rates (Costandi, 2016, p. 130). Costandi further notes that children from underprivileged backgrounds have less gray matter in the hippocampus (involved with memory) and demonstrate changes in activity in the amygdala and prefrontal cortex, which are involved in attention and emotional regulation. He concludes that "growing up in poverty has severe and persistent effects on brain development that can affect both mental and physical health in adulthood." So Daniel's context included structural dimensions that complicated his own ability to empathize with his classmates of color, both enabling them and distorting them. We will describe below the ways in which racial differences in themselves make empathic connections more difficult, but first we sketch our newer understandings of empathy itself.

In healthy development and rich interpersonal environments, as distinct from abusive or neglectful contexts, children demonstrate an increasing capacity to recognize first that others have thoughts and feelings as they do, and then later to speculate about what those contents might be—what cognitive scientists call "theory of mind." One insight into how human brains develop this capacity arose from the discovery of mirror neurons in the 1990s. First detected in macaque monkeys and then confirmed in humans, approximately one-third of the motor neurons that would be involved in initiating and planning a particular movement become active when subjects are watching the movement performed by someone else. The mirror neuron system is active when viewing faces for emotional content too, suggesting that the developing human brain unconsciously "rehearses" a facial expression and then "reads out" how the brain's own body responds affectively. It is a rapid, automatic process by which the brain mimics an expression and says, in essence, "if my face looked like that, this is what I would be feeling." Fortunately this process generally functions without prompting and enables human interaction and understanding in most of our day-to-day encounters. Further confirmation of this process appeared in studies that noted diminished mirror neuron systems in the brains of autistic children; other studies also discovered that patients with damage to the regions of the brain that monitor the body's own internal world (somatosensory) were unable to determine accurately the feeling states of faces of others (for a fuller treatment, see Hogue, 2010). We feel within our own bodies before we imagine what others are feeling.

Key to healthy development of the human brain and to the ability to engage in intimate relationships later in life is the presence of a consistent nurturing presence in the young child's life during the critical window of early brain development. There is, however, evidence that even persons who did not experience such relationships can, over time, repair both the psychological and neurological deficits of earlier years. This takes place most auspiciously within consistent, dependable relationships of care, enabling persons to develop a "learned attachment" and enter more fully into satisfying relationships (Schore, 1994). Daniel likely experienced such a relationship with his pastoral counselor, though broadening and enriching his relationships with others in his life will provide opportunities for healing beyond that professional relationship.

Relationship needs, of course, are critical not only for persons who have suffered neglect or abuse early in life. Healthy human beings need and seek relationships of care, particularly at times of stress or turmoil. The research noted here suggests that throughout life our brains are being reshaped by our experiences, particularly by our intimate social relationships. Such data underscore the imperative for pastoral caregivers to attend to and nurture relationships of care and trust within congregations, couples, families, and friendships, as well as tending to the relationships each develops with parishioners and clients. In processes that echo those early relationships of intimate care, empathic pastoral relationships serve as "containers" and integrators of sufferers' thoughts and feelings.

Empathic engagement was a critical capacity for Daniel's counselor: without entering into his emotional world she would have been unable to form the kind of connections with him that would provide a safe place for the deep exploration that his panic attacks called for. We don't know much about the quality of Daniel's relationship with his parents or caregivers in childhood, but he had few, if any, intimate relationships now. His relationship with the counselor likely provided hints about what deeper emotional connections can feel like; that relationship may also have motivated some of his reaching out to others. It became apparent as well, though, that Daniel's capacity for empathy with others had faced some roadblocks.

## Engaging Race

In conversations with his pastoral counselor, Daniel encountered his own conflicted feelings about race. Startled when he recalled the trauma of his classmate's beating, he was brought face to face with his own implicit bias. He saw himself as unbiased, and may have even claimed not to "see color." Now he felt shame.

Here again recent neuroscientific research deepens our understanding of his experiences. Psychologists have long noticed marked discrepancies between subjects' self-report of racial bias and their responses on implicit measures of bias. Most participants, regardless of race, tend to associate negatively charged words and guns with black faces, and positively charged words and tools with white faces (Bartholow and Henry, 2010, p. 872). These associations are confirmed by functional magnetic resonance imaging (fMRI) tests, which detect a trigger of the brain's alarm system when exposed to African American faces, even among subjects who report having no bias and who normally respond in culturally sensitive ways. That's the bad news.

But there is also good news. Researchers at the University of Missouri detected an automatic, unconscious "Response Conflict" system in the brain that registers when subjects experience an implicit values conflict (Bartholow and Henry, 2010). People who consciously rejected overt forms of racism had apparently developed new neural connections that override the initial bias even before subjects become aware of it. Racial typing, they conclude, is quite difficult to unlearn, but the brain can develop mechanisms to reverse, if not eradicate, racist responses. Human bodies and brains interact in shaping interpersonal and intercultural relationships, but the brain's ability to change (a process known as neuroplasticity), with new experiences, serves as a powerful ally in struggles against racism.

Empathy turns out to apply most effectively to one's own cultural group; neurobiologically and cognitively, our capacities for empathy drop off significantly the higher the degree of racial or cultural difference that we encounter in other persons. The positive outcomes of empathy for members of one's own group are counterbalanced by hostility toward those outside the group (Chiao et al., 2008). A small body of neuroscientific research is exploring distinctive brain "signatures" that appear when viewing persons of one's own race or culture, and brain structures activated when viewing persons of a different cultural group. This literature provides an intriguing glimpse into the ways our religious and life practices may shape interracial relationships. Two particular research threads will illustrate: perceptions of individual facial differences in other racial groups and the brain's management of internal conflict between personal values and racial associations (for a fuller treatment, see Hogue, 2015).

The human brain is particularly attuned to the human face. Two structures within the visual processing areas of the brain (the fusiform gyrus and the posterior cingulate cortex) play an important role in detecting and responding to other faces (Ito and Bartholow, 2009, p. 524). These structures are more active when individuals perceive racial characteristics like their own than when they perceive racial characteristics that differ. We tend to be much better at distinguishing faces within our own racial group than within other racial groups. We don't start out that way, but our capacity to distinguish other-race faces diminishes early in life. Three-month-old Western European children, for instance, were able to distinguish faces in four racial groups, but nine-month-olds could only recognize faces in their own cultural group (Kelly et al., 2007). Rather than an innate racial bias, however, this narrowing of focus appears to be a function of the racial groups to which children are exposed. That is, children adopted from other racial groups developed the capacity to distinguish faces in their adoptive parents' culture (Sangrigoli and De Schonen, 2004). Young children exposed to other racial groups do not experience this loss of ability to distinguish faces in the groups they have encountered, and the effect in children who have known only one racial group can be reversed with later exposure to other racial groups. Race becomes a more determining factor in interpersonal relationships when there is little or no previous experience with that cultural group.

The recognition that racial associations become deeply embedded in our brains, and are difficult to change, provides a measure of grace. This may open Daniel, and people like him, to respect the power of race in shaping our relationships and to consider more honestly their own implicit biases. At the same time they suggest a partial remedy: our personal and religious practices can also reshape our brains to interrupt, if not completely eradicate, those associations. We can deepen those brain changes through respectful, curious encounters with persons of other races. While the racial changes in Daniel's neighborhood during his childhood and adolescence gave him opportunity for regular encounters with persons of color, by his own admission there was very little opportunity for students of different racial groups to know each other. So Daniel's attempt to locate his former classmate, his decision to reflect more honestly on his own reactions and participate in his church's shared ministry with an African American congregation, his attending more closely to black colleagues, all represent concrete practices that can change his mind from the inside out. And Daniel's resolve serves as a reminder to pastoral leaders about the critical need for cross-racial dialogue and shared community ventures that build relationships, break down racial barriers, and address systems of injustice that victimize and marginalize.

### Religious Practices and Living in Community

Many practices of pastoral care occur within personal, one-to-one relationships with caregivers like Daniel's counselor. But our religious communities provide even larger, more variegated networks for relationship and for religious practices that can deepen the integration of thought and feeling, of self and other. Practices of worship, prayer and meditation, education, fellowship, and service broaden the horizons of our connectedness with others, and, for many, with God. Heart, mind, and body may reclaim their unity in the presence of others, gathered to worship One who embraces all, transcending the threatened loneliness of existence.

Daniel attended worship regularly, though he reported few close relationships there, and he described his experience in recent years as "going through the motions." He wasn't exactly sure why he continued to go—force of habit, he suspected, or simply familiarity. But there was also some unnamed draw that got him out of bed on Sunday mornings. As he reflected more carefully with his counselor, it occurred to him that simply sitting quietly in the presence of others, in contrast to so much of his time alone, gave him a vague sense of connectedness in spite of the lack of deep personal contact. Singing familiar hymns grounded him. He would also find himself in prayer, which he seldom did by himself, but which he recalled having done frequently in his youth and early adulthood.

An old adage proclaimed that "prayer changes things," and the neurosciences are documenting that, at the very least, prayer changes our brains. One of the most studied relationships between practice and brain changes involves meditation (Siegel, 2007; Newberg and Waldman, 2009; Bingaman, 2014). One reason for the volume of research on meditation is its accessibility: since meditation is generally practiced in place, rather than moving around, meditators can practice within the restricted confines of fMRI machines. Experienced meditators, from both Eastern and Western (Christian) traditions, demonstrate significant brain differences from non-meditators, and mindfulness training programs of even a few months produce measurable brain shifts. Such practices are labeled "top-down" approaches because they begin with conscious thought and intention, such as in contemplation, and over time, regularly practiced, they reshape brain and body.

Yet there is also increasing evidence that behavior and physical movements shape our brains as effectively as do thoughts, working from the "bottom-up" from body to mind (Hogue, 2003; Roozeboom, 2016). Our ritual practices, particularly those that involve physical gestures and movement, rely on what memory researchers call procedural memory—learning how to do things. We first learn these practices intentionally and with effort, much like a musician learning scales and exercises through careful repetition. Over time they become automatic and we look beyond the movements to their message, to the realities they both reveal and create. Effortful scales and chord progressions are transformed into beautiful sonatas or soulful jazz improvisations; ancient prayer formulas reverently memorized open us to transcendent truths and ground us in a great "cloud of witnesses." These constitute our experiences of transcendence and spiritual formation (d'Aquili and Newberg, 1999). In worship, what we do, even more than what we say or think, changes us. Standing and sitting, making the sign of the cross, passing the peace—all of these practiced movements shape our spiritual, emotional selves and join us to our fellow worshipers.

As pastors and practical theologians grapple with the unconscious and feeling dimensions of living, we are confronted with the limits of human logic. Instead of helping suffering persons think differently about their circumstances, we are better served by helping them develop regular practices that serve to form and re-form themselves and their communities. Boston University neuroscientist Patrick McNamara notes that religious experiences open possibilities for personal and spiritual transformation:

> ... the circuit which mediates religiousness ... appears to regulate or control many other areas of the brain. Therefore when we undergo religious experiences and engage this circuit the circuit in turn is sending messages to these other widespread areas of the brain thus making substantial behavioral and cognitive changes more likely. (McNamara, 2015, p. 133)

While the depth and durability of such changes remain to be studied further, it seems clear that our religious and social practices have dynamic interactions with our brains that are not yet fully understood or tapped.

In our ritual practices our stories, our feelings, and our connections with others are embodied and reunited. Practical theologian James K. A. Smith describes the futility of focusing merely on the cognitive worldviews (i.e. semantic and autobiographical memories) of those we serve—instead we should attend more carefully to what they desire, what they love. He recognizes the critical role of ritual (liturgical) processes, both secular and sacred, and the ways in which they shape the "desires of our hearts." "That's the kind of animals we are, first and foremost: loving, desiring, affective, liturgical animals who, for the most part, don't inhabit the world as thinkers or cognitive machines ... we worship before we know—or rather, we *worship in order to* know" (Smith, 2009, p. 34).

## Embodying Pastoral Theology

In this era, we cannot overlook the impact neuroscientific findings are having on parishioners, our clients, on other clergy, and on the public at large. To be sure, we must avoid the dangers of reductionism and extrapolating too far, especially from neuroscientific claims made in the popular press. But we can detect several themes arising from these discoveries that confirm and challenge our assumptions about the human condition, our theological anthropologies, our understanding of the imago dei.

First, they underscore the physicality of emotional and religious experiences. Mind and soul cannot be separated from our bodies, emphasizing the unity of human personhood. Contemporary Christian theology challenges the strict dualisms of soul and body that were shaped by the Greek philosophical traditions which Paul incorporated in early theological formulations. Our minds and souls are not disembodied selves, held prisoner in sinful bodies: we are created as mind–soul–body unities. Rather than a spirit that ascends to heaven at the time of death, Christian hope lies in the Resurrection of the body, firmly connecting body and soul. This conviction calls for a revaluing of the body rather than its neglect or even denigration as the "seat of all sinful passions." Our bodies are to be respected and cared for, not tamed, abused, or neglected. This reminder that our bodies are "temples of the Holy Spirit" (I Corinthians 6:19) prompts religious leaders to faithful forms of self-care as well as attending to the health of those for whom they provide care.

Second, these findings illuminate the power of unconscious, affective, and even addictive behaviors and strategies that all humans employ and require. "For I do not do the good I want, but the evil I do not want is what I do. Now if I do what I do not want, it is no longer I that do it, but sin that dwells within me" (Romans 7:19–20). Far from being the "captains of our own souls" or the "masters of our own fates," we are reminded of the powerful forces of creation that direct our lives in unseen ways. Such recognition can breed despair or denial of responsibility for our own actions. But more faithfully, such recognition informs our understanding of human sin, of the fallibility of reason and will, and humbles our pretensions of self-control. "In the long run, in the house of the brain and memory, we are still only partially the master" (Markowitsch and Welzer, 2010, p. 110).

We are enculturated to distrust and even demonize emotions for their "unruliness." Yet neither head nor heart alone can be blamed for the distorted images of ourselves and our relationships that separate us from ourselves and each other. Either can mislead us. Such discoveries should call us to humility about our judgments and our claims to truth. They also remind us that reason and feeling, interwoven within the inner recesses of our brains, work most wholesomely in concert. Without joy and sorrow, reason becomes unreasonable; without reason, emotion is misguided. And we cannot create this integrated self alone.

Because, third, these findings remind us that we are not alone, that we cannot live in any sense fully unto ourselves. We require each other; each is indeed "flesh of my flesh and bone of my bone." The "social brain" is formed in relationships, nurtured in relationships, and healed in the context of relationships. Families, friendships, and faith communities are essential contexts to the nurturing of children, the formation of youth, and the sustaining of adults throughout the lifespan. Practical theologians who have advocated particularly for children (Couture, 2000; Miller-McLemore, 2003; Mercer, 2005) will find further support for the necessity of sustained, dependable networks of care.

Finally, understanding brain function can assist parishioners and clients in participating in their own healing. Such knowledge is never a substitute for empathic pastoral and congregational relationships that have significant potential to reshape troubled lives; nor is it always a necessary dimension of pastoral conversations. But where such interpretation can underscore the reality of embodied change in emotional and spiritual healing, neuroscientific insights add depth to self-understanding, to changes of the heart, and to comprehension of our shared physical and biological similarities to the rest of creation.

These discoveries then offer this picture of the imago dei, however imperfectly its traces echo in any one of us: we are inveterate storytellers, creating narrative worlds and living in them; we are passionate feelers, filled with fears, desires, longings, and hope; we are seekers of relationship, longing for connection and belonging, profoundly shaped by the presence and absence of others; and we are in fact creatures of habit, formed and transformed by the practiced, embodied rituals of our lives.

## Looking Forward

Much of the neuroscience research directly relevant to relationships of care has focused on dyadic relationships: between parent and child, pastoral therapist and client, pastor and parishioner, partners. Research is emerging about the impact of social media on human relationships that deserve pastoral attention. But more importantly, what remains to be addressed are the ways brains are shaped by the broader cultural, gendered social networks that constitute the "living human web." How do the in-group/outgroup constraints on empathy play out in our religious communities? What remedies might there be for the growing outbreaks of racist, sexist, heterosexist rhetoric in the US and elsewhere? What hope can be found for the flourishing of human beings in an increasingly polarized world? That is, in what ways can the neurosciences engage the critical questions being raised elsewhere in this volume? Science and theology speak different languages, but the dialogue provides a critical voice.

Pastoral theologian Emanuel Lartey notes the claim by anthropologists Kluckholn and Murray that "[e]very human person is in certain respects: 1) like all others; 2) like some others; and 3) like no other" (Lartey, 2003, p. 34). The neurosciences focus primarily on shared human (biological) realities, the ways in which all human beings are alike. It must also be remembered, though, that culture, gender, race, and class also shape human brains, as does individual experience. There is not space in this single chapter to develop the ways in which such powerful forces interact with human brains, but we must avoid overstating our similarities at the expense of the rich diverseness of human experience that our adaptive brains make possible.

The costly procedures and advanced knowledge to do neuroscientific work of value to these questions lies beyond the scope of any current religious organization or movement. Most of the resources that support such research come from large government projects such as the National Institutes of Health and of Mental Health and presidential task forces, or from large medical and pharmaceutical companies seeking to provide treatments for specific neurological concerns or answer questions of scientific interest. We have little role in shaping the direction of the research itself. But we do have a responsibility to attend to the issues being raised, the questions being asked, and the implications being drawn from this massive and growing body of scientific research. The neurosciences have yet to solve many of the larger questions we face, such as polarization, racism, militarization, and violence, and they may never do so, though writers like d'Aquili and Newberg (1999) suggest they could. But they do provide important evidence of the critical need for families and communities that nurture children, strengthen human relationships, care for the ill and the aging, and help build beloved communities. They underscore our common humanity (including the limits of empathy) in ways that could help bridge racial, sexual, and cultural divides. Pastoral leaders and practical theologians need at least basic knowledge of the human brain, its role in illness and suffering as well as healing, and the implications of this critical work for understanding the destructive power as well as the creative forces present in the evolving human brain and in our world. Constantly we are being bombarded with new insights into an ages-old question: what is humanity that God is mindful of us?

## References

Ashbrook, James. 1995. *Minding the Soul: Pastoral Counseling as Remembering.* Minneapolis, MN: Fortress Press.

Ashbrook, James and Carol Albright. 1997. *The Humanizing Brain: Where Religion and Neuroscience Meet.* Cleveland, OH: Pilgrim Press.

Bartholow, Bruce and Erika Henry. 2010. "Response Conflict and Affective Responses in the Control and Expression of Race Bias." *Social and Personality Psychology.* Volume 4, Issue 10, 871–888. DOI:10.1111/j.1751-9004.2010.00299.x.

Beauregard, Mario and Denyse O'Leary. 2007. *The Spiritual Brain: A Neuroscientist's Case for the Existence of the Soul.* New York: HarperOne.

Bingaman, Kirk. 2014. *The Power of Neuroplasticity for Pastoral and Spiritual Care.* New York: Lexington Books.

Chiao, Joan, Tetsuya Iidaka, Heather Gordon, Junpei Nogawa, Moshe Bar, Elissa Aminoff, Norihiro Sadato, and Nalini Ambady. 2008. "Cultural Specificity in Amygdala Response to Fear Faces." *Journal of Cognitive Neuroscience.* Volume 20, Issue 12, 2167–2174.

Costandi, Moheb. 2016. *Neuroplasticity.* Cambridge, MA: MIT Press.

Couture, Pamela. 2000. *Seeing Children Seeing God: A Practical Theology of Children and Poverty.* Nashville, TN: Abingdon Press.

Damasio, Antonio R. 1994. *Descartes' Error: Emotion, Reason, and the Human Brain.* New York: G. P. Putnam's Sons.

Damasio, Antonio R. 1999. *The Feeling of What Happens: Body and Emotion in the Making of Consciousness.* New York: Harcourt Brace & Co.

d'Aquili, Eugene and Andrew Newberg. 1999. *The Mystical Mind: Probing the Biology of Religious Experience*. Minneapolis, MN: Fortress Press.

Hebb, Donald. 1949. *The Organization of Behavior: A Neuropsychological Theory*. New York: Wiley & Sons.

Hogue, David. 2003. *Remembering the Future, Imagining the Past: Story, Ritual and the Human Brain*. Cleveland, OH: Pilgrim Press.

Hogue, David. 2010. "Brain Matters: Neuroscience, Pastoral Theology and Empathy." *Journal of Pastoral Theology*. Volume 20, 25–55.

Hogue, David. 2015. "Imaging the Other: Neuroscientific Insights into Human Experiences of Culture and Race." In *Complex Identities in a Shifting World: Practical Theological Perspectives*, edited by Pamela Couture, Robert Mager, Pamela McCarroll, and Natalie Wigg-Stevenson. Zürich: Lit Verlag.

Hogue, David. 2017. "Because We Are: Practical Theology, Intersubjectivity and the Human Brain." In *Practicing Ubuntu: Practical Theological Perspectives on Injustice, Personhood and Human Dignity*, edited by Olehile A. Buffel, Jaco Dreyer, Yolanda Dreyer and Malan Nel. International Academy of Practical Theology. Zürich: Lit Verlag.

Ito, T. and Bruce Bartholow. 2009. "The Neural Correlates of Race." *Trends in Cognitive Sciences*. Volume 13, Issue 12, 524–531. DOI:10.1016/j.tics.2009.10.002.

Jeeves, Malcolm. 2013. *Minds, Brains, Souls and Gods: A Conversation on Faith, Psychology and Neuroscience*. Downers Grove, IL: IVP Academic.

Jeeves, Malcolm and Warren Brown. 2009. *Neuroscience, Psychology, and Religion: Illusions, Delusions, and Realities about Human Nature*. Templeton Science and Religion Series. West Conshohocken, PA: Templeton Press.

Kandel, Eric. 2006. *In Search of Memory: The Emergence of a New Science of Mind*. New York: W.W. Norton.

Kelly, David, Paul Quinn, Alan Slater, Lee Kang, Ge Liezhong, and Olivier Pascalis. 2007. "The Other-Race Effect Develops During Infancy: Evidence of Perceptual Narrowing." *Psychological Science*. Volume 18, Issue 12, 1084–1089. DOI:10.1111/j.1467-9280.2007.02029.x.

Lartey, Emmanuel. 2003. *In Living Color: An Intercultural Approach to Pastoral Care and Counseling*, 2nd revised edn. London: Jessica Kingsley.

Markowitsch, Hans J. and Harald Welzer. 2010. *The Development of Autobiographical Memory*. New York: Psychology Press.

McNamara, Patrick. 2009. *The Neuroscience of Religious Experience*. New York: Cambridge University Press.

McNamara, Patrick. 2015. "Neuroscience Can Contribute to Pastoral Care and Counseling." *Sacred Spaces*. Volume 7. American Association of Pastoral Counselors.

Mercer, Joyce. 2005. *Welcoming Children: A Practical Theology of Childhood*. St. Louis, MO: Chalice Press.

Miller-McLemore, Bonnie. 2003. *Let the Children Come: Reimagining Childhood from a Christian Perspective*. San Francisco, CA: Jossey-Bass.

Neuger, Christie. 2001. *Counseling Women: A Narrative, Pastoral Approach.* Minneapolis, MN: Fortress Press.

Newberg, Andrew and Waldman, Mark. 2009. *How God Changes Your Brain: Breakthrough Findings from a Leading Neuroscientist.* New York: Ballantine Books.

Panksepp, Jaak. 2012. *The Archeology of Mind: Neuroevolutionary Origins of Human Emotions.* New York: W.W. Norton.

Roozeboom, William. 2016. *Neuroplasticity, Performativity, and Clergy Wellness: Neighbor Love as Self-Care.* New York: Lexington Books.

Sangrigoli, Sandy and Scania De Schonen. 2004. "Recognition of Own-Race and Other-Race Faces by Three-Month-Old Infants." *Journal of Child Psychology and Psychiatry.* Volume 45, Issue 7, 1219–1227. DOI:10.1111/j.1467-9280.2007.02029.x.

Schacter, Daniel. 1997. *Searching for Memory: The Brain, the Mind, and the Past.* New York: Basic Books.

Schore, Allan. N. 1994. *Affect Regulation and the Origin of the Self: The Neurobiology of Emotional Development.* Hillsdale, NJ: Lawrence Erlbaum Associates.

Schore, Allan. N. 2012. *The Science of the Art of Psychotherapy.* New York: W.W. Norton.

Siegel, Daniel J.. 2007. *The Mindful Brain: Reflection and Attunement in the Cultivation of Well-Being.* New York: W.W. Norton.

Siegel, Daniel J. 2015. *The Developing Mind: How Relationships and the Brain Interact to Shape Who We Are*, 2nd edn. New York: The Guildford Press.

Smith, James. 2009. *Desiring the Kingdom: Worship, Worldview, and Cultural Formation.* Grand Rapids, MI: Baker Academic.

Whitehead, Jason. 2015. *Redeeming Fear: A Constructive Theology for Living into Hope.* Minneapolis, MN: Fortress Press.

3

# Class Power and Human Suffering

Resisting the Idolatry of the Market in Pastoral Theology and Care

*Bruce Rogers-Vaughn*

## Introduction and Literature Review

This chapter focuses on class, not because it assumes oppressions rooted in class take priority over other forms of suffering, but because class has been neglected, especially since the "neoliberal turn" in capitalism that has emerged since the 1980s. This means that thinking about class has never been more important than today, nor more likely to be misunderstood. In contemporary discourse, the word "class" conjures up notions regarding socio-economic status, education level, social prestige, and cultural distinction. These associations are obscure and misleading. They distract us from the power differentials this term signifies. Class is not a neutral or descriptive expression. Rather, it names a form of oppression intrinsic to capitalism, in which dominant elites use their economic, political, and cultural power to subjugate and stigmatize people who do not possess such power. The purpose of this dominance is the generation of wealth and maintenance of control for those at the top of the class hierarchy. The term also refers to the resistance arising from those who endure this oppression. When I assert that class has been neglected, therefore, I am talking about the moral significance of class antagonism.

However, the dramatic rise in economic inequality that accompanies global neoliberalization has rekindled attention to class. This is reflected in pastoral and practical theology, as these fields have reoriented themselves to matters of public concern. Nevertheless, the manner in which we attend to class has been imprecise, ambivalent, and bifurcated. Only within the past five years have pastoral and practical theologians begun to undertake a thoroughgoing analysis of class. Here I review how class has appeared in the literature during the past three decades, attending to its imprecision and divided approach, and identify the new trajectory. In succeeding sections I indicate the directions this might take.

*Pastoral Theology and Care: Critical Trajectories in Theory and Practice,*
First Edition. Edited by Nancy J. Ramsay.
© 2018 John Wiley & Sons Ltd. Published 2018 by John Wiley & Sons Ltd.

Before proceeding, I must identify my own social location and personal sources of interest in this subject. I am a white, heterosexual male, a Protestant minister who grew up in the Free Church tradition (Baptist) in the Deep South (USA). I was fortunate to receive an advanced education, and have enjoyed a long career as a professional pastoral counselor and as a teacher in a theological school located within an elite private university. All of this adds up to substantial privilege. I have lived my life in overlapping systems that generally favor people like myself, at the expense of women, people of color, those who identify as gay, lesbian, bisexual, transgender, queer, and intersex (GLBTQI), religious minorities, and other marginalized populations. Simultaneously, there have been countercurrents in my experience that set me against myself. First, I grew up in southern Appalachia, in a working class family and poverty-stricken communities. I come from a long line of union activists, sustenance farmers, and manual laborers. I am the first person in my extended family to graduate from college, much less earn a doctoral degree. Working in the academy, I am acutely aware of the "imposter syndrome" that many academics from the working class have described (Ryan and Sackrey, 1996). Second, I was born physically disabled. I was severely "club-footed" in both feet, a condition that took years to correct. Prior to late adolescence, I frequently endured bullying due to my inability to participate in the physical activities that were so highly valued in my culture, especially for boys. Even though this disability is no longer visible to others, I continue to navigate its complications. Finally, I am a descendant of lower class European immigrants who settled in Appalachia. Many of these intermarried with Native Americans. There are several members of the Cherokee Nation in my direct lineage. As I grew up, I frequently heard stories about our "Cherokee roots," and sympathetic references to how Native Americans had been treated. These narratives made a deep impression upon me, as they were incongruent with the patriotic rhetoric that otherwise surrounded me. Today they open my heart to decoloniality and postcolonial theory, and to seeing neoliberalization for what it is—a global neocolonial process. Although they do not reduce my privilege, these countercurrents have sensitized me to asymmetries of power in society and the world, and how these power differentials impact the wellbeing of communities, relationships, and individual subjectivity. So, as I enter the seventh decade of life, I find these concerns at the focus of my research and writing. By the time our discipline shifted in the direction of public theology, I was predisposed to embrace it.

The move toward public theology began in the 1980s and 1990s. Charles Gerkin's book, *Widening the Horizons* (1986), broadened the scope of pastoral theology to include the social context of suffering. Within practical theology this move has come to its most developed articulation in the work of Elaine Graham (1996, 2013). Today virtually all progressive pastoral and practical theologians operate within this paradigm. However, public theology did not just appear in the last three decades. During the Industrial Revolution, pastoral theologians were engrossed with interpreting the social injustices of their time, including class exploitation, through a theological prism known as the "Social Gospel." Today's public theology is in alignment with that movement, but set now in the context of financial capitalism rather than industrial capitalism.

Following the Gilded Age, class vanished from pastoral discourse, and did not reappear until the revival of public theology. In the dominant approach, however, class is often named, but rarely theorized. Wendy Brown (1995), observing that liberals in the academy have largely accepted capitalism, raises this concern: "Could we have stumbled upon one reason why class is invariably named but rarely theorized or developed in the multiculturalist mantra, 'race, class, gender, sexuality'?" (p. 61). This holds true for most public pastoral theology. Joyce Ann Mercer (2012) notes that pastoral theologians "name 'race, class, and gender' as categories, but go on to address only race and/or gender in the substance of their work." She concludes: "In each instance, class issues are improperly elided with race and gender, in a move that subsumes and silences class relations within these other identity categories" (p. 433).

I offer two examples of this majority position, both collections of essays by public pastoral theologians. The first is *Pastoral Care and Counseling: Redefining the Paradigms* (Ramsay, 2004). Although there are abundant references to other forms of subjugation, there are only scattered references to class in this volume. One contributor acknowledges: "Class continues to be one of the most neglected perspectives in pastoral theology." She foresees this will change: "Critiques of capitalism and general economic practices, class structures and distribution of wealth and resources" will constitute a future trajectory of the field (Neuger, 2004, pp. 76, 82). Here the issue is identified, but only as a potential. The other volume is *Injustice and the Care of Souls* (Kujawa-Holbrook and Montagno, 2009). It contains 22 essays on oppressions rooted in differences concerning race, gender, religion, age, sexuality, disability, and so on. There are no chapters on class as a form of oppression. Brown's "multiculturalist mantra" appears throughout the volume, but in no instance is class defined or theorized. These two volumes typify the mention of class in public pastoral theology, coupled with a stunning silence about what is being mentioned. Class is concealed rather than revealed.

The argument I put forward in this chapter is that adequate definitions and discourses about class already exist, but pastoral theology has not yet appropriated them. Thus, although she pinpoints the problem, Mercer (2012) does little to remedy it. Noting an "instability of definition," as well as "the absence of a public discourse and vocabulary with which to talk about class differences" (p. 434), she ranges across a number of practical theological works having to do with economic injustice and poverty. The insinuation is that to discuss these matters is to address class. This is simply not the case.

Meanwhile, a handful of pastoral theologians have begun to thoroughly analyze class, an effort that of necessity requires a detailed critique of capitalism.

The first intimations of this appeared in Archie Smith's *The Relational Self* (1982), as well as in the work of Judith Orr (1997), and in James Poling's *Render Unto God* (2002). Each of these pastoral theologians identifies capitalism as a system of exploitation. Poling's book, which includes a historical overview of capitalism, represents a pivot to a new trajectory concerning class in public pastoral theology. However, like Smith and Orr, he does not attempt an analysis of class.

In 2008, the speculative bubble built upon housing debt burst, initiating a global financial crisis. In response, scholars representing many disciplines have intensified their critical assessments of neoliberal capitalism, including its iterations of class. Subsequently, in the US, at least four pastoral theologians have extended the work begun by Smith, Orr, and Poling. Philip Helsel (2015) argues that class is not about socio-economic status, poverty, educational level, or cultural taste. Rather, it is about the flow of power between social classes, or class antagonism. Helsel explores the impact this is having on mental illness and its treatment. Congruent with this understanding of class, Cedric C. Johnson (2016) examines the impact of neoliberalization on African Americans in the US. His book is an analysis of the ongoing entanglement between racism and class struggle. My own work (Rogers-Vaughn, 2014, 2016) analyzes how neoliberalization is transforming human suffering, including class conflict. I argue that current alterations to class struggle call on us to reconsider intersectionality theory and "diversity." Without a thorough understanding of the emerging mutations of class, we are left with versions of identity politics that simply accommodate neoliberalism (2016, pp. 144–161). Ryan LaMothe (2015, 2016) also investigates class as the antagonism between classes, with attention to how this is adversely affecting the subjectivities of both the capitalist and the working classes. In *Care of Souls, Care of Polis* (2017), he contends for a "political pastoral theology" that includes a detailed assessment of how the class dynamics appearing under neoliberal governance are not only characterized by conflict, but *neglect*. This means that neoliberalism both undermines and distorts care. What these four pastoral theologians share is a critical retrieval of Marxist analyses of class. The arc is toward an examination of how class dynamics appear under financial capitalism, as opposed to the industrial capitalism of Marx's time, along with implications for contemporary pastoral practice.

Within the pastoral and practical theological literature, this new trajectory has gained little traction outside the US. I have encountered two exceptions. One is the UK. In *Pastoral Care and Liberation Theology* (1994), practical theologian Stephen Pattison argues that liberation theology challenges the individualism that has characterized mainstream practices of pastoral care in Europe and North America. While sensitive to oppressions based upon race and gender, Pattison's integration of pastoral care with liberation theology retains the latter's use of Marxist theory and its emphasis on class conflict.

He argues that the increasing economic inequality throughout the world challenges practical theologians to give more attention to class antagonism in their analyses and practices of care. More recently, Eric Stoddart (2014) calls for the deconstruction and radicalization of practical theology. Such an approach would be "well equipped for enabling critical discipleship that is attuned to a world in the disturbing times of global capitalism" (p. xv). Stoddart uses *The Wiley-Blackwell Companion to Practical Theology*, edited by Bonnie Miller-McLemore (2012), as a "case study" of established practical theology. He argues that the 56 chapters in this collection, with a few exceptions, are silent concerning "the neoliberal and imperialist elephant in the room" (Stoddart, 2014, pp. 108–119). Although Stoddart does not undertake an analysis of class, he appeals to a critical retrieval of liberation theology—not as it has been appropriated in liberal theological education, but as it is taught and practiced in "laocratic movements" throughout the world (pp. 90–107). These movements are not limited to Latin America or sub-Saharan Africa, but appear also among the oppressed populations within Britain, Europe, and the US. Without consistently naming it as such, Stoddart is describing collective responses by people who have been exploited by class elites. By implication, the "radical practical theology" he proposes places class antagonism at the forefront of theological reflection. He approvingly cites Rebecca Chopp who, critiquing the "revised correlation method" that arose in the US, accuses mainstream practical theology of compliance with "bourgeois existence" (Chopp, 1987/2009). In effect, Chopp, like Stoddart, accuses practical theologians of siding with the ruling and middle classes.

The other exception is South Africa. What the US and South Africa share is a history of civil rights movements that yielded hard-won freedoms for people of color, rapidly followed by a neoliberal revolution that replaced social solidarity with individual meritocracy. The result is a restoration of political and economic power to their white populations. This involves an intensification of class struggle carried out predominately, although not exclusively, upon racial lines. Practical theologian Nadine Bowers Du Toit (2016) observes that South Africa has one of the highest rates of economic inequality in the world. The recent increasing unrest in South Africa, she notes, is largely about class antagonism, which she identifies as "the elephant in the room" in the theological discourse within South Africa. She calls upon religious leaders to replace the current "theology of assistance" with the previously dominant Apartheid-era "theology of resistance," undergirded by liberation theology. Similarly, Stephan de Beer (2015) pleas for the "(un)shackling" of cities and universities in South Africa from their neoliberal bondage. With an implicit sensitivity to class conflict, he too calls for a return to liberation theology and its emphasis on solidarity.

I have not attempted an exhaustive assessment of the works in pastoral and practical theology that have some peripheral relationship to class. Such a review would be both unwieldy and unedifying. Rather, my focus has been quite narrow. Leaving aside writings about economic injustice, poverty, or consumerism, I have highlighted only those works that talk explicitly about class. Even so, readers will no doubt know of authors I have overlooked. The advantage of this narrow approach is that the trajectory of these disciplines with regard to class is made more visible. What arises now is a trip "back to the future." If pastoral theologians in the first Gilded Age talked so passionately about class, how did we come to a place where we ignored this? And when we did take it up again, why was it in such a vague and evasive manner?

## Forgetting Class

Contemporary historians frequently compare the inequality of "the first Gilded Age," with that of "the second Gilded Age." The first began during the late 19th century, culminating in the global unrest that rocked the industrialized world through the 1920s. We are now deeply embedded in the second. Discussions of class dominated the first Gilded Age, but are virtually absent from the second (Fraser, 2015).

During the first Gilded Age, churches openly took sides in class struggle. While no monolithic "working-class Christianity" emerged, "class was nevertheless among the most important lines of demarcation running through the Gilded Age church and workers were far more likely than their social betters to believe that God sides decisively with the poor" (Carter, 2015, p. 7). Concerns about class preoccupied pastoral theologians during this period. Gladden (1898/1910) begins *The Christian Pastor and the Working Church* with the statement: "This book is intended to cover the field of what is known as Pastoral Theology" (p. v). The remainder of this book, however, bears only a faint resemblance to the pastoral theology of today. One reason is that he gives little attention to gender and race. Another reason concerns his preoccupation with class. Gladden asserts: "The separation of classes threatens the disruption of existing society, and the overturn of all our institutions" (pp. 32–33). His solution was to try to make peace between the factions, to "teach them to respect one another and care for one another" (p. 38). This was not a radical proposal, as it left the extreme power disparities between workers and the ruling class intact. Other religious leaders were far more forceful. Rauschenbusch (1907/2007), for example, spoke openly about "a war of conflicting interests which is not likely to be fought out in love and tenderness" (p. 330). In a few short decades, such frank talk about class would disappear from public conversation in the US.

If the first Gilded Age was a time of rebellion, the second Gilded Age has become "the age of acquiescence" (Fraser, 2015). Discussions about class have virtually disappeared. How has this happened? First, a panic occurred in reaction to the Bolshevik Revolution and socialist movements world-wide. In the US, opposition to the New Deal labeled anything resembling European-style social democracy as "un-American." This soon led to a "linguistic cleansing," in which the use of terms such as "class" and "class struggle" were purged from public discourse (p. 200). Investigations by the US Congress into unions eradicated their more radical elements. In this environment, "Class talk was just not tolerated" (Zweig, 2012, p. 52). Second, the broad prosperity following World War II was engrossed with upward mobility and consumerism. Those who discussed class exploitation therefore "seemed stuck in an earlier era" (Zweig, 2012, p. 52). Third, political concessions made to the South in order to get New Deal legislation passed effectively kept blacks and women from joining unions (Cowie, 2010, pp. 236–238). Consequently, "for many the working class came to be identified as only reactionary white men" (Zweig, 2012, p. 54). Fourth, the fall of the Soviet Union dispelled the notion that there is any alternative to capitalism. To some, this represented the "end of history," the arrival of a capitalist utopia (Fukuyama, 1992/2006). One result has been the acceptance of different outcomes for different classes as part of the natural order.

Finally, pre-existing tensions in the labor movement with regard to gender and race made progressive movements easy prey for the neoliberal turn that began in the 1970s and 1980s.[1] Neoliberal rationality, with its emphasis on individual freedom rather than solidarity, was able to drive a wedge into the social justice movement, splitting off demands for justice based on cultural identities from those calling for economic justice (Fraser, 1997; Duggan, 2003; Harvey, 2005). While reinscribing new and malignant versions of racism and sexism, neoliberal reason nonetheless retains the culture side of this divide, celebrating it in terms of "multiculturalism" and "diversity" (Rogers-Vaughn, 2016). Meanwhile, the economics side of this split is expunged, and with it any possibility of meaningful appeal to class struggle. The term "class" becomes an empty cipher. At best, it is a static marker of socio-economic status. "Class came to mean 'the poor,' who were in turn said to be women and minorities" (Zweig, 2012, pp. 54–55). This ideological divide is a distinguishing feature of neoliberalization.

This partitioning has serious consequences. First, it obscures the fact that the working class is not equivalent to either whiteness or maleness. The working class in the US is disproportionally female, black, and Hispanic. If any class embodies white supremacy and patriarchy, at least in the US, it is mainly the ruling class. As an indicator, chief executives in this country are primarily male (74.5%) and non-Hispanic white (89.2%) (Zweig, 2012, p. 34).

Second, class differences *within* various identity groups have often undermined efforts seeking justice for those same groups. "The solidarity of race or gender has never been complete because class differences have been, and continue to be, real and important among people of any identity" (Zweig, 2012, p. 132).

Third, much of the discussion of class today is carried out by white men. Often these men do not listen well enough to women and racialized others (hooks, 2000, p. 7). Addressing class conflict does not resolve racism and sexism: "To be most effective, working class politics needs to complement and incorporate these other movements" (Zweig, 2012, p. 133).

Finally, the economics/culture split elides the struggles of white working class men, as well as poor whites generally. Without a meaningful discourse of class struggle, these people are lumped in with a monochromatic and monolithic whiteness. "This type of politics is a recipe for alienation and anger among white men, dividing the working class and creating needless hostility toward the justifiable demands of women and minorities" (Zweig, 2012, p. 55). This does not mean that white working class people do not participate in white privilege. The point, rather, is that the power of white supremacy is unevenly distributed by class. Its chief architects live not in Appalachian shacks, trailer parks, and low-rent areas, but in gated communities and corporate boardrooms.

## Class in Everyday (Neoliberal) Life: Structure and Dynamics

Class is tied to the nature of production, and how capital exploits workers for increased profits (Zweig, 2012, pp. 9–10). The conditions under which we work have changed immensely since the 1980s. I begin, then, with a snapshot of working life today. Most critiques of neoliberalism emphasize its oppression of the poor, the working class, the young, and minorities. These appraisals are compelling and necessary. However, in order to illustrate the current pervasiveness of class antagonism, I reproduce here an exhibit of how today's capitalism is eroding the so-called middle class, even among the majority white population within the US. I follow this case with an analysis of the structure and dynamics of class under the conditions of neoliberalization.

Bill and Sheryl are a white couple who have been married for 20 years (Leicht and Fitzgerald, 2014, pp. 18–19). Both are 45 years old. They are active participants in a Catholic parish and in their community. They are parents of two children, one already in college and the other in high school. Bill is a computer software engineer, while Sheryl is a social worker employed by the state. They own an attractive four-bedroom home in a suburb of Cleveland, Ohio (USA). Their two cars are paid off, but are now well-worn and require frequent repairs. "By most middle class standards, Bill and Sheryl seem to have it made" (p. 18). However, despite appearances, their economic condition is abysmal. Bill lost his job at a large firm ten years ago, when his company was taken over during a leveraged buyout. Since that time, he has been unable to secure employment. He is now an independent consultant. He has no benefits or paid time off, and makes a fraction of the annual salary of $55,000 he once earned.

Meanwhile, Sheryl works for the county where they live. This job provides their health insurance. However, their state government has adopted neoliberal austerity policies, cutting welfare programs and declaring "war on the poor." Since this is the population she serves, Sheryl finds herself trying to help more people with diminishing resources. This not only makes her job more stressful, but she hasn't had a raise in five years. However, faced with poverty-stricken and homeless people every day, Sheryl feels she has no reason to complain. She says to her kids: "At least we're not sleeping under bridges" (Leicht and Fitzgerald, 2014, p. 19). To make matters worse, the county, coping with reduced funding by the state, is considering eliminating her unit in order to consolidate services.

As a consequence of these changes in their work lives, "Bill and Sheryl have been cannibalizing their economic assets to keep their middle class lifestyle afloat" (Leicht and Fitzgerald, 2014, p. 19). Sometimes they must resort to buying groceries on credit. They now owe more than $15,000 on their credit cards. In addition, when their son started to college, they assumed a second mortgage, as well as a home equity line of credit. When the global speculation on housing crashed in 2008, their home lost so much value that they now owe more than it is worth, despite having lived there for 15 years. If Sheryl loses her job with the county, they will fall over an economic cliff.

This couple is representative of the decline of the middle class in the US. "Bill and Sheryl are trapped in a cycle of work, layoffs, debt, payments, and taxes that will never end" (Leicht and Fitzgerald, 2014, p. 19). The neoliberal practices that have transformed their lives impose a perpetual debt servitude (pp. 20, 25–52, 68–90). How can this happen when "the economy has continued to grow by leaps and bounds?" The answer is that middle class earnings have stagnated, while consumer credit has loosened. This means we are "loaning domestic consumers money they could otherwise be paid" (p. 29). The result has been a staggering redistribution of wealth to those who were already affluent—the investor class. So, while the economy has been growing in the US, literally all the added wealth during the past four decades has gone to the top 0.1 percent (Zucman, 2016).

Indebtedness is not simply a plague of the middle class. Debt now governs workers globally, and is especially pernicious for populations of color (Chakravartty and Ferreira da Silva, 2013). Debt even governs those of the underclass who cannot take out personal loans, because the escalating sovereign debts of nation states create impoverishment for most of their inhabitants (Lazzarato, 2012, p. 32).

What sense are we to make of this case? While discriminations rooted in cultural identities are often quite apparent, class is much harder to point to. And yet, like the unseen power of the wind, class blows through the details of Bill's and Sheryl's lives. We can witness its effects, but not the thing in itself. This is because class has to do with powers that are *distal* to individuals and families (Smail, 2005, pp. 26–34). Unconsciousness is largely external, rather than simply internal. Understanding class in its particularities, then, is a special instance of "making the unconscious conscious."

So, what is class? First, we must be clear that to talk about class is to talk about capitalism. Capitalism cannot exist without a division between owners and investors (capitalists), and everyone else (workers and debtors). Therefore, unlike other forms of oppression, such as racism, class originates in the structure of capitalism, rather than in discrimination or prejudice: "racism is a necessary condition for the reproduction of 'race', but 'class-ism' is not a necessary condition for the reproduction of class" (Sayer, 2005, p. 94).

Neither is class equivalent to social stratification. It is not simply about cultural tastes, socio-economic status, poverty, or education. Class is ultimately about *power*. Zweig (2012) asserts: "When I talk about class, I am talking about power. Power at work, and power in the larger society. Economic power, and also political and cultural power" (p. 1). Attention to power discloses the trinitarian *structure* of class: economic power, political power, and cultural power. These are, of course, interrelated.

Most reviews of neoliberalism emphasize economic inequality. In the US, for example, economic inequality began rising around 1980, and now equals the levels seen during the first Gilded Age. The top 1 percent of households currently controls 42 percent of the total wealth, while the bottom 90 percent collectively owns just 23 percent (Zucman, 2016).[2] Oxfam International (Hardoon, 2017) documents that neoliberalism has had a similar impact globally. Beginning in 2015, the richest 1 percent of earth's population has held more wealth than the remainder of humanity. "Eight men," the report confirms, "now own the same amount of wealth as the poorest half of the world" (p. 2).[3]

This degree of inequality is matched in the political dimension. The proliferating economic power of the capitalist class allows them unconstrained access to the powers of government. Growing inequality is not primarily attributable to increased technology or globalization, as is often claimed, but to the seizure of state power by global elites (Hacker and Pierson, 2010; Reid-Henry, 2015). Large corporations and staggeringly wealthy individuals are able to impose their will on legislation, as well as controlling the courts and penal systems. Extreme inequality means that neither the working class nor the dwindling middle class have significant political influence (Gilens, 2012; Gilens and Page, 2014). The result is a hollowing out of democracy. Moreover, inequality disproportionally impacts women and people of color, signifying the critical role of class power in the (re)production of racism and sexism (Stephanopoulos, 2015).

Neoliberalization occurs not only in the economic and political dimensions, but is also a cultural process (Rogers-Vaughn, 2016, pp. 42–46). Class power in the cultural dimension has to do with the ability to determine values not reducible to economics. Neoliberalization modifies these values in accord with its emphasis on *competition, entrepreneurship,* and *individual responsibility*

(Duggan, 2003; Dardot and Laval, 2009/2013; Brown, 2015). Under the pressure of radical inequality, this has destructive consequences. First, powerful and wealthy individuals are intensely idealized, even by members of the working classes. Second, competition divides the social world into a very few "winners," and a multitude of "losers." Finally, individuals are made to be responsible for their own failures. Like Bill and Sheryl, we are left with no reason to complain. Thus, economic and political inequality are mirrored in *psychological* inequality. This leads inevitably to a global pandemic of depression and addiction, as vast populations attempt to cope with responsibility for their own struggles (Alexander, 2008; Walker, 2010; Rogers-Vaughn, 2014).

But it is insufficient to talk about class simply as a structure. As the preceding paragraphs imply, there are also *dynamics* involved. The power structures are dimensions of a *system* in which the classes are entangled with each other. This brings us to consider *class conflict*. The masses are relatively powerless *because* class elites have subsumed most of the power unto themselves. This brings attention to the power imbalance between the small "top" and the much larger "base" of the new class structure (Wysong et al., 2014, pp. 31–37). This conflict appears in all three dimensions of class power. In the economic ecology, this materializes as the stagnation of wages during a period when productivity has dramatically increased. Under finance capitalism, however, the role of debt becomes ever more central. Debt is *the* defining economic feature of neoliberalism (Lazzarato, 2012; Davies, 2016). A new phase of capitalism has emerged since the recession of 2008, which Davies (2016) calls "punitive neoliberalism." Here debt is not simply utilitarian, but is "heavily moralized," becoming a form of punishment. The plight of Bill and Sheryl has become normative. As cultural power this appears, at the base of the class structure, as a psychology of depression and self-recrimination (Davies et al., 2015). Meanwhile, at the top, the other side of this cultural conflict appears as hatred and disgust toward these internal "enemies" (Davies, 2016). In the political dimension, this is acted out, on the part of the elites, through the adoption of policies designed to exact vengeance. The "austerity politics" now engulfing the globe epitomizes this phase.

One symptom of this class struggle is the balkanization of labor. Division within the working class is fostered by the interests of the capitalist class: "Segmented labor markets, ethnic rivalry, racism, sexism, xenophobia, and informalization all work against solidarity" (Johnson, February 2016, para. 77). Meanwhile, the economics/culture split occurring under neoliberalization leaves no path for public appeal except through neoliberal versions of identity politics, which focus on discrimination without reference to class conflict:

> An unspoken risk inherent in the monopolitics of "diversity" was that white guys, too, would avail themselves of their own form of identity politics, taking shelter from the storm of cultural conflict in the politics of nostalgia, resentment, and authority. (Cowie, 2010, p. 240)

This "politics of resentment" is apparent in the support for Trump (Cramer, 2016; Hochschild, 2016).

This division within labor impedes care. Caring for people like Bill and Sheryl will be hampered without a solidarity that embraces difference. Meanwhile, since the election of Trump, debates among progressives have devolved into tired repetitions of "race versus class" and "gender versus class." Class conflict is entangled with racism and sexism. It is not an either/or matter. They rise and fall together (Rogers-Vaughn, 2016). Until we grasp this, the solidarity that embodies care will continue to elude us.

## Class Struggle: What Does Pastoral Theology Have to Do with It?

What light does a public pastoral theology shed on neoliberal capitalism, and on the alterations to class dynamics it has engendered? This question demands both a broad-ranging and deep analysis. I will consider this question from my own perspective as a Christian theologian who acknowledges the Jewish roots of this tradition, restricting my response to three interrelated concerns that suggest paths for further inquiry: how this system corrupts our relationship with the Eternal, transforms social power into money, and erodes our dependency upon and obligation to other people. All three disruptions bear directly upon a pastoral theological assessment of class, and the fruits of these alterations are evident in the lives of Sheryl, Bill, and their human cohorts throughout the world.

The analysis of class in the preceding section indicates that Sheryl and Bill are ensnared in a web of power not of their own making. The corporate takeovers, austerity politics, suppressed wages, and sprawling structure of debt production that transfers value from this couple to the capitalist class are dimensions of neoliberal processes that make their lives precarious and, no doubt, produce sufferings that arise from shame (Helsel, 2015, pp. 121–154). What could justify this system? Neoliberal ideology claims that capitalism and class are simply natural, and that Bill and Sheryl must accept personal responsibility for their own undoing. This quickly brings us to the core of the problem. The valuation of values is the central conundrum of theology: "The fundamental problem is this: what is worth the sacrifice of flesh and blood, of time, attention, and devotion?" (Goodchild, 2009, p. 239). To this question capitalism responds: *the accumulation of wealth*. This is the supreme value, to which everything else must be sacrificed. If the production of wealth means that millions of people will die or suffer exploitation, or the earth is plundered, then that is simply the price of progress. *Capitalism is a system that enriches and empowers a few at the expense of many, and this fact lies at the heart of class difference.*

The Jewish and Christian scriptures directly contradict such thinking. The Hebrew Bible insists that the earth and all its inhabitants belong to God, subverting all ultimate claims to private property. In the Gospels, Jesus is emphatic: "You cannot serve God and wealth" (Matt. 6:24). Jesus proclaims woes upon the rich and blessings upon the poor (Luke 6:20–26). He asserts: "It is easier for a camel to go through the eye of a needle than for someone who is rich to enter the kingdom of God" (Mark 10:25). The Gospel is decidedly not "good news" to the wealthy. "It was not, however, the subjective enjoyment of wealth that was his target; it was wealth as a principle of power or judgment" (Goodchild, 2009, p. 5). It was, in other words, the placement of wealth as the chief value. In the discourse of the Hebraic traditions—Judaism, Christianity, and Islam—wealth displaces God as the supreme good, and this is the essence of *idolatry*. Idolatry occurs whenever our desire, in the effort to secure ourselves in the face of tragic existence, no longer *strives through* the mundane to the Eternal, but *comes to rest* in the ordinary object (Farley, 1990). This is the origin of sin, or human evil. Whenever we posit something familiar in the place of the Eternal, given our innate awareness of the fragility of the mundane, we become willing to sacrifice anything to protect the idol. The idol—in the case of capitalism, wealth accumulation—becomes absolute. Capitalism thus becomes a religion (Rogers-Vaughn, 2016, pp. 78–90). This is a religion that demands human sacrifice. It practices what Harvey Cox (1999) calls "reverse transubstantiation": "Things that have been held sacred transmute into interchangeable items for sale" (para. 9–10). Are these the kinds of sacrifice we wish to be making?

In the "secular" religion of capitalism, then, the laboring classes and the poor are laid upon the altar as a sacrifice. This involves not only a corruption of our relationship with the Eternal, but also the transformation of social power into money. Not all social power is evil. Love, care, compassion, the desire for justice, worship of the Eternal—all these are forms of social power. They move us in one direction rather than another. Under capitalism such powers are not necessarily monetized, but they are transmuted into or replaced by the power money conveys. As a valuation of values, money delivers access to other forms of power—military force, information, the molding of public consciousness, the capacity to prioritize through selective funding, and so on (Goodchild, 2009, pp. 12–13). Furthermore, especially in the case of neoliberalism, money is produced as debt. Finance capitalism is a system based on the production and trading of debt (Lazzarato, 2012). "The physical expression of worship and devotion has mutated from the offering, through the tithe and the tax, to the interest payment" (Goodchild, 2009, p. 237). Despite its abstract quality, money as debt nonetheless exacts payment in the form of human lives: "The value of money is still paid for in flesh and blood." Moreover, a finance economy makes us complicit in one another's suffering: "Whenever one spends money, one spends a portion of the substance, wealth, and life of those who have undertaken loans" (p. 236).

The shift from industrial capitalism to finance capitalism transforms class struggle. Marx emphasized the antagonism between owners of the means of production and workers. While such conflict still exists, it has been overtaken by the new credit economy. Today's dominant form of class conflict is not that between owners and workers, but between investors and debtors. In a debt system, it is not just one's work that is exploited, but one's very self. Debt is a contract on one's future work: "The credit economy is a network of contracted servitude" (Goodchild, 2009, p. 236). Here we do not just surrender the surplus value of our labor. We lose our freedom. We do not simply owe. We are owned. This is the ultimate "reverse transubstantiation," as human beings are transmuted into money upon the altars of the finance system.

But debt servitude goes much further than this. Debt "is premised on an assumption of equality" (Graeber, 2011, p. 86). Thus, we presume that people take on debt as a free, unencumbered choice. This means we accept that we have a moral obligation to repay the debt. This has two immediate consequences. Graeber identifies the first:

> If history shows anything, it is that there's no better way to justify relations founded on violence, to make such relations seem moral, than by reframing them in the language of debt—above all, because it immediately makes it seem that it's the victim who's doing something wrong. (p. 5)

This ignores that, under finance capitalism, the vast majority of debt in the world has been taken on under duress. Among nation states, those most in debt (relative to their wealth) are the very ones who were exploited under colonialism. International financial institutions, promulgating neoliberal policies, have imposed tremendous amounts of debt on "developing economies," leaving us now with a neocolonialism (Chakravartty and Ferreira da Silva, 2013). We might also recognize that the truism "everyone must always repay their debts" is patently not true. Following the 2008 financial crisis, for example, the US government, under the ideology of "too big to fail," dissolved the debts of many large banks and corporations. This, in turn, cancelled out the losses for their investors. "As it turns out, we don't 'all' have to pay our debts. Only some of us do" (Graeber, 2011, p. 391). This crisis disclosed that even the inviolability of debt repayment may be suspended for class elites, but never for those lacking their political power. The moral obligation of debt repayment is unevenly distributed by class.

This injustice is repeated at the level of individuals. It is clear, for example, that Sheryl and Bill did not take on debt as an unencumbered choice. The erosion of their wages required the acceptance of debt if they were to continue caring for themselves and their children. Moreover, those who take on debt generally accept the ideology of free choice and individual responsibility. This leads to the second consequence. Unpayable debt—the "infinite debt"

(Lazzarato, 2012, pp. 77–81) typical under neoliberal governance—now constitutes a pervasive form of moral injury. Theologians Brock and Lettini (2012) investigate the moral injuries of soldiers, who violate their own consciences as they follow orders under the pressure of combat. These individuals identify their own being as the source of great injustice. One result is that combat veterans account for 20 percent of all suicides in the United States (p. xii). A similar pattern appears in the moral injury of debt where, again, those who cannot repay the debt feel that they alone are responsible. As with combat veterans, suicide is a common result (Leech, 2012, pp. 55–56).

Again, a refusal of money as the governing power of society, including the imposition of debt, is prominent in Christian scripture. Jesus, exhorting his disciples to love even their enemies, repeats the Golden Rule: "Do to others as you would have them do to you." He then interprets the meaning: "If you lend to those from whom you hope to receive, what credit is that to you? Even sinners lend to sinners, to receive as much again. But love your enemies, do good, and lend, expecting nothing in return" (Luke 6:31, 34–35). Here a loan does not impose a debt, much less interest. It is, to the contrary, the equivalent of a gift. In his typical fashion, Jesus takes economic terms and turns them on their heads. In the Parable of the Unforgiving Servant (Matt. 18:23–35), the king forgives an unpayable debt of a servant, only to cast him into prison when this same man refuses to forgive a lesser debt. This same sentiment appears in the Lord's Prayer, still recited in Christian worship throughout the world: "And forgive us our debts, as we also have forgiven our debtors" (Matt. 6:12). This posture toward debt was taken up in classical Christian theology. Charging interest, referred to as "usury" in the language of the period, was either forbidden or sternly restricted by Aquinas, Luther, Calvin, and Zwingli, among others (Wykes, 2003; Savage, 2011). In much of Christian thought, even salvation is framed in starkly economic terms. The word "redemption," and the reference to Christ as "Redeemer," regards salvation as the cancellation of an unpayable debt, or the recovery of what had been given up for a loan (Graeber, 2011, pp. 80–82). Understood in context, redemption is "really more a matter of destroying the entire system of accounting" (p. 82). In sum, refusing the power of money and its capacity to rank people and bind them in debt would mean the end of the class system as we know it.

This brings us to the third consideration. Not only does neoliberal capitalism corrupt our relationship with the Eternal and transform social power into money, it also distorts our relationships. As already noted, neoliberal governance turns us all into entrepreneurs competing with each other in the marketplace. A society ruled by the iron law of competition subjects everyone to the risk of redundancy and abandonment. "Competition yields winners and losers; capital succeeds by destroying or cannibalizing other capitals" (Brown, 2015, p. 64). By replacing the notion of exchange with competition, neoliberal governance does not posit members of different classes as having conflicting interests that can be negotiated. Instead, they are simply enemies. Commenting on how neoliberal-ism shifts class antagonism, LaMothe (2017) asserts: "care in this context is cor-rupted by recognizing the Other as enemy" (p. 219).

We cannot reconcile this with the message of Jesus as recorded in the Gospels. I could cite many of Jesus' sayings to support this, but I will use only the one for which he is perhaps most famous, the Parable of the Good Samaritan (Luke 10:25–37). The story opens with a lawyer asking Jesus how he might inherit eter-nal life. Jesus asks him what is written in the Law. The lawyer answers: "You shall love the Lord your God with all your heart … and your neighbor as yourself." Jesus says, "You have the right answer; do this, and you will live." The lawyer then asks the inevitable: "And who is my neighbor?" Jesus responds with the now familiar story. A man is traveling from Jerusalem to Jericho and gets mugged and left for dead. First a priest passes by, then a Levite, neither of whom stop to help. Amy-Jill Levine (2014) observes that Jesus is following a pattern, the "rule of three." So, his audience is expecting a third figure to come by. They are not to be disappointed. However, Levine notes that this is a familiar list for Jewish listen-ers. If you say "priest" and then "Levite," she states, then "anyone who knows anything about Judaism will know that the third person is an Israelite" (p. 95). The hearers, then, must presume the next passerby will be an Israelite, who will stop and help. Instead, there is a shocking turn. The next man is a Samaritan, a despised enemy. Levine quips: "In modern terms, this would be like going from Larry and Moe to Osama bin Laden" (p. 95). Jesus then asks the stunned lawyer who was neighbor to the distressed man, and he answers: "The one who showed him mercy." The story assumes that human relationships are based upon obliga-tion, care, and dependency. We are not entrepreneurs in competition. We are neighbors obligated to care, and to accept care from others, regardless of who they are. The emphasis is not on individual meritocracy, but *shared life*.

If we combine the Parable of the Good Samaritan with the previous sayings of Jesus regarding wealth and debt, a portrait emerges for understanding class. LaMothe (2017) reflects:

> … the ministry of Jesus and the early church represent a movement toward a society structured and dominated by relations of mutual respect and forms of distribution and exchange that mitigate class, clas-sism, and class conflict. (pp. 212–213)

Jesus' vision, he concludes, is a community "where there are no classes, where there are no categories of poor and rich" (p. 229). Meanwhile, a neoliberal world is one that depends upon class and economic inequality. This brings me to the next question. What will be the role of religion and theology in a global economy dominated by an economic elite? What form does pastoral care assume in such a climate?

# Pastoral Care: Promoting, Accommodating, or Resisting Class Structure?

Although we remain in an "age of acquiescence" (Fraser, 2015), there are now signs of awakening. One indicator is the increasing interest in class in religious and theological studies. A collection of essays with the revealing title: *Religion, Theology, and Class: Fresh Engagements after Long Silence* (Rieger, 2013) is a noteworthy example. The authors make a strong case that theology and religious practices are never non-aligned regarding class. At the very least, to be silent in a context of extreme inequality is to take sides with those in power. But the impossibility of neutrality goes further, including the ways specific religious ideas and practices promote, reform, or resist neoliberal capitalism and its class formation (Dreher and Smith, 2016). As theologians and religious devotees, we are always taking sides in class struggle, even when we are unaware.

Bringing all this to bear upon pastoral care, we must acknowledge that care is also never class-neutral. Generally, the pastoral care practiced in religious movements that promote neoliberalism reinforces the values of the ruling class. The elite's doctrine of individualism, for example, privatizes both suffering and care. It urges us to look for the origins of suffering only within ourselves. We are responsible to manage this suffering individually, using whatever resources are at our disposal. In this instance, care may take rather harsh forms. If Bill and Sheryl become depressed, addicted, or just "stressed out," they may be told to "get it together" and to "tough it out," in the belief that hard work will eventually be rewarded. They might also be admonished for taking on so much debt, and told that it is their moral duty to repay it. Faith demands sacrifices to powers that are "higher" than themselves—to God, their employers, and their creditors.

In religious groups trying to reform and thus accommodate neoliberalism, pastoral care takes forms most progressives accept as normal. These congregations adopt a kinder, gentler individualism. Suffering and care remain privatized, but caregivers attempt to comfort or in some way ameliorate the pain. The usual outcome, however, is that sufferers receive just enough help to remain conformed to a system that produced the pain to begin with. Frequently, this means managing their pain as a chronic condition (Cazdyn, 2012).

What form does pastoral care assume in religious movements that resist neoliberalism and its enhancement of class power? Here care includes but is not limited to empathic presence and acts of compassion. Suffering is interrogated for its meaning, a meaning that is likely relevant not just for the suffering individual, but for the entire collective. How is this so? Because suffering has been reconnected with its social context. In effect, pain becomes a commentary on what is happening within the collective, between the collective and its social surround, and/or in the world at large. Specifically, it makes conscious the destructive power differentials that pervade human systems. Moreover, what the suffering offers is not simply cognitive. It is revelatory, but its meaning is not limited to information. Suffering also involves emotions. These are no longer simply "owned" by the individual, as they are in contemporary capitalism. Rather they are turned back out again, and point to the origins of the suffering. Not only that, but the suffering and its accompanying affects constitute an embryonic resistance—a passion that is amplified when heard in the context of the group's solidarity. Thus, it is a resource for both the content and the *desire* for change. Clearly, neither suffering nor care in this context are privatized. Individuals no longer suffer in isolation, nor are they alone responsible for "getting better." Such care is no longer just a discrete task. It is not simply something the congregation does. The solidarity it nurtures is caring in itself.

This religious community constitutes what LaMothe (2017) calls "an *alter-capitalist ecclesia.*" I have said that a pastoral care that resists class structure *interrogates* suffering. This requires an explicitly educative dimension. Class power, as I have noted, is mostly hidden from us. Thus, "An *altercapitalist ecclesia* can educate its members and Others about the origins of class and income inequalities" (LaMothe, 2017, p. 227, emphasis in original). This returns us, finally, to the mission of a public pastoral theology. This sort of theology does not settle for descriptive analyses. It takes sides:

> A political pastoral theology engages not simply in the prophetic moral suasion of those in the upper classes but also in prophetically critiquing the very economic and political systems that create the so-called upper classes. (LaMothe, 2017, p. 229)

Likewise, a care of souls that resists neoliberalism embodies a utopian spirit that strives toward a community that dismantles the forms of oppression designated by the term "class" (Rogers-Vaughn, 2016, pp. 228–237).

## Conclusion

The continuing inattention to class in this "second Gilded Age" poses a serious problem. Popular appeals to "diversity" leave us with ideals of social justice that are compromised unless they simultaneously address the inequalities of class power. In light of this, religious leaders, congregations, and pastoral theologians must wonder why we have not been more vocal on this matter, compared with the substantial emphasis on class conflict by the Social Christianity that appeared in the US during the Industrial Age. The story, however, remains unfinished. Carter (2015) provides a fitting conclusion for where we now find ourselves:

Now, in the early decades of the twenty-first century, American capitalism appears once more poised to overwhelm American democracy. ... It remains to be seen whether present-day believers will quietly abide this state of affairs, or whether it will at some point call forth a generation of prophets comparable to those that visited Gilded Age Chicago. (p. 182)

Under neoliberal expansion, what Carter says about Chicago and the US now goes for the entire planet. Today the need for a prophetic movement is global. We shall see.

## Notes

1 I have documented the neoliberal turn in *Caring for Souls in a Neoliberal Age* (2016, chap. 2).
2 A video illustrating US wealth distribution is available at www.youtube.com/watch?v=QPKKQnijnsM&list=FLucdX5GEDe5ykVaPeXI-HGQ (accessed March 26, 2017).
3 The global increase of economic inequality over the past five decades has been visually summarized by a series of maps created by the University of Texas Inequality Project. The maps are available at http://utip.gov.utexas.edu/ (accessed March 26, 2017).

## References

Alexander, Bruce K. 2008. *The Globalization of Addiction: A Study in Poverty of the Spirit*. New York: Oxford University Press.

Bowers Du Toit, Nadine. 2016. "The Elephant in the Room: The Need to Re-discover the Intersection between Poverty, Powerlessness and Power in 'Theology and Development' Praxis." *HTS Theological Studies*. Volume 72, Issue 4, 1–9. DOI:10.4102/hts.v72i4.3459.

Brock, Rita Nakashima and Gabriella Lettini. 2012. *Soul Repair: Recovering from Moral Injury after War*. Boston, MA: Beacon Press.

Brown, Wendy. 1995. *States of Injury: Power and Freedom in Late Modernity*. Princeton, NJ: Princeton University Press.

Brown, Wendy. 2015. *Undoing the Demos: Neoliberalism's Stealth Revolution*. Brooklyn, NY: Zone Books.

Carter, Heath W. 2015. *Union Made: Working People and the Rise of Social Christianity in Chicago*. New York: Oxford University Press.

Cazdyn, Eric. 2012. *The Already Dead: The New Time of Politics, Culture, and Illness*. Durham, NC: Duke University Press.

Chakravartty, Paula and Denise Ferreira da Silva, Eds. 2013. *Race, Empire, and the Crisis of the Subprime*. Baltimore, MD: Johns Hopkins University Press.

Chopp, Rebecca S. 1987/2009. "Practical Theology and Liberation." In *Formation and Reflection: The Promise of Practical Theology*, edited by Lewis S. Mudge and James N. Poling, pp. 120–138. Minneapolis, MN: Fortress Press.

Cowie, Jefferson. 2010. *Stayin' Alive: The 1970s and the Last Days of the Working Class*. New York: The New Press.

Cox, Harvey. 1999 (March). "The Market as God: Living in the New Dispensation." *The Atlantic*, Volume 283, Issue 3. Available at:. www.theatlantic.com/magazine/archive/1999/03/the-market-as-god/306397/ (accessed March 27, 2017).

Cramer, Katherine J. 2016. *The Politics of Resentment: Rural Consciousness in Wisconsin and the Rise of Scott Walker*. Chicago, IL: University of Chicago Press.

Dardot, Pierre and Christian Laval. 2009/2013. *The New Way of the World: On Neo-Liberal Society*. Translated by Gregory Elliott. London: Verso.

Davies, William. 2016 (September/October). "The New Neoliberalism." *New Left Review*. Volume 101, 121–134.

Davies, William, Johnna Montgomerie, and Sara Wallin. 2015. *Financial Melancholia: Mental Health and Indebtedness*. London: Political Economy Research Centre, Goldsmiths, University of London. Accessed www.perc.org.uk/perc/wp-content/uploads/2015/07/FinancialMelancholiaMentalHealthand Indebtedness-1.pdf (accessed January 3, 2017).

de Beer, Stephan. 2015. "The University, the City and the Clown: A Theological Essay on Solidarity, Mutuality and Prophecy." *HTS Theological Studies*. Volume 71, Issue 3, 1–12. DOI:10.4102/hts.v71i3.3100.

Dreher, Sabine and Peter J. Smith, Eds. 2016. *Religious Activism in the Global Economy: Promoting, Reforming, or Resisting Neoliberal Globalization?* London: Rowman & Littlefield International.

Duggan, Lisa. 2003. *The Twilight of Equality? Neoliberalism, Cultural Politics, and the Attack on Democracy*. Boston, MA: Beacon Press.

Farley, Edward. 1990. *Good and Evil: Interpreting a Human Condition*. Minneapolis, MN: Fortress Press.

Fraser, Nancy. 1997. *Justice Interruptus: Critical Reflections on the "Postsocialist" Condition*. New York: Routledge.

Fraser, Steve. 2015. *The Age of Acquiescence: The Life and Death of American Resistance to Organized Wealth and Power*. New York: Little, Brown and Company.

Fukuyama, Francis. 1992/2006. *The End of History and the Last Man*. New York: Free Press.

Gerkin, Charles V. 1986. *Widening the Horizons: Pastoral Responses to a Fragmented Society*. Philadelphia, PA: Westminster Press.

Gilens, Martin. 2012. *Affluence and Influence: Economic Inequality and Political Power in America*. Princeton, NJ: Princeton University Press.

Gilens, Martin and Benjamin I. Page. 2014. "Testing Theories of American Politics: Elites, Interest Groups, and Average Citizens." *Perspectives on Politics*. Volume 12, Issue 3, 564–581. DOI:10.1017/S1537592714001595.

Gladden, Washington. 1898/1910. *The Christian Pastor and the Working Church.* New York: Charles Scribner's Sons.

Goodchild, Philip. 2009. *Theology of Money.* Durham, NC: Duke University Press.

Graham, Elaine L. 1996. *Transforming Practice: Pastoral Theology in an Age of Uncertainty.* Eugene, OR: Wipf and Stock Publishers.

Graham, Elaine. 2013. *Between a Rock and a Hard Place: Public Theology in a Post-Secular Age.* London: SCM Press.

Graeber, David. 2011. *Debt: The First 5,000 Years.* Brooklyn, NY: Melville House Publishing.

Hacker, Jacob S. and Paul Pierson. 2010. *Winner-Take-All Politics: How Washington Made the Rich Richer—And Turned Its Back on the Middle Class.* New York: Simon & Schuster.

Hardoon, Deborah. 2017. "An Economy for the 99%." (Oxfam briefing paper). Oxford: Oxfam International. Avaibable at:https://www.oxfamamerica.org/explore/research-publications/an-economy-for-the-99-percent/ (accessed March 26, 2017).

Harvey, David. 2005. *A Brief History of Neoliberalism.* Oxford: Oxford University Press.

Helsel, Philip Browning. 2015. *Pastoral Power Beyond Psychology's Marginalization: Resisting the Discourses of the Psy-Complex.* New York: Palgrave Macmillan.

Hochschild, Arlie Russell. 2016. *Strangers in Their Own Land: Anger and Mourning on the American Right.* New York: The New Press.

hooks, bell. 2000. *Where We Stand: Class Matters.* New York: Routledge.

Johnson, Cedric. 2016 (February 3). "An Open Letter to Ta-Nehisi Coates and the Liberals Who Love Him." *Jacobin.* Available at: https://www.jacobinmag.com/2016/02/ta-nehisi-coates-case-for-reparations-bernie-sanders-racism/ (accessed April 17, 2017).

Johnson, Cedric C. 2016. *Race, Religion, and Resilience in the Neoliberal Age.* New York: Palgrave Macmillan.

Kujawa-Holbrook, Sheryl A. and Karen B. Montagno, Eds. 2009. *Injustice and the Care of Souls: Taking Oppression Seriously in Pastoral Care.* Minneapolis, MN: Fortress Press.

LaMothe, Ryan. 2015. "The Willie Lomans of a Market Society: Addressing Political-Economic Sources of Suffering in Pastoral Counseling." *Journal of Pastoral Care and Counseling.* Volume 69, Issue 2, 102–112. DOI:10.1177/1542305015586774.

LaMothe, Ryan. 2016. "Plutocratic Fears and Fantasies: Projective Identification and Enactment in a Market Society." *Pastoral Psychology.* Volume 65, Issue 1, 61–77. DOI:10.1007/s11089-015-0659-z.

LaMothe, Ryan W. 2017. *Care of Souls, Care of Polis: Toward a Political Pastoral Theology.* Eugene, OR: Cascade Books.

Lazzarato, Maurizio. 2012. *The Making of Indebted Man.* Translated by Joshua D. Jordan. Los Angeles: Semiotext(e).

Leech, Garry. 2012. *Capitalism: A Structural Genocide*. London: Zed Books.

Leicht, Kevin T. and Scott T. Fitzgerald. 2014. *Middle Class Meltdown in America: Causes, Consequences, and Remedies*, 2nd edn. New York: Routledge.

Levine, Amy-Jill. 2014. *Short Stories by Jesus: The Enigmatic Parables of a Controversial Rabbi*. New York: HarperOne.

Mercer, Joyce Ann. 2012. "Economics, Class, and Classism." In *The Wiley Blackwell Companion to Practical Theology*, edited by Bonnie J. Miller-McLemore, pp. 432–442. Chichester: Wiley-Blackwell.

Miller-McLemore, Bonnie, Ed. 2012. *The Wiley Blackwell Companion to Practical Theology*. Chichester: Wiley-Blackwell.

Neuger, Christie Cozad. 2004. "Power and Difference in Pastoral Theology." In *Pastoral Care and Counseling: Redefining the Paradigms*, edited by Nancy J. Ramsay, pp. 65–85. Nashville, TN: Abingdon Press.

Orr, Judith L. 1997. "Hard Work, Hard Lovin', Hard Times, Hardly Worth It: Care of Working-Class Men." In *The Care of Men*, edited by Christie C. Neuger and James N. Poling, pp. 70–91. Nashville, TN: Abingdon Press.

Pattison, Stephen. 1994. *Pastoral Care and Liberation Theology*. Cambridge: Cambridge University Press.

Poling, James N. 2002. *Render Unto God: Economic Vulnerability, Family Violence, and Pastoral Theology*. Eugene, OR: Wipf & Stock.

Ramsay, Nancy J., ed. 2004. *Pastoral Care and Counseling: Redefining the Paradigms*. Nashville, TN: Abingdon Press.

Rauschenbusch, Walter. 1907/2007. *Christianity and the Social Crisis in the 21st Century: The Classic That Woke Up the Church*, edited by Paul Rauschenbusch. New York: HarperOne.

Reid-Henry, Simon. 2015. *The Political Origins of Inequality: Why a More Equal World is Better for Us All*. Chicago, IL: University of Chicago Press.

Rieger, Joerg, Ed. 2013. *Religion, Theology, and Class: Fresh Engagements after Long Silence*. New York: Palgrave Macmillan.

Rogers-Vaughn, Bruce. 2014. "Blessed Are Those Who Mourn: Depression as Political Resistance." *Pastoral Psychology*. Volume 63, Issue 4, 503–522. DOI:10.1007/s11089-013-0576-y.

Rogers-Vaughn, Bruce. 2016. *Caring for Souls in a Neoliberal Age*. New York: Palgrave Macmillan.

Ryan, Jake and Charles Sackrey. 1996. *Strangers in Paradise: Academics from the Working Class*. Lanham, MD: University Press of America.

Savage, Brenda K. 2011. "Echoes from Geneva: Finding John Calvin's Socio-Economic Interests in the Modern World." Rollins Scholarship Online. Available at: http://scholarship.rollins.edu/cgi/viewcontent. cgi?article=1001&context=mls (accessed March 20, 2017).

Sayer, Andrew. 2005. *The Moral Significance of Class*. Cambridge: Cambridge University Press.

Smail, David. 2005. *Power, Interest and Psychology: Elements of a Social Materialist Understanding of Distress.* Ross-on-Wye: PCCS Books.

Smith, Archie, Jr. 1982. *The Relational Self: Ethics and Therapy from a Black Church Perspective.* Nashville, TN: Abingdon.

Stephanopoulos, Nicholas O. 2015. "Political Powerlessness." *New York University Law Review.* Volume 90, 1527–1608.

Stoddart, Eric. 2014. *Advancing Practical Theology: Critical Discipleship for Disturbing Times.* London: SCM Press.

Walker, Carl. 2010. *Depression and Globalization: The Politics of Mental Health in the Twenty-First Century.* New York: Springer Science + Business Media.

Wykes, Michael. 2003. "Devaluing the Scholastics: Calvin's Ethics of Usury." *Calvin Theological Journal.* Volume 38, Issue 1), 27–51.

Wysong, Earl, Robert Perrucci, and David Wright. 2014. *The New Class Society: Goodbye American Dream?* 4th edn. Lanham, MD: Rowman & Littlefield Publishers.

Zucman, Gabriel. 2016. "Wealth Inequality." In *State of the Union: The Poverty and Inequality Report 2016*, pp. 39–44. (Special issue of *Pathways: A Magazine on Poverty, Inequality, and Social Policy*). Stanford, CA: Stanford Center on Poverty and Inequality. Available at:http://inequality.stanford.edu/sites/default/files/Pathways-SOTU-2016-2.pdf (accessed March 26, 2017).

Zweig, Michael. 2012. *The Working Class Majority: America's Best Kept Secret,* 2nd edn. Ithaca, NY: Cornell University Press.

# 4

# Postcolonializing Pastoral Theology

Enhancing the Intercultural Paradigm

*Emmanuel Y. Amugi Lartey*

## Introduction

In this chapter I shall be focusing on the disciplines of pastoral theology and pastoral care as I trace the emergence of a trajectory of postcolonial criticism in the work of pastoral theologians, especially emphasizing the work of those whose cultural and historical heritage, like my own, is traceable to the African continent.[1] I shall explore pathways in postcolonial thought and practice that seek to enhance an engagement with the cultural heritage of the formerly colonized in ways that lift up subjugated knowledge for the purpose of a more authentic future in which suppressed ways of being and knowing are represented and clearly articulated at the table of all pastoral theology. I write from the region of the United States of America that is referred to as the Deep South, where for the past 16 years I have lived, taught, researched, and provided pastoral care and counseling. I was born in Ghana, then known as the Gold Coast, in the dying years of British colonial rule on the African continent. My own experience growing up, living and teaching in Africa, and then studying and teaching for over a decade in Britain, and now since 2001 here in the US, informs everything I have to say and has had a marked influence on my perspectives and views. Moreover, I have had the honor and privilege of traveling internationally and engaging in research and study in different parts of the world, including extensively in Africa, in Asia, the Caribbean, and South America. My experience has typically been in intercultural communities located in the various countries I have worked in. Coming from a minority ethnic group in my home country, and then sharing the life space and existential realities of minorities— black British, African Americans, and people of color—has given me a particularly keen sense of the experience of being marginalized. However, as a professor and religious leader, privilege and power have not been absent from my experience as well. In this regard marginalization and recognition,

*Pastoral Theology and Care: Critical Trajectories in Theory and Practice*,
First Edition. Edited by Nancy J. Ramsay.
© 2018 John Wiley & Sons Ltd. Published 2018 by John Wiley & Sons Ltd.

oppression and valuing, resentment and respect, rejection and acceptance, have in curious ways been the hallmarks of my existence and social location.

Since the mid-1980s a steady stream of works from pastoral theologians have embraced and operated through a lens that has been described as "intercultural." In this approach a concerted effort is made to seriously promote a dialogical and interactive study and practice of ministry and pastoral care, drawing upon theories and practices from different cultures. The underlying premise of this effort is equal respect for all cultures and all people as bearing the image and likeness of God. The *modus operandi* of intercultural pastoral care and counseling has entailed respectful dialogue between participants from different geographic and social locations in which each purports to learn from the other. If all people are created in and bear the image of God then all have a contribution to make in the presentation of the God of all creation and in the care of all humanity. It goes without saying that if there is to be genuine intercultural interaction among pastoral practitioners, there indeed needs to be recognition and respect for each participant's cultural and religious heritage. Such, however, was not the case from the beginnings of interaction between Europeans and peoples of the rest of the world. When Europeans ventured out of their shores beginning in the 15th century CE it was in a mode of conquest and control of trade, economics, culture, and religion. European civilization sought to dominate and impose its own values on all everywhere it went. European imperialism and colonialism were fueled by views of superiority and patronage.

The colonial project with its inherently oppressive and de-facing characteristics in relation to cultures different from itself has left the partners in intercultural interaction who originate from the former colonies unable to truly engage the colonizers and their descendants from an equal epistemological and political base. Psychiatrist and political activist, Frantz Fanon perhaps most clearly analyzed the deleterious effect of colonialism upon Africans. In *The Wretched of the Earth*, a seminal text that, although predating formal designations of "postcolonial criticism", articulates very well the core values of postcolonial thought. He declared, "Colonialism is not satisfied merely with holding a people in its grip and emptying the native's brain of all form and content. By a kind of perverted logic, it turns to the past of the oppressed people, and distorts, disfigures and destroys it" (Fanon, 1990, p. 169).

Intercultural efforts flounder on the very existence of the inherent inequalities between the partners in dialogue. The playing field is far from level and one of the teams of players has been severely injured prior to the start of the match. As Sugirtharajah, a towering figure in postcolonial studies, puts it in language that describes lingering images of Africa which persist even today, "for colonialism the vast continent of Africa was a 'haunt of savages' replete with 'superstitions and fanaticisms', and was held in contempt and cursed by God" (Sugirtharajah, 2002, p. 17). Intercultural interaction will never bear fruits that are useful all round so long as these social, political, and epistemological disparities exist.

Participants in the intercultural dialogue whose origins lie on the side of the formerly colonized need the uplifting strength and empowerment of their own resources in order to be enabled to relate to the descendants of the colonizers on an equal or at least more fulsome and authentic footing. Herein lies the need for postcolonial theory and practice.

The task postcolonializing activities seek to accomplish entails critique, validation, recovery, and construction. They aim to facilitate the formerly colonized person's authentic participation in intercultural engagement. Postcolonial criticism uncovers the logic of colonialism's constructions of the colonized and demonstrates its inadequacy and misrepresentation of the people and cultures encountered. It also critiques the hegemony and "control over" that is embedded in much of the discourse of relations between nations and cultures. Because of the pervasive, often pernicious, and latent power of the colonial project to the personhood of the colonized, an important aspect of postcolonial criticism and one of its objectives is the "de-colonizing" of the thought, theory, and practice of colonized experience. Postcolonial interpretations of the realities of the colonized validate and revalue their humanity and begin to underscore and strengthen the formerly colonized people's capacity for authentic selfhood.

The task of recovery is often one of a process of re-appropriation of subjugated knowledge and epistemology. Such resurgence requires both historical and constructive research and crafting. Subjugated knowledge needs to be re-appropriated, validated, and put to work in the construction of new realities, theories, and practices able to forge a new consciousness and new orientation to life for all in the future. Postcolonial thought thus requires both courage and creativity.

## How Postcolonial?

The term *postcolonial* has many and varied usages in different disciplines. More often than not it indicates not just a chronological ordering of relations in reference to what follows the colonial, but rather a discourse about existing orientations and in critique of ongoing international relational realities. Generally, it is employed in an attempt to capture two particular features of international and intercultural relations historic and contemporaneous. First, postcolonial studies have been about an analysis of the various strategies employed by colonizers to construct images of and to exercise dominance over the colonized. This form of study undertaken mostly by scholars from the historic colonizing nations can and has been very sharply criticized.[2] Second, postcolonial criticism has referred to the study of the agency of the colonized in making use of and transcending colonial strategies of dominance, subjugation, and demeaning in order to articulate and assert their dignity, self-worth, and identity, and to empower themselves. Sugirtharajah, whose work has been pioneering in the field of postcolonial biblical and Asian studies, describes postcolonial criticism "as signifying a reactive resistance discourse of the colonized who critically interrogate dominant knowledge systems in order to recover the past from the Western slander and misinformation of the colonial period" (Sugirtharajah, 2002, p. 13). This way of using the term has led to a flurry of studies and texts mostly by nationals of the former colonized nations. It is important to note that in this latter way of analysis the critique has included that of the "colonized" themselves and the ways they have at times internalized the images and projections of their interlocutors, as Sugirtharajah puts it postcolonial criticism "also continues to interrogate neo-colonizing tendencies after the declaration of independence" (2002, p. 13).

## Postcolonial Criticism in Pastoral Theology and Care

One of the first publications in the field of pastoral theology and pastoral care to explicitly make reference to postcolonial theory and practice in the sense outlined was *Pastoral Care from a Third World Perspective: A Pastoral Theology of Care for the Urban Contemporary Shona in Zimbabwe*, Tapiwa Mucherera's doctoral thesis published in 2001. Mucherera identifies the existence of deep psychological and spiritual scars needing healing within his formerly colonized Zimbabwean compatriots. Psychiatrist Frantz Fanon's answer to the scars of colonization was a call to Africans to recover their history and reassert their identity, dignity, and culture (Fanon, 1990). Mucherera called for pastoral caregivers with "integrative consciousness," by which he meant caregivers who understood both the traditional African and the Western worldview and were able to integrate these in treatment modalities.

Mucherera's second monograph *Meet me at the Palaver*, published in 2009, lifts up a tried and tested ancient African approach to communal conflict management and education—the village gatherings referred to as "palavers"—and demonstrates how African wisdom operates more adequately in dealing with the HIV/AIDS pandemic plaguing the continent than individualistic Western logo-centric approaches. Drawing on holistic communal narratives and oral story-telling modes of communication, Mucherera takes seriously African attention to spirit, body, and mind, in quest for healing of souls.

The *Journal of Pastoral Theology* has in recent years regularly featured articles that represent postcolonializing discourse. The Society of Pastoral Theology's 2007 annual study conference held in San Juan, Puerto Rico, had as its main theme "Doing Pastoral Theology in a Post-Colonial Context." Articles generated from this conference published in the *Journal of Pastoral Theology* address very squarely the complex and intriguing postcolonial relations within the South, Central, and North American context. This conference was itself evidence of the desire on the part of members of the Society for Pastoral Theology, most of whom are US nationals, to engage decidedly in and seek to study long-standing postcolonial pastoral theological theories and practices promulgated by Central American peoples. In that issue (2007) of the *Journal of Pastoral Theology*, Professor Héctor López-Sierra, pointing to the subversive survival skills (la *brega*) and resilience of Hispanic Caribbean religious subjects, speaks of their need to "reinvent ourselves" (López-Sierra, 2007, p. 60). In the midst of the liminality and hybridity of the Hispanic Caribbean lived experience he argues that "one of the results of that *brega* has been to make our myths and customs survive through the subaltern worldviews and practices of popular religions, spirituality, and multiple religious belongings or 'affiliations' of the peoples" (p. 61). He further points to a postcolonial methodology in which his people "raise an 'ironic syncretic voice' that starts with the criticism and deconstruction of Iberian-European and North American hegemonic God-talk, and ends by subverting the institutionalized story of 'official' Christianity from the hybrid and 'syncretic rhetoric' of 'popular' religion, spirituality, and contemporary socio-cultural knowledges" (p. 61). As López-Sierra shows, Hispanic Caribbean postcolonializing pastoral theology has been going on "ironically" for a long time. Its two-fold methodology, both clear and intriguing, is as follows:

1) Criticize, deconstruct, and subvert the Iberian Europeans and North American hegemonic God-talk.
2) Utilize "the hybrid and syncretic rhetoric of official Christian ecclesial establishment discourse and tradition, 'popular' religion and spirituality, and contemporary psycho-socio-cultural knowledge." (p. 77)

Such deconstructive and constructive strategies are present in all forms of postcolonial pastoral theology and pastoral care.

In 2013 my text *Postcolonializing God: An African Practical Theology* was published, in which I explore historic examples of postcolonializing activities undertaken by different leaders of colonized and formerly colonized peoples. These activities are discernible, if latent, in much of African Indigenous (independent) Christianity and latterly more so in the religious pluralism that is evident in the growth of mystical and inter-religious movements on the African continent and in the diaspora. In direct reference to pastoral care, I raise the centrality of spirituality, the crucial function of building healthy communities, and the transformation of cultures that have been and continue to be key goals of postcolonial pastoral practice, about which more will be found later in this chapter. That same year Melinda McGarrah Sharp offered a work based on her experience as a Peace Corp volunteer in Suriname, South America, titled *Misunderstanding Stories: Towards a Postcolonial Pastoral Theology* (2013). McGarrah Sharp squarely faces a very real challenge of encounters across cultures unexplored in earlier works, namely misunderstandings and conflicts.

Drawing thoughtfully on resources from pastoral theology, ethnography, and postcolonial studies, she provides a valuable resource for relating across cultural difference especially where conflict and misunderstanding rise to the fore. An important methodological recognition that is common to both Mucherera with reference to Zimbabwe (East Africa) and McGarrah Sharp in reference to Surinam (South America) is the pursuit and exploration of narrative as a significant analytic category highly valued within the subjugated knowledge repertoire and practice of colonized people across the world.

In terms of methodologies of pastoral theological research and engagement with the agency of postcolonial subjects, Hee-Kyu Heidi Park demonstrates the two-fold action of postcolonial criticism in, first, unearthing the epistemological assumptions and reductive essentializing tendencies in phenomenology, and, second, in constructive mode, drawing on feminist standpoint theory, indigenous research, and postcolonial theories to propose "a pastoral theological phenomenology that allows the postcolonial person, as a person characterized by hybridity and mimicry, to reflect on the power dynamic within the self and to stand on the bracket as his or her standpoint" (Park, 2014, pp. 3–14). Postcolonial critical studies make room for the complexity of postcolonial experience to find both authentic standpoint and voice at the table.

In a similar postcolonial turn Congolese American pastoral theologian Fulgence Nyengele engages in what is a third feature of postcolonial study, namely the articulation and enhancement of subjugated knowledge. Nyengele lifts up subjugated knowledge in the form of the Southern African concept of *Ubuntu*, bringing it in critical dialogue with the recently articulated discipline of positive psychology "to recover African ancestral wisdom and put it to the positive service of the world" (Nyengele, 2014, pp. 4–28). A significant recent example of this turn to subjugated knowledge and to *Ubuntu* precisely in the field of practical theology was the 2015 International Academy of Practical Theology conference, which was held in Pretoria, South Africa. Twenty-two thoughtful papers from the conference containing reflections on *Ubuntu* as it relates to justice, personhood, and human dignity in southern Africa as well as across the globe are contained in the book edited by Dreyer et al. and titled, *Practicing Ubuntu: Practical Theological perspectives on Injustice, Personhood and Human Dignity* (2017).

Korean American theologian Hee An Choi in *A Postcolonial Self: Korean Immigrant Theology and the Church* (2016), extends postcolonial discourse into the realm of the experience of minorities within the US Western colonial metropolis. As Sugirtharajah, following Madsen argues, "since a sense of commonality runs through the writings of the Third World and American minority writers based on experience of 'imperial domination, cultural catastrophe, genocide, and erasure' (Madsen) there is no justification for excluding their texts" (Sugirtharajah, 2002, p. 35) from considerations of postcolonial discourse. Choi explores how Korean immigrants work to create a different identity in response to life in the US. She discusses how a Korean ethnic self differs from Western norms. She then examines theological debates over the concept of the independent self, and the impact of racism, sexism, classism, and postcolonialism on the formation of this self. The book concludes with a look at how Korean immigrants, especially immigrant women, cope with the transition to US culture, including prejudice and discrimination, and the role the Korean immigrant church plays in this. Choi's work provides an illuminating analysis of postcolonial Korean experience and acts as a resource for postcolonial Asian American pastoral care and counseling.

*Postcolonial Practice of Ministry: Leadership, Liturgy and Interfaith Engagement* edited by systematic theologian Kwok Pui Lan and pastoral theologian Stephen Burns (2016), a ground-breaking text exploring various aspects of practical theology and ministry through postcolonial lenses, was published in 2016. This comprehensive collection of essays, international in scope, covers the various disciplines of practical theology and includes chapters on the "Dynamics of interfaith collaborations in postcolonial Asia" (Jonathan Tan), "Womanist interfaith dialogue: Inter, intra, and all the spaces in between" (Melanie Harris), "Table habits, liturgical *pelau*, and *dis*placing conversation" (Michael Jagessar), and "Church music in postcolonial liturgical celebration" (Lim Sewee Hong). The first section of the book, headed, "Pastoral leadership" contains illuminating pastoral theological articles by Emmanuel Lartey, Melinda McGarrah Sharp, Mona West, and Stephanie Mitchem, all engaging in postcolonial critical discourse in the arena of the spiritual care of individuals and communities.

## Themes in Postcolonial Pastoral Theology

In terms of the emerging trajectory of postcolonial pastoral theology, care and counseling, three main thematic issues are discernible. These are:

1) voice
2) epistemology
3) praxis.

## Can the Subaltern Speak? Voice, Access, Space[3]

Spivak's poignant question draws attention to the complex realities of the silencing and the silence of the economically dispossessed. The issue clearly is not the ability of the subaltern to speak but rather whether they are given the space or the permission to voice their own views or whether Western intellectuals will be the only ones permitted to speak on behalf of the dispossessed and colonized. In postcolonial pastoral theological discourse four types of speaking by the formerly colonized are recognized and discussed. These are mimicry (or imitation), improvisation, innovation, and polyvocality.

## Imitation

*Imitation* (Homi Bhabha's "mimicry") in which the colonized speaks in the very form and "voice" of the oppressor, in my experience is adopted as a strategy to fulfill different objectives. Being able to reproduce the colonizer's speech "to the letter" convinces the colonizer that the colonized, far from being incapable, incompetent or even subhuman, actually possesses all the capabilities of the colonizer. However, as Bhabha argues, mimicry because it always contained an element of mockery, remained menacing to the colonizer always causing uncertainty as to what the colonized was actually trying to convey, and ominously suggesting that the colonized may actually have had an edge over the colonizer (Bhabha, 1984, p. 86).The colonized can "play the oppressor's part." Mimicry as a strategy for the subversion and overthrow of colonialism has become a postcolonial way of life, at times far exceeding even the practice during the colonial period. In Africa we are left especially in the churches with the repetition of the doctrines and negative attitudes of the colonizers toward all things African, to the detriment and neglect of these rich traditions. Many of the traumas suffered by persons of African descent result from inauthentic imitation of the discourse and belief patterns foisted upon us in colonization. Mimicry as a postcolonializing strategy needs reconsideration for its potential to subvert the crucial tasks of recovery, and uncovering of subjugated knowledge can render it counterproductive. Mimicry functions as a defense mechanism needed for the protection of vulnerable souls, yet often masks the painful reality of inauthentic existence. Pastoral caregivers and counselors seek to promote the authentic selfhood of clients and parishioners. In this task though they often have to plow on through and work with the defenses of mimicry.

## Improvisation

In improvisation persons utilize whatever they can find at hand to make the most of an inadequate situation. Improvisation is the creed of the slave, the colonized, the un-free, who must make the most of what is available. The colonized, slaves, and people kept under domination have used incredible skills to improvise. Improvisation is the art of survival. Improvisation is the "muddling through" that is the lived experience of so many former colonized people. Improvisation in music, art, and literature bears witness to the ingenuity and social fortitude of the oppressed. In terms of the colonial experience it seems to me that the colonized and especially the enslaved utilized improvisation to good effect as a survival strategy. As the need arose for the formulation of ceremonies at times especially of gathering, slaves no doubt used whatever was at hand, and whatever they could call to memory in the crafting of rituals of encouragement, memorial, and renewal. With limited resources of education in the languages of the colonizer, the colonized were still able, as for instance in the establishment of independent indigenous churches on the African continent and in the Caribbean and elsewhere, black churches and other black spiritual movements, to form social institutions that resembled those of the colonizers while infusing them with the philosophies and cultural content of their African heritage.

Improvisation as a colonial and postcolonial activity differs from mimicry in that it includes substantial content from the cultural heritage of the colonized. As a postcolonializing exercise improvisation goes much further than imitation. It entails a degree of independence and unconcern with the gaze of the colonizer. In slavery it happened mostly away from that gaze. In colonialism it took place decidedly in contexts in which the influence of colonizers was very limited. Thus, improvisation became a significant strategy of the free in which their dignity and capabilities were expressed and endorsed from within themselves and their own communities. Improvisation continues to be a significant postcolonializing activity, but that of those whose resources in both colonial and indigenous terms, are limited. So long as access and opportunity remain limited, improvisation will continue to be an important feature of the postcolonial discourse in pastoral theology. There is a sense in which the intercultural paradigm currently functions for persons from outside Europe and the US with an improvisational voice. The full function of interculturality therefore awaits the third type of speech.

## Creativity

In creativity the colonized has great facility in both their own arts and those of the colonizer. The creative person has inner freedom that is born of confidence in different spheres and fields of knowledge. Mucherera referred to this as "integrative consciousness" (2001). Such confidence comes from a variety of sources. The creative person is neither afraid of the sanctions of an authority nor has anxiety at the gaze of any legitimizing forerunner. Creativity is what postcolonial pastoral theology craves and calls for. Innovation is the language of postcolonial pastoral theologians who have attained maturity. Postcolonial pastoral theologians are increasingly finding their own authentic voice, and are thus more able to make more substantial contributions to the discipline and practice of pastoral care and counseling. They call for and produce new forms of being, institutions, and practices. They weave together disparate materials into innovative forms and practices. Moving beyond improvisation, which implies utilizing the leftovers and whatever is available in and from the colonial project in the formulation of structures that are implicitly temporary, creativity requires the generation and utilization of new practices, methods, and materials in the development and promotion of substantially different forms of activity that go beyond the status quo inherited or established as standard by colonizers. This is what Héctor López-Sierra has referred to as "reinventing of self."

## Polyvocality

Postcolonial pastoral theologians recognize, operate out of, and highly value *polyvocality*. They recognize and encourage many voices to speak and be heard on the subjects under consideration. Never satisfied with solely one perspective on any subject, the postcolonial pastoral theologian actively seeks out voices other than their own, especially submerged, ignored, or rejected voices, to be invited to the table, and there to articulate their own authentic voice. Subjugated voices with submerged often despised knowledge are given room at the postcolonial table. Educated, middle class, liberal, progressive voices are not the only ones invited to speak. Nor is there an attempt to silence the speech of the uneducated, differently able, or different. Such recognition and encouragement is vital to the postcolonial project. It is precisely the silencing, suppression, denial, or ignoring of voices because of their difference from the dominant ones that has led to the need for postcolonial activity. Postcolonial pastoral theologians seek to make possible the contributions of a rich variety of voices recognizing the infinite value of such at the table of new forms of the pastoral care and counseling needed in these times.

# Knowledge and Epistemology

*The second set of issues that postcolonial pastoral theologians are occupied with has to do with knowledge and epistemology.* Questions such as the following are beginning to be addressed. What specifically do the colonized know and how different is it from Western knowledge? What does postcolonial or de-colonial practical knowledge really look like? Four features of postcolonial pastoral epistemology are apparent.

First, it is recognized that postcolonial activities in pastoral theology need to be *counter-hegemonic*, insurgent even subversive in nature and character. That is to say that postcolonial pastoral theology operates out of a counter-hegemonic epistemology. Such ways of knowledge by their very nature call into question hierarchy, dominance, and hegemony in human relations. Where patterns of dominance have solidified into oppressive structures that stifle or threaten to squeeze the life out of clients, postcolonial pastoral theologians actively support insurgency and may be deemed subversive by the powers that be. They essentially problematize, disrupt, and attempt to subvert dominant structures with a view to the establishment of more equable relations between and among people.

Through recognition of domestication on the part of many who suffered the brutal suppression and selective valorizing processes of colonialism, and of the nature of domesticated discourse, it is possible to discern counter-hegemonic patterns and strategies sometimes deeply embedded within domesticated discourse. It is also possible to recognize more overt forms of counter-hegemonic activities.

Second, postcolonial pastoral care is politically *strategic*. In other words it brings into critical focus the dialogical nature of relations between theory and practice, and results in actions with transformative intent in the world. I have described this kind of knowledge in line with liberation theologians as "praxiological or practical-and-theoretical with an action-for-change orientation" (Lartey, 2013, p. xvi). The kind of knowing referred to here is knowledge gained through action. An example of this that I have utilized in therapy is dance and rhythmic movement. Drawing from ethnographic research I have engaged in with African religious healers, I elaborate on, in a chapter titled, "Knowing through moving: African embodied epistemologies," African embodied ways of knowing self, other, and God. With reference to the Anlo-Ewe people of South-East Ghana and Togo, I explain how "*proprioception*, the term used to describe the sensory information that contributes to the sense of position of self and movement, seems to mark the key to human ontology and epistemology in African traditional and African Diasporan religious practice" (Lartey, 2016b, p. 102). As I have listened intently and participated in the rituals and practices of African religious practitioners, what has been most fascinating for me is that in place of a logo-centric, word-based theory from which is derived particular healing and care practices, African priest healers seem to know through a different means, one more bodily, more incarnational, and especially more kinesthetic. Movement, rhythm, and dance are for them powerful symbols and signals that are cathartic in themselves and also convey important messages that can assist in calling the desired states of being into existence.

Third, postcolonial practical knowledge recognizes its *hybridity* and participation in multidimensional discourses and practices. Such knowledge is intrinsically *variegated* and *plural*. *Diversity* is a hallmark, characteristic feature and desired end of postcolonial pastoral theological processes. As such, it is *messy*, in that it questions and disrupts sharp and clear boundaries between materials, recognizing the often arbitrary lines of demarcation that are drawn, and calling for attention to complexity and *metissage* in the approach to all matters. Sharp demarcations and neat contents are not to be found in postcolonializing discourse and practices. They are therefore also and always ambiguous and at times contradictory, full of contestation and controversy, wary of over-privileging any one form over all others.

Fourth, postcolonial pastoral theology is *dynamic* in nature. Epistemological dynamism recognizes that issues are in a constant state of change and flux. As such, postcolonial pastoral theologians attempt to engage in analyses that reflect time, change, and movement. Analyzing moving structures can be daunting. However, recognizing that social reality is inevitably fluid is a sign of maturity not to be rejected. Postcolonial pastoral theological practices presuppose and therefore prepare for change.

## Practices of Care

*The third issue postcolonial pastoral theologians reflect on has to do with practices of care. What does pastoral care look like when it is informed by postcolonial theory and practice?*

In order to address this in concrete terms consider the following case.

### Case Study

Kofi (40) and Ama (36) have been married for 10 years. They have two daughters (Afia, 8) and Adjoa, 6). For as long as Ama can remember she has felt sad, unwanted, and a sense of not belonging. For the past several years Ama, whose marriage relationship began very well, has felt closed up ("caged," her words) in her relationship with her husband. Recently relations between Kofi and Ama have been rather cold and she has experienced feelings of jealousy that have been heightened by a dream in which she saw Kofi in the company of a female work colleague of his. Kofi has had health challenges and has been in and out of hospital to see his doctor. No diagnosis of his condition has yet been offered. Kofi has an uncle who is an herbalist and who has offered to assist him using African "traditional" medical means. One of Ama's aunts belongs to a group that engages in "meditation" and other Eastern religious practices. She has often invited them to attend sessions with her. All of the extended family attends church regularly as well. Relations in the extended family are generally good, with each agreeing to live and let live. Kofi and Ama are staunch members of a local protestant church, where Ama is in the choir and Kofi often leads prayer services. They are the least tolerant in their extended family, feeling that their relatives are not "faithful Christians" because they engage in religious practices that seem to them to be outside of their Christian faith. Two days before, their youngest daughter Adjoa fell heavily on a concrete floor during a game with her friends in break time at school. It was not clear whether she had been pushed, tripped, or simply had missed her step and stumbled on the uneven floor. She has been admitted at the hospital with a severe head wound and concussion. Kofi and Ama make their way to see their pastor, who is a trained counselor.

In responding to the experiences of Kofi and Ama in terms recognized and lifted up in postcolonial pastoral theology, three concerns are uppermost: the centrality of spirituality in the practice of pastoral care and counseling; the need for the promotion of healthy communities; and the goal of cultural transformation.

## Spirituality is Central in the Practice of Pastoral Care and Counseling

Postcolonial pastoral theologians (Schipani, 2003; Mucherera, 2009,) clearly articulate the need for spirituality to be centrally placed in the practices of pastoral care and counseling. At the core of African anthropologies lies a central organizing aspect of the human personality variously designated (e.g. Akan, *okra*; Gã, *kla*; Ancient Egypt, *ka*; Yoruba, *ori*), which refers to a God-given essence that is received or uniquely chosen in the divine realm prior to a human being's entry onto the earth plane. This spiritual inner reality serves as the core or key driving force of a human being's life purpose, character, or personality. This component of one's personality links one with the divine while also being the core of one's psychology. African traditional healers and diviners locate their activities very often centrally in this aspect of a human's being. Any approach to the care of persons within an African environment that does not address this central feature, or that has nothing to offer that dimension of a person's experience is fundamentally flawed and doomed to failure. Pastoral caregivers within such social and cultural spaces are called upon to engage this "spiritual" element if their work is to scratch where their clients itch. As such, postcolonial African pastoral caregiving attends primarily to the spiritual center and soul of clients. They come to the soul and the psychological theories and the therapeutic practices that follow from them only after they have paid attention to the spiritual core and center. In Kofi and Ama's case, therefore, addressing the spiritual becomes key. The pastoral counselor invited them first to reflect on and relate their concerns in terms of their spiritual perceptions. What inspired their marriage in the first place? What was the nature of their spiritual life, as they saw it, together? What about individually? How would they characterize their relationship with God and significant spiritual persons in their lives growing up? What roles did parents, uncles, aunties, mentors, teachers, and spiritual leaders play in shaping and forming their worldview and understanding of marriage as a spiritual phenomenon? In addressing these questions there is no sense in which a sharp division is maintained between a "religious" as opposed to a "secular" life. In keeping with African traditional world-sense in which no such dichotomizing is sustainable, questions about spiritual life encompass the psychological and social.

Postcolonial pastoral care within African social environments (including African diasporan spaces) finds ways of challenging the psychological reductionism that seems to have been the modus operandi of Westernized approaches to pastoral care and counseling. Postcolonial pastoral care centers spirituality integrally and crucially. Spirituality instead of psychology becomes the major cognate discipline for pastoral care. However "spirituality," understood in the African sense I am discussing, is a synthetic concept. Postcolonial pastoral approaches re-adopt this African sense and engage the spiritual core essence of persons recognizing that this essence has divine as well as psychological, social, and ecological dimensions to its complexity. As such, while privileging the divine, these approaches explore the inter-relationships between the divine, the psychological, the sociological, and the ecological. By ecological I make reference to relations with the natural world: the earth, geographical features such as rivers, rocks, mountains, the flora and fauna, and the world of animals. Postcolonial pastoral care, certainly within an African context, then, is about helping persons fulfill the life purpose and plan they chose and agreed to in the divine realm prior to their birth and entry onto this human plane of existence. It is about discerning and utilizing their "spirituality" to navigate the issues of their life successfully in ways that will contribute to the wellbeing of the human community. So Kofi and Ama are invited to examine their individual and relational lives in relation to their understandings of life purpose, destiny, and vocation in life. They are encouraged to explore the extent to which occurrences in their lives, such as the accident suffered by their child, may be understood as spiritual acting out of tensions and challenges of a spiritual nature. Notions that it is possible for behaviors to be manifestations of spiritual, and not only psychological or social dynamics, are important in postcolonial pastoral care.

However, too sharp cause-and-effect couplings are also subject to question. The logic of the spiritual realm of our lives does not follow a simple physical, rationalistic, reductionist pattern. There is room for unforeseen, unrecognized, or unexpected outcomes in the spiritual realm. Openness to alternative explanations and complexity remains necessary in these spiritual explorations. The key is to explore and examine all perceptions, thoughts, dreams, inclinations, hunches, or assumptions that may be of a spiritual nature, leaving no feelings or thoughts unreviewed. Such thoughts in relation to Ama's dream, Kofi's undiagnosed physical ailments, and Adjoa's fall are all on the table, taken seriously, and examined for any spiritual inferences or implications associated with them.

## Individuals Cannot Be Well in Isolation: Building Healthy Community

Postcolonial pastoral care and counseling emphasize the deeply *interactional*, *interpersonal*, and *intersubjective* nature of the human. Postcolonial pastoral theologians emphasize the social and global nature of phenomena and encourage approaches to subjects that engage interactively with all of people's experience in the discourse on any subject. In other words they engage analytically and relationally with the agents as well as the practices they wish to critique and transform. Relationality is valued especially when it is set within an ethical framework of equality and respect.

For Kofi and Ama this means that the pastoral counselor invites them to explore their relational world in its totality and complexity. Relations with all relatives within the extended families are fair game. A systematic approach is taken, beginning with close family, through church communities, and then living neighborhood, workplace communities, and ethnic group and even national affinity groups are all allowed to be discussed. Within a cultural setting that, on the one hand, values community, and on the other is wary of harm that comes to one through relations, it is crucial that the quest for healthy relations be examined critically. This was exemplified in Adjoa's fall in which there was a lack of clarity as to whether she was pushed, tripped, or whether it was purely "accidental."

Postcolonial pastoral care is about community building. A central motivation for these approaches to pastoral care is a communal relational one. One of the downsides of the drive for the autonomous, self-directed, personally morally responsible, rational, logic-centered individual envisaged and imposed by the Westernizing colonial social agents was the loss of community and the socially and relationally integrated persons that traditional African morals upheld. This is not an argument for one to replace the other, which sadly was the effect of colonialism. Had there been a greater respect for the communal values of the colonized, a better balance would have been sought between the rugged rational individual and the socially responsible communal person. Pastoral counseling in Kofi and Ama's situation required a careful exploration of what healthy community might mean in their specific circumstances. Postcolonial pastoral counseling is directed at the fostering of communities within which acts of care and counseling have meaning and significance, and within which persons may thrive as individuals as well as participants in relational networks to which they may contribute. Pastoral practices and pastoral counseling are the natural outflow of these communities of care. Healthy communities—like healthy families—produce healthy people. Individuals who receive excellent therapy and whose inner lives are repaired only to return into unwholesome social circumstances will soon be re-infected and need to return for individual therapy. It is the growth of healthy societies that will lead to the stabilization of healthy persons. An individual cannot be well in a society that is toxic and that allows illness to fester. In any case there is the need for attention both to the care of individuals and the care of communities if there is to be an encompassing delivery of health.

The aim of postcolonial pastoral care is the cultivation of communal spaces in which all people can be safe, nurtured, and empowered to grow. The focus on individual therapy to the exclusion of communal care follows the pattern of an ineffectual colonialism. Postcolonial pastoral care sets individual therapy within a community-building paradigm that privileges the growth of persons as social beings and communal participants who seek the wellbeing of total groups. Pastoral caregivers, by virtue of their recognition of the importance of communal space and communal resources, will be at the forefront of the struggle for safety in community. They will seek to establish places of safety for all persons at risk of molestation, violence, discriminatory, or oppressive practices of any sort. This will mean a keen eye for potential danger evident in the social climate. Aware of the fact that societies can be manipulated and mobilized in ways that are oppressive of minority groups, they will be searching through social and public policy making processes for any hints of legislation that could prove harmful to certain groups. They will in such instances be willing to organize against such policies ever becoming law.

They will be mobilizing resources for the provision of safe houses for women at risk of violence, and the staffing of such premises with suitably trained personnel. They will be engaging in the political processes of the communities in which they are in the interest of disadvantaged and marginalized groups. This means that a crucial part of the pastoral caregiver's art is listening for the voices of the marginalized of whatever kind. Such voices are frequently very loud by their absence. So pastoral caregivers will be attuned to the voices of the silenced and the silence of the voiceless. Pastoral caregiving includes advocacy for social justice. And pastoral caregivers do not shy away from participating in and engaging the political process in the interest of the creation of humane communities. The goal of pastoral care is always the creation of healthy communities in which *all persons* can live humane lives. Human dignity is premised upon social institutions and processes of nurture and growth.

With Kofi and Ama, the conversations revolve around what healthy community might look like within their extended families. The extent to which they are open and flexible enough to permit difference of opinion and ritual practice in terms of religious or spiritual observance is a measure of the health of their family. Work communities also need to be examined by the same token. Is the school a safe place for the children? Does Afia, their older daughter about whom not much is heard in this case study, have a voice? Is she considered important only in as much as she can be seen to provide role modeling and leadership for her younger sibling? Or does she matter in her own unique right?

## It Takes the Whole World: Transforming Cultures

Postcolonial pastoral care has to do with the transformation of cultures. Postcolonial pastoral theologians see pastoral care really functioning as a liberating human activity, in line with divine activity. As such, it aims at changing underlying assumptions about human communities, about divine presence and activity, and about human wellbeing. Accordingly, postcolonial pastoral care aims not merely at the personal transformation of individuals, but rather at changing the total ecology of the world, the nature of relations between and among peoples. Communities, and therefore individuals, are set within cultures. Whole cultures can promote and maintain healthy communities which, in turn, nurture individuals who are well. Cultures in which the signs, symbols, tendencies, ideologies, and covert assumptions are disrespectful of human persons and death-dealing cannot produce healthy communities. Communities that result from the postcolonial pastoral care activities and practices referred to do bear the hallmarks and characteristics of health, safety, and human dignity, interpersonal, communal, and inter-communal wellbeing.

What needs to change within Kofi and Ama's world and cultural context for there to be greater health and wellbeing for all? This line of examination makes possible a re-examination of the entire assumptive world within which they operate and the opportunity to interact with ideas, concepts, and worldviews that may be foreign or alien to that in which they have been and are living. In postcolonial pastoral care, clients are invited to imagine a world that is completely different from the one they live in and to explore what the nature of their relational patterns might be in such a world.

In Kofi and Ama's pastoral therapy, a time came when they were allowed to craft a play—they were both creative artists—compose music, and then actually dance out in expressive form their vision of a renewed more healthy communal existence. This was done in clear recognition and as an ode to an epistemic turn that postcolonial practical thinking values. Creativity, ritual, and movement can be vehicles of knowledge and transformation that words alone cannot accomplish.

## Conclusion

Postcolonial pastoral theology is charting a trajectory in which the upliftment of the forgotten, denied, suppressed, and subjugated in a range of different practices of pastoral care and counseling becomes a reality. Its aim is not to supplant or replace Western forms of the discipline, but rather to be an authentic partnering voice in what needs to be a global phenomenon in which voices from throughout the world are able to contribute their wisdom and where such contributions are valued and respected. Postcolonial pastoral theology and pastoral care operate under a vision of empowered communities of the oppressed former colonialized peoples of this world. This vision of global responsibility inspires postcolonial theorists and practitioners to recover subjugated knowledge and to revalue silenced people. The table can be enriched. The disciplines of pastoral care and counseling can be more relevant to a world that is diverse and polyvalent—not by a one-size-fits-all monolithic endeavor but instead by a polyvocal, communal, respectful practice of the care of persons.

# Notes

1 In this essay I stay within the discipline of pastoral theology understood as exploring the theological underpinnings, implications, and practices of pastoral care and counseling. In this regard I would define practical theology as encompassing the four disciplines of religious education, liturgy and worship, homiletics, and pastoral theology.

2 For a detailed summary of the most trenchant critiques, see Bart Moore-Gilbert. 1997. *Postcolonial Theory: Contexts, Practices, Politics*. London: Verso, pp. 5–33.

3 Spivak's oft-quoted essay with the title, "Can the subaltern speak?" was published first in Cary Nelson and Lawrence Grossberg's (1988) *Marxism and the Interpretation of Culture*. New York: University of Illinois Press.

# References

Bhabha, Homi. 1984. *The Location of Culture*. London/New York: Routledge.

Choi, Hee An. 2015. *A Postcolonial Self: Korean Immigrant Theology and Church*. New York: State University of New York Press.

Dreyer, Jaco, Yolanda Dreyer, Edward Foley, and Malan Nel, Eds. 2017. *Practicing Ubuntu: Practical Theological Perspectives on Injustice, Personhood and Human Dignity*. Zürich: Lit Verlag.

Fanon, Frantz. 1990. *The Wretched of the Earth*, trans. C. Farrington. London: Penguin Books.

Kwok, Pui Lan and Stephen Burns, Eds. 2016. *Postcolonial Practice of Ministry: Leadership, Liturgy and Interfaith Engagement*. Lanham, MD: Lexingon Books.

Lartey, Emmanuel. 2013. *Postcolonializing God: An African Practical Theology*. London: SCM.

Lartey, Emmanuel. 2016b. "Knowing through Moving: African Embodied Epistemologies." In *Sensing Sacred: Exploring the Human Senses in Practical Theology and Pastoral Care*, edited by Jennifer Baldwin, pp. 101–113. New York: Lexington Books.

López-Sierra, Héctor E. 2007. "Towards a Spanish-speaking Caribbean, Postcolonial, Macro-ecumenical, and Trans-pastoral Practical Theological Method." *Journal of Pastoral Theology*. Volume 17, Issue 2, 57–81. DOI:10.1179/ jpt.2007.17.2.005.

McGarrah Sharp, Melinda. 2013. *Misunderstanding Stories: Toward a Postcolonial Pastoral Theology*. Eugene, OR: Pickwick Publications.

Moore-Gilbert, B. 1997. *Postcolonial Theory: Contexts, Practices, Politics*. London: Verso.

Mucherera, Tapiwa N. 2001. *Pastoral Care from a Third World Perspective: A Pastoral Theology of Care for the Urban Contemporary Shona in Zimbabwe*. New York: Peter Lang.

Mucherera, Tapiwa N. 2009. *Meet Me at the Palaver: Narrative Pastoral Counseling in Postcolonial Contexts*. Eugene, OR: Cascade Books.

Nelson, Cary and L. Grossberg. 1988. *Marxism and the Interpretation of Culture*. New York: University of Illinois Press.

Nyengele, M. Fulgence. 2014. "Cultivating Ubuntu: An African Postcolonial Pastoral Theological Engagement with Positive Psychology." *Journal of Pastoral Theology*. Volume 24, Issue 2, 4-1-4-35. DOI:10.1179/jpt.2014.24.2.004.

Park, Hee-Kyu Heidi. 2014. "Toward a Pastoral Theological Phenomenology: Constructing a Reflexive and Relational Phenomenological Method from A Postcolonial Perspective." *Journal of Pastoral Theology*. Volume 24, Issue 1, 3-1-3-21. DOI:10.1179/jpt.2014.24.1.003.

Schipani, Daniel. 2003. *The Way of Wisdom in Pastoral Counseling*. Elkhart, IN: Institute of Mennonite Studies.

Sugirtharajah, R.S. 2002. *Postcolonial Criticism and Biblical Interpretation*. Oxford: Oxford University Press.

5

# Caring from a Distance

Intersectional Pastoral Theology amid Plurality Regarding
Spirituality and Religion

*Kathleen J. Greider*

> *I am only able to get close to a stranger if I am capable to bear his
> remoteness.*
>
> (Bernhard Waldenfels, cited in Rohr, 2006, p. 30)

In this chapter, using the lens of plurality regarding spirituality and religion, we
reflect on situations where we are called to care amid distances created by our
differences. Our exploration is in four parts: contextualization; related devel-
opments in Christian pastoral theology and care (PT&C); reflection on a case
exemplifying care amid distances affected by plurality regarding spirituality
and religion; and future steps.

## Contextualizing Matters

My commitment to these emphases mirrors the spiritually and religiously
diverse context of Claremont School of Theology (CST) and southern
California. For over two decades, students from diverse traditions have enrolled
at CST, especially due to desire to offer chaplaincy. Our classrooms and their
clinical placements have been laboratories for creating theory/practice in
PT&C informed by but not restricted to the field's Christian origins. This work
also has personal foundations, especially the role of religion in my experience
of economic vulnerability and marginalizing illness in my family of origin, and
learning I sought from feminism and anti-racism training about navigating
asymmetries of power and privilege. I am further informed by experience of
plurality within my religious tradition, Christianity. Learning from other spiritual and religious traditions has helped me navigate distances and divisions I
experience among Christians and leads me to anticipate that readers of this
volume from other traditions will have insights that enrich my own.

*Pastoral Theology and Care: Critical Trajectories in Theory and Practice,*
First Edition. Edited by Nancy J. Ramsay.
© 2018 John Wiley & Sons Ltd. Published 2018 by John Wiley & Sons Ltd.

## Caring from a Distance?

Within liberating traditions of Protestant Christianity, pastoral theologians develop theory/practice that offers caring responsiveness to suffering, interwoven with socio-political engagement informed by caregiving, with commitment to disrupt oppressive systems and decrease the misuses of power that cause suffering. Pastoral theology conceived in this way has been characterized by an intercultural commitment to engage particularity, diversity, and asymmetries in social locations. All this draws attention to the distances between us whenever we apprehend the actual, existential, embodied otherness of others—gaps between us that cannot be closed.

Increased clarity about these gaps implies limits to empathy. Trying to articulate the needed evolution in empathy, David Augsburger offers "interpathy," which increases our attention to difference as we imaginatively engage others' realities (1986, 2014). Whatever terminology is used, contemporary theory/practice in PT&C is grounded in the recognition of complex difference and in confidence, theologically argued, that with enough caring intentionality it is possible to comprehend and make connections with those from whom we are most distant. And, of course, even as we are Other to one another, embodied particularities of wildly differing cultures and worldviews, we experience care. I presume the possibility and value of making caring connections amid difference and distance.

Still, growing awareness of the severity of polarization—globally, in everyday encounters, in our most personal relationships—confronts us with gaps that are persistently, poignantly, painfully unbridged. As surely as we know positive potentials of relationality, we know dispiriting disconnections (also theologically understandable). The differences and distances we appreciate also challenge us, especially when we experience them as unexpected, unwanted, inexplicable, or violating. Whether we call it empathy or interpathy, excessive optimism about human capacity for care amid differences and distances is not warranted. Wisdom requires wrestling with the real limits of our capacity for empathy and interpathy, and with the cost of our denial of those limits.

Differences and distances do not need to be disconcerting or divisive, of course. But when they are, and when neither referral nor abstention from caregiving are adequate, how do we offer care? How do we offer care if closeness, similarity or, especially, agreement and shared affirmations cannot provide sufficient bases for our care? Especially, given intersecting systems of oppression and privilege, what might it mean to offer care that intentionally makes space for distances and divisions, as compared to bridging or transcending them?

## Intersectional Pastoral Theology

Intersectional pastoral theology synthesizes intersectionality theory's emphasis on social justice (Ramsay, 2014, p. 455) and pastoral theology's emphasis on relational justice, to the benefit of both. Justice is created through a web of ethical non-violent social and interpersonal relations grounded in values that serve the common good and abundance of life for all. Justice itself is holistic—subjective and social, interpersonal as well as systemic, enacted at the micro and macro levels. Widespread justice will be attained only through eradication of the cycle of violence, which is fueled by abuse and neglect in interpersonal relationships and by injustice at the systemic level.

Intersectional pastoral theology takes intersectionality seriously in both methodological and phenomenological ways. Relative to our focus, methodologically, intersectional theory analyzes and strategizes with attention to the interactional nature of our personal, group, social, *and religious* locations relative to asymmetrical systems of power and privilege. Phenomenologically, we will focus on plurality regarding religion and spirituality but will resist treating those differences like a special or isolated case of distance or aspect of identity. We will treat religion as sometimes distinguishable, but never separable from, other intersecting aspects of culture and interculturality itself.

## Spirituality and Religion: Plurality, Location, Power/Privilege, Violation

The phrase "plurality regarding spirituality and religion" carries a wide range of meanings. First, religious plura*lism*—the ongoing intentional work of constructive relationality between persons and communities of differing religious identities—is largely beyond our scope. Rather, our focus is mainly on plura*lity*, the mere fact of diverse opinions and identities regarding spirituality and religion, which so often bring distances into sharp focus. Spirituality and religion are aspects of culture where differences between us remain relatively concrete—dress, rituals, prayer practices. Further, plurality regarding spirituality and religion is often fundamental to the affective and cognitive challenges associated with differences and distances: old traditions eclipsed by radical revisions, and secularism; spirituality unamicably divorced from religion; disdainful breaches between conserving and liberating religious camps. In the realm of spirituality and religion, otherness remains obvious and intercultural competence is in its infancy.

The phrase also signals the variety of positions taken vis-a-vis spirituality and religion. That is, whether we are appreciative of religion or ambivalent or antagonistic, or consider ourselves spiritual but not religious, or call ourselves agnostic, atheist, humanist, or are simply uninterested, all these are *locations* relative to religion. From this point on, I refer to all these positions collectively as *religious location*, like notions of social location and personal location (Greider, 2015).

As with our social and personal locations, analysis of power dynamics relative to religious location is a foundational aspect of caring and just relationality. In the US, we benefit from a developing discussion in which *religious privilege*—asymmetry of power in religious location—is being analyzed, a notion that parallels male privilege and white privilege. From his religious location in Judaism, Lewis Schlosser (2003) offered an early examination of the dominance and advantages enjoyed by Christians in the US, where Christian privilege accrues from numerical dominance but even more from the dominance of Christians in positions invested with socio-political and economic power/privilege. In the US, all Christians enjoy religious privilege, to greater or lesser degrees. These dynamics operate professionally, as can be seen in the power/privilege enjoyed by Christians in PT&C.

*Violation* traceable to religious location illustrates the danger of not caring for those with whom we cannot agree. Blaming violence on religious extremism is common. But this is scapegoating. Of all kinds of cultural difference, those related to religious location are most likely to bring out non-negotiable, conflicting values that quickly bring us to the limits of our capacity for peaceable inclusion of difference—disagreements related to parenting, sexuality, and gender are prime examples (Miller-McLemore and McGarrah Sharp, 2010; McGarrah Sharp, 2013). Mutual contempt simmers in the distancing near-silences between religious right and left. Attitudes of religious superiority intersect with racism, nationalism, sexism, and other oppressive systems and attitudes to make our divisions increasingly dangerous—from the vitriolic polarization noted above to religiously fueled microaggressions and hate crimes. The toxicity between us, no matter where we like to place ourselves on the spectrum of attitude toward religion, fuels destructiveness.

### Description of the Case: Parents Circle-Families Forum

Reflection on lived experience and narrative are widely considered to be basic elements for informative scholarship in PT&C. Thus, we turn here to reflection on Parents Circle-Families Forum (PCFF), which describes itself as "a joint Palestinian Israeli organization of over 600 families, all of whom have lost a close family member as a result of the prolonged conflict."[1] Here we focus on the "thick description" prized in practical theologies and in a later section turn to reflection on the case. I choose this case because it exemplifies our foci: caring from a distance amid plurality of religious location; phenomenological intersectionality; and human experience for which PT&C has particular responsibility—in this case, death and mourning complicated by other forms of human violation and divisiveness.

Limits and benefits attend my choice. Obviously, it is far beyond the limits of a chapter to convey or argue the Palestinian–Israeli conflict; basic understanding of the situation must be assumed.[2] Moreover, like PCFF, which strives to be pro-Israeli, pro-Palestinian, and pro-solution, our emphasis is on living and working with the conflict, not on arguing sides. I am in important ways an outsider in this conflict and still implicated; this case exemplifies situations where, though we may not be immediately involved, we still have obligations due to intersectionality, history, globalization, and/or religion. My authority for reflecting on PCFF is limited by my very modest firsthand experience of their work and of Israel/Palestine. Importantly, then, though our method is not technically among the empirical methods increasingly used in practical and pastoral theology, study of this case allows for a value of empiricism: it is based on data accessible for readers' further investigation, mainly, two documentary films, and the PCFF website. Care is central to pastoral theology, and participants in PCFF convey that they experience being cared for; nonetheless, care is not the focus of PCFF and can only indirectly illuminate the complications we encounter when functioning as identified religious leaders and caregiving professionals.

Finally, precisely because it is a situation of unvarnished intersectionality, spirituality and religion are rarely distinct dynamics, forcing us to practice moving beyond single-axis analyses and ferret out more subtle dynamics. Religion is so embedded in these holy lands and intertwined with all aspects of life and the conflict that it is part of every interaction even when not explicit. PCFF participants rarely speak of religion as a distinct entity, perhaps because in this region religion is ubiquitous, not a distinct category. And paradoxically, when PCFF participants do seem to speak explicitly about religion, they are not necessarily speaking religiously, and vice versa. The simple matter of self-naming provides an example. Participants in PCFF mostly refer to themselves as Palestinians or Israelis. Almost always, though unstated, Palestinian = Arab and Muslim, Israeli = Jewish. However, many PCFF Israelis are culturally Jewish but not religious. Important minorities within the Palestinian participants in PCFF are non-observant Muslims or practicing Christians. Further, given that religion is present but mostly implicit in PCFF, other religious communities may be represented in PCFF even though I encountered no explicit reference to them.

As its first name conveys—Bereaved Families Forum—PCFF roots itself in death and grief related to the conflict. Videos of PCFF participants telling the story of their losses show people weighted with the grief of bereavement multiplied: killing of multiple loved ones across generations; conflict-related suicide of bereaved loved ones; for the Palestinians especially, preventable deaths because treatment was not reachable. Violence mars religion and religion magnifies losses when deaths coincide with religious holidays. They are engaged in work for peace, yes, but they are no less scarred and anguished. It is important to remain clear-eyed that PCFF is a story of destruction as much as it is a story of work toward peace.

Bereaved families visit the homes of other bereaved families to share stories, describe their experience of PCFF meetings, and invite families to give it a try. Willing family members come to meetings jointly facilitated by Palestinian and Israeli bereaved family members. Basic communication guidelines are offered and modeled, and the facilitators guide the bereaved family members to create among themselves the kind of space in which they can also slowly create the difficult dialogues that are needed. The team tells the stories of how their loved ones died in the conflict and then the story of their experience of dialogue and work in PCFF. The team makes the main expectation clear: participants are asked to listen to each other and strive, not necessarily to agree, but to understand. PCFF facilitators from both sides express this core commitment—Israeli Daneilla Kitain, bereaved mother: "Our identity won't suffer if we listen to someone else's pain, and vice versa" (Ben Mayor et al., 2012); Palestinian Ali Abu Awaad, bereaved brother: "I don't have to love Israelis to make peace with them" (Avni et al., 2007). A variety of learning modes are used: separate orientation meetings; in small groups and plenaries, participants tell their stories of loss and bereavement and listen to the stories of others' suffering; exercises designed to help participants imaginatively experience the experience of the other; education about the history of the region and its peoples; and guided visits to sites of pain in the other sides' history. Most fundamentally, these meetings aim to provide a space where participants experience the complexity and humanity of their adversaries and begin to comprehend the existence of multiple realities and truths. Especially, they experience unexpected, compelling narratives from the other side that mirror their own, especially persuasive claims to the land and undeniable injustices. Slowly, conflict-filled conversations emerge—about the physical violence and other violations, historical and current, that divide them and led to the deaths of their loved ones. The excruciating honesty is understood as necessary grounding if sufficient trust and cooperation for peace work is eventually to be built.

It is difficult to convey how stunning the PCFF meetings are for participants. For the large majority, especially younger participants, PCFF meetings are often their first person-to-person encounter with the humanity of the other side and almost none has experienced the dialogue and cooperation they witness between the Palestinian and Israeli PCFF facilitators. Most basically, they have not engaged because of frequent language difference—Hebrew and Arabic. (Simultaneous translation is needed in all meetings.) Even if they share language, a workplace, or neighborhood, it is increasingly the case in the region that Israelis and Palestinians rarely encounter one another outside the roles they play in the conflict—they are to each other the more and less powerful, soldier and resistors, oppressors and oppressed, occupier and occupied, settlers and refugees—and all these roles carry valence relative to religion. They lack the most basic conflict-relevant information about each other: that Israelis—females as well as males—are mandated to serve two years in the military after high school; that Palestinians regularly spend hours trying to pass through checkpoints when they need to enter Israel for work or school; that there are everyday people on both sides who believe in the peace process and are working for a solution. Consequently, participants regularly report initial PCFF meetings to be utterly bewildering.

We will use the overarching, single-identity nomenclature they most commonly use for the other side—Israel/Israeli/Jewish and Palestine/Palestinian.

However, intersectional theory helps us comprehend the depth of the confusion they experience: their realities are astonishingly de-centered and their identities complexified. The alienating dualistic dynamics of the primary conflict between Palestinians and Israelis are invaded by new perception of additional circumstances suffered and endured by the other side. Indeed, the common assumption that there are (only) two sides to a conflict is destabilized. The meetings disclose the mindboggling range of peoples present with their diverse personal and communal experiences of the conflict and the attendant asymmetries of power and privilege: women and men; divisions between Jews, from secular to ultra-Orthodox; the minority of Arabs living in majority-Jewish Israel and of Christians living in majority-Muslim Palestine; Muslims navigating diversity of observance among themselves; differing grief of parents, spouses, siblings, and extended families, complicated by the age cohorts they represent; differences in education, financial vulnerability, ways of self-expression.

The mission of PCFF is to increase peace and stop the bereavement. Having watched truth and reconciliation processes around the world, they see themselves as starting that work preemptively, frustrated by their politicians' failure to work out peace accords. Several statements recur as expressions of their mission. They work because of "the unbearable thought of yet another family joining the 'dreaded club of the bereaved'": they want no one else on either side to suffer as they are suffering. They talk to each other because "it won't stop until we talk": not talking, whether in formal peace negotiations or in everyday life, fuels more violence and bereavement. Their public witness leverages on behalf of peace the moral authority of having lost a family member to the conflict: "If we who lost what is most precious can talk to each other, and look forward to a better future, then surely you can, too." To work toward these ends, PCFF takes into the community the model of the face-to-face meetings between bereaved families. "Our most important ongoing daily work," PCFF says, is the many forms of Dialogue Meetings they offer in the community for Israeli and Palestinian youth and adults. These programs allow participants to hear the personal narratives and joint message of an Israeli and a Palestinian representative from the PCFF and then to raise their concerns and questions in free-ranging discussion.

Thus, creating opportunities for difficult dialogue remains the core from which all other PCFF projects emerge, even when the project also has other goals: public art installations to concretize the dialogue; Palestinian women engaged in economic development, assisted by Israeli women; the Blood Relations program—Israelis donating blood for Palestinians, Palestinians donating for Israelis. During the most recent years of violence, PCFF has taken dialogue meetings to Facebook, and to the streets. PCFF members set up tents and chairs in urban spaces and invite passersby—Jews and Arabs—to join the discussion. In every case the goal is to reach skeptics and critics.

Given the particularities of grief, compounded by the volatility of the conflict, it is to be expected that PCFF has critics, about which they are transparent. The PCFF website provides a link to writings by Israeli Arnold Roth, bereaved father, that articulate what are likely to be common critiques: PCFF misrepresents and disrespects bereaved families whose expression of grief and political views differ from PCFF; PCFF's characterization of the conflict is naïve and not balanced, favoring the Palestinian narrative; PCFF's accounting of membership, activities, and use of funds is suspect (Roth, 2014). These critiques are an example of distancing and irreconcilable differences; they are important and, at the same time, do not need to derail us from learning from those who find value in their experience of PCFF.

Reprisal also evidences such criticism. Numerous participants convey that they pay a harsh cost for their involvement in PCFF, especially from their own people. Palestinian Bushra Awad, bereaved mother:

> Some of the [Palestinian] people accept what I am doing and some of them don't. The ones who are against what I am doing are telling me I am selling the blood of my son. But I am not selling the blood of my son and I will never do that. And I'll never forget my son. I am buying the blood of my other children that are still alive. (Kang, 2015)

## PT&C and Plurality in Religious Location: Developments thus Far

Turning to relevant PT&C literature, it is important first to emphasize that there is a multilingual international discussion none of can fully engage. We can glimpse it through conferences and publications sponsored by guilds and described on specific pages of their websites, for example: "Publications" of the Society for Intercultural Pastoral Care and Counseling (SIPCC, n.d.) and of the International Association for Spiritual Care (n.d.); and "Papers" of the International Council on Pastoral Care and Counselling (ICPCC, n.d.). Only English-language literature in PT&C is engaged here. Plurality of religious location has been most substantially addressed in PT&C scholarship through four themes: interculturality in global perspective, especially internationalization; hybridity; postcolonialism; and interfaith chaplaincy.

Substantial engagement with diverse spiritual and religious worldviews arguably first appeared where concern for *interculturality in global perspective* was strong. David Augsburger's *Pastoral Counseling across Cultures* (1986) had groundbreaking effect through combined emphases on interculturality, international scope, and engagement of multiple religious traditions. At about the same time, concern for cultural diversity led to participation of persons from religious traditions not previously represented in guilds such as SIPCC and

ICPCC—particularly Buddhism, Judaism and, later, Islam (Elsdörfer, 2013). Especially, the Christian professionals were confronted in these face-to-face encounters with the relationally destructive effects of their unexamined Christian privilege, insufficient education in other traditions, exclusivist Christian theologies, and, in Christian pastoral care, culturally biased assumptions about soul and spirit, communication, caring relationality, and wellbeing.

Even in their earliest work, Emmanuel Lartey (1997) and Siroj Sorajjakool (2001) personified and led development in the Christian PT&C literature of an emerging synthesis: interculturality, internationalization of scope, and engagement of plurality in personal religious location. Their work and this synthesis evolved into another relevant development: literature engaging *hybridity* in religious and spiritual practice. This literature explores the phenomenon in which persons and communities engage more than one religious or spiritual tradition (e.g. Greider, 2011; Lee, 2011; Bidwell, 2018, forthcoming).

As early as 2002, Lartey observed a number of "post-phenomena" affecting PT&C: postcolonialism, post-Christian, and "post-pastoral" (p. 1), the latter signaling the field's shift away from the Christian terminology of "pastoral care" to "spiritual care." All these effects, along with religious hybridity, are reflected in *Postcolonializing God* (2013), in which Lartey demonstrates how profoundly PT&C is challenged and transformed when Christianity is not assumed and plurality of religious location is taken seriously.

By far the largest portion of resources in PT&C addressing plurality of religious location is motivated and informed by *interfaith spiritual care* (IFSC) and chaplaincy. Chaplains' work in public settings—health care, military, prisons, education—requires spiritual care offered amid direct, daily experience of plurality in religious location. A substantial portion of the resources address preparation for IFSC, not only of students but also of seasoned professionals who received their formal education and certification with little attention to IFSC. Face-to-face encounter within groups of religiously diverse chaplains is especially valuable in classrooms and professional organizations because in such settings caregivers do not need to prioritize the experience of careseekers and can instead focus on their own reactions to religious plurality. English-language resources from the Netherlands (Ganzevoort et al., 2014) and Germany (e.g. Temme, 2011; Weiß, 2011) help us glimpse a global emphasis on such interreligious continuing education in IFSC.

Several book-length treatments help us characterize other resources for IFSC too numerous to cite exhaustively. Dagmar Grefe's *Encounters for Change* (2011) offers the most comprehensive examination of interfaith education and cooperation for the purpose of caregiving, using primarily social psychological and theological analyses. Especially pertinent for our purposes is that Grefe unflinchingly pursues a straightforward question throughout her analysis— "What keeps us apart?" In the gaps, she sees us that we: use social categories that assume too much alikeness; see the best in our "clan" and the worst in others; lack sufficient consciousness of prejudicial stereotypes and systemic discrimination; and allow our realistic fears to be exaggerated. *Intercultural and Interreligious Pastoral Caregiving* (Federschmidt and Louw, 2015) offers an overview of the international discussion SIPCC has created through 20 years of international seminars. It valuably interweaves multireligious perspectives—Christian, Jewish, and Muslim authors—with a global purview—authors from 11 countries. Similarly, *Encounter in Pastoral Care and Spiritual Healing* (Louw et al., 2012) is a window into the contributions of ICPCC and shows how even where Christian location predominates among the authors, integrity in self-reflexivity and interculturality inevitably brings plurality of religious location into discussion.

Authored and edited publications by Leah Dawn Bueckert, a Canadian, and Daniel Schipani, an Argentinian living in the US, comprise the largest share of the IFSC literature. They address foundational, crucial issues for IFSC: prayer, Christian biblical foundations, care for language, ethics of care, practical theological method, pastoral theological reflexivity, and competencies for the sake of cultivating wisdom (Bueckert and Schipani, 2011b). *Interfaith Spiritual Care* (Schipani and Bueckert 2009) helps us identify two major emphases in the literature overall. We find resources that strive to build for IFSC somewhat generalizable models, best practices, rationale, and competencies for education and certification. Also, we find resources that address IFSC in specific national and religious contexts. *Multifaith Views in Spiritual Care* (2013) exemplifies Schipani's leadership in this area; as editor and coauthor he drew together an international group of scholar-practitioners who articulate IFSC from seven spiritual/religious traditions.

## What is in a Caring Distance?: Learning from the Case

What can we learn from PCFF about caring amid plurality of religious location? Space allows us to consider only their foundational activity—face-to-face encounters between bereaved Israelis and Palestinians. Because spirituality and religion are not usually explicit in PCFF and always intersecting with other dynamics, our reflections will emphasize existential, philosophical, and relational concerns arguably at the heart of spirituality and religion. Three themes emerge that address common concerns in PT&C and provide some counterpoint to its commonly emphasized goals:

- Irreparable devastation: attends to death and mourning, and complements emphases on healing and wholeness.
- Inescapable finitude: attends to limits and losses, and complements emphases on empowerment, possibility, and growth.
- Living and working with enemies: attends to just relationality and care, and complements emphases on forgiveness, reconciliation, and conflict resolution.

This reflection is done with respectful acknowledgment of the many Palestinian and Israeli bereaved family members not involved in PCFF, especially those who critique the PCFF approach. They evoke essential, nagging questions. For example, when injustice kills, how is non-violence morally adequate? Intersectionally, what power/privilege might make choice or rejection of the PCFF approach more possible or likely? Interculturally, how do we create enough space for the endless intersecting variety of personal, familial, and cultural circumstances that tax our inclusivity? From a PT&C perspective: if care and increased cooperation for peace are experienced between Palestinians and Israelis involved in PCFF, and publicized, why does that care and cooperation not persuade or attract the majority?

## Irreparable Devastation: Futility and Remorse

PT&C prioritizes excellence in supporting those suffering death and mourning. Relevant to this, the case raises a helpful question: do our emphases on healing and wholeness give sufficient attention to devastation that cannot be repaired, specifically, to the irreparability of lost lives and devastation of grief? As we will see, PCFF participants challenge caregivers to temper our optimism about healing and interrogate our rhetoric that gives preference to wholeness over living amid persistent brokenness.

Of course, anything we learn from the case of PCFF is, at its core, learning from the devastation of death and mourning. Its lifeblood is, paradoxically, irreversible loss. PCFF participants are devastated by their loss, but that by itself does not distinguish them from bereaved family members who disregard or refuse PCFF. The radical decision to participate in PCFF appears to be a turning point, compelled by a new conviction: the old ways of being in the conflict will never repair the devastation suffered by their families and cultures. Two themes can be identified inherent in this conviction: futility and remorse.

PFCC participants convey a poignant experience of *futility* with regard to the death of their loved one and the conflict itself. Many speak of the pointlessness of their loved one's death: it accomplished absolutely nothing; the conflict grinds on the same way as before, only killing more. It seems these families are together first and foremost because for them, though they are enemies, the wastefulness of the conflict is more intolerable. Especially, the strategies of violence used in the conflict are futile. Some protest that officials use the killings politically, to justify more violence, more bereaved families. PCFF aligns itself with the tradition of non-violence, though the common argument participants voice is not that violence is wrong but that it is ineffectual. Palestinian Jalal Khudari, whose mother, two siblings, and friend were killed in the conflict, speaking about his first meeting of Israeli and Palestinian families: "All spoke about pain, and of what we had not gained with violence."

The strategy of violent revenge—though they see it as a natural drive—is especially futile. Israeli Rami Elhanan, bereaved father, describes his first impulse as "an urge for revenge that is stronger than death." But also:

> When the first madness of anger passes, you begin to ask yourself penetrating questions: if I kill someone in revenge, will that bring my baby back to me? And if I cause someone pain, will that ease my own pain? And the answer is absolutely "No."

Palestinians speak of the futility of self-destructive revenge, understanding but rejecting the rationalization of suicide missions. Mazen Faraj, bereaved son:

> It's easy to walk up to a soldier and kill him or go to some organization and obtain explosives. To do a huge terror attack in Tel-Aviv or Jerusalem, blow myself up and kill lots of Israelis but … I believe that … I may have lost my father, but I didn't lose my head. (Avni et al., 2007)

Expressions of *remorse* also distinguish the bereavement of PCFF participants. Remarkable self-reflexivity is demonstrated by participants throughout PCFF materials, perhaps no more than in this example: they examine how their action or inaction before their bereavement might have contributed to the violence that eventually killed their loved ones. Especially, they feel remorse for having been uninvolved in working to increase peace. Indeed, remorse led to the creation of PCFF. During an interview about why he created PCFF, founder Israeli Yitshak Frankenthal, bereaved father, speaks of such remorse:

> After Arik was murdered, I understood that I had failed as a father. … I had brought a son into the world but he did not live—not because he was sick, but because there was no peace. Because I didn't do anything to promote peace. (Ahituv, 2014)

The irreparable devastation of death, and grief complicated by futility and remorse, leaves many without clarity about how to function, even to stay alive. But then, some bereaved families say, the eventual discovery of the work of PCFF was for them "a reason to get up in the morning." Such discovery of a reason to keep living is long in coming and does not repair the devastation. Still, it is life-saving.

What can we learn? Caring from a distance is capacity to acknowledge devastation beyond our comprehension, to lament brokenness that cannot be undone, much less wholly healed, especially death. We admit with sufferers the natural, powerful, tantalizing impulse toward revenging the death of their loved one, and join in the search within ambivalence for strength to resist the pull of retaliation. This is difficult territory for many caregivers. In my tradition, and despite the high value caregiving places on self-reflexivity, progressive Christians often balk at accompanying sufferers into the realities of futility and remorse, and speak precipitous words of hope or absolution. Such "care" may well be a luxury rooted in privileged life experience that distances us from the devastation others suffer and cannot escape.

## Inescapable Finitude: Humanness and Invitation

PT&C prioritizes excellence in supporting those suffering the limits and losses inherent to our human condition. Relevant to this, the case raises a helpful question: do our emphases on empowerment, possibility, and growth give sufficient attention to the inescapability of limited power, lost possibilities, and the unavoidable finiteness of our human condition? As we will see, PCFF participants challenge caregivers to see in the gaps between us actual differences of opportunity and capacity and question strategies for care that fail to account for all that is not within reach.

PCFF materials convey that for participants, the experience of futility and remorse in the devastation of bereavement often evolves into increased cognizance of finitude's inescapability. Of course, the devastation of their loved ones being killed is a jolting confrontation with what is surely the most inescapable aspect of human finitude—mortality, the transience of human life, including their own limited time. Additionally, PCFF participants convey awareness of living in inescapable finitude through at least two other emphases: a heightened sense of the humanness of self and others, which, in turn, increases openness to invitations to meet their enemies.

PCFF narratives suggest that confronting the very *humanness* of humanity lays a foundation that seems later to embolden participants for the countercultural action of meeting with the enemy. Their humanness comes through in numerous forms. Participants convey being rocked by experience of their vulnerability—loss has broken into their lives like a thief, robbed and ransacked them, made plain the illusions of control, safe space, protection, security. They are humbled people, not in self-effacing ways, just very aware of their limits. Lack of pretense allows a transparency and authenticity about the humanness of struggle and the struggle to be humane.

Being grounded in realism about the inescapability of their own finitude seems to prepare them for encountering the finitude of other humans and experiencing appreciation when others exceed the most minimal expectations: Palestinian Hanim Sbieh, bereaved sister, thanks other participants at a PCFF meeting, saying "I think finding a person who's willing to think about you is a great achievement" (Ben Mayor et al., 2012). They openly admit lack of understanding and even, remarkably, a dawning awareness of their ignorance about the enemies they thought they understood all too well. A Palestinian Christian, Imad Amin Abu Nssar, tells of learning by happenstance, after participating in a demonstration that turned into rock-throwing, that Israelis had been protesting with him and protected him from Israeli soldiers:

> For me it was a big surprise. It was the first time that I met Israelis who were not interrogators or soldiers or settlers. It sounded strange when one introduced himself as a university lecturer, the other as a student and the third as an engineer.

Eventually, Israeli Rami Elhanan, bereaved father, wrestled with his ignorance about his enemy, posing "penetrating questions" to himself about the suicide bomber who killed his daughter and her friends and allowing some curiosity about his enemy to emerge.

> During a long and slow, difficult and painful process you gradually reach the other road, and you try to understand: what occurred here? What can drive someone to such anger and despair as to be willing to blow himself up together with little girls? And most important: what can you, personally, do to prevent this intolerable suffering from others?

And then, they experience an *invitation* from a PCFF member to meet other bereaved families from among their enemies. In this terrain of irreparable devastation and inescapable finitude, how can they accept this invitation? Perhaps the confrontation with futility, remorse, and humanness of self and Other has the paradoxical effect of nursing desperation, and then desire for some different experience. Perhaps the known danger of the enemy has been relativized by their battle with finitude's other dangers. Somehow, intrapsychic, interpersonal, and psychosocial ground is cultivated for encountering the other side more directly, even allowing the choice to expose one's bereaved self to the enemy.

Sometimes the invitation is between persons on the same side of the conflict, which can allow for easier trust, and candor. Rami Elhanan remembers that it took a year to be ready to accept his invitation to a PCFF meeting, which came from another Israeli, PCFF founder Yitshak Frankenthal.

> He suggested that I come to a meeting of the "bunch of crazies" and see with my own eyes. Not wanting to offend him, and also because I was a bit curious, I went.

Here we can see the synergy of Elhanan's budding curiosity combining with Frankenthal's non-pressuring, even lighthearted tone. The preposterousness of such people meeting—"crazies"—is complemented by a significant but simple request—"see." The invitation is modest: try, once, to approach your enemy human-to-human. The minimalism of the invitation, so important for making the impossible possible, foreshadows the oft-repeated expectation of PCFF meetings: not to agree with the enemy, much less love or even forgive, but to listen, to try to understand.

Sometimes, though, the invitation comes from, and is the first encounter with, the enemy. Frequently, Israelis extend the invitation to Palestinians, one way in which prevailing power dynamics are acknowledged and challenged early in PCFF processes. It is impressive to Palestinian participants, though ambiguously so, when Israelis take the initiative and first risk, venture into wary Palestinian neighborhoods, reject domination and instead choose to expose themselves by offering their stories of bereavement, risk extending such preposterous invitations. After becoming active in PCFF, Israeli Rami Elhanan, bereaved father, went to a Palestinian home to meet a bereaved family and invite them to try a PCFF meeting. Palestinian Osama Abu Ayash, bereaved brother of the family being visited, recounts a rocky experience often echoed in PCFF narratives:

> I saw an Israeli car parked nearby the house of my sister and her husband Razi. I asked who the visitors were. When I heard that they were Jews I said to Razi: how can you bring home Jews who killed your brother, have you forgotten his blood? He told me that his visitors had lost dear ones in a terrorist attack. "Please," he said, "they are here, enter and speak to them. If they don't find favor in your eyes, you can leave." I said that I will not leave and it is they who will go and not return. However, when I entered I met someone by the name of Rami Elhanan who respectfully stood to greet me. He shook my hand. I felt as though he was about to kiss me. I asked: "What are you doing here? Aren't you afraid?" He said: "Aren't we all human beings?" He started to tell me how he had lost his beloved daughter and how much he missed her. He encouraged me to speak about our pain. He told me that he recognizes the Palestinian pain and feels that it is imperative that a Palestinian state be established. It is necessary to put a stop to the occupation. He told me that he is working to that end with the Forum of bereaved families, both Palestinian and Israeli. Rami spoke about the Forum, its members, objectives and activities. His words were strong and convincing. I also told him about our loss. He invited us to join the Forum, to become members. ... I agreed to become a member of the Forum at that moment.

Certainly, decisions to choose PCFF this quickly are rare. And it is essential not to sentimentalize this moment: personal loss, compounded by the long disaster engulfing the region, has brought PCFF participants so low that they do the unthinkable—they stop waiting for the ceasefire and, unarmed, walk toward the enemy amid danger. Still, as we turn our attention to reflection on what happens in the meetings, we will encounter in different forms the startling power of a PCFF mantra: "[The killing] won't stop until we talk." And when they do begin to talk, PCFF members appear to experience on both sides what Mazen Faraj, bereaved son, articulates from a Palestinian perspective:

> [The meeting] was completely strange for me. They wanted to hear, they wanted to listen, they wanted to talk with you. Not like with Israeli soldiers, or in an investigation. Not as intelligence agents or that you are working with them. No. They want to talk as humans.

Discovering humanity where we had only seen inhumanity, risking invitation to meet, can be the fruit of accepting finitude's inescapability.

What can we learn? Caring from a distance means not distancing ourselves from the realities of mortality, which, despite our denial of death, is not a distant threat. We know that fears and limits that seem to us unrealistic or exaggerated are fed by actualities we cannot know. We refuse grandiose hopes, refuse to ignore that we can barely know the constraints sufferers endure. Our awareness of sufferers' smallest accomplishments is heightened, limits and losses having turned them into achievements, for which we offer respect. Our invitations are gentle, our expectations modest, both spoken only because we have taken the risk we ask of the other.

### Living and Working With Enemies: Validating Pain and Multiplying Truths

PT&C prioritizes excellence in supporting those suffering conflict and injustice. Relevant to this, the case raises a helpful question: do our emphases on forgiveness, reconciliation, and conflict resolution give sufficient attention to situations where the continuation of conflict is necessary to establish justice and, thus, the capacity for living and working constructively amid conflict is urgent? PCFF participants challenge caregivers to ferret out tendencies we have toward conflict avoidance or privileged sentimentality about peacemaking and to develop values and practices necessary to support those who must live with their enemies and with that which is unforgivable, irreconcilable, or unresolvable. Space allows for attention to only two themes, chosen for their role in evoking cooperation among these adversaries: mutual processes of validating pain and multiplication of narratives of truth.

Israeli Rami Elhanan recalls his initial experience of Palestinians at a PCFF meeting of bereaved families:

> And then I saw an amazing spectacle! Something that was completely new to me. I saw Arabs getting off the buses, bereaved Palestinian families: men, women and children, coming towards me, greeting me for peace, hugging me and crying with me. ... And I distinctly remember, a respectable elderly woman dressed in black from tip to toe and on her breast a locket with a picture of a kid, about six years old...

This experience exemplifies many others where PCFF participants allow insight to break into their stereotypes of the Other—ignorance yields to amazed recognition of the ordinary humanity of their enemy. One of Elhanan's most detailed perceptions is recognizing that behind the ubiquitous black veil is an old woman grieving a child lost to battle. Suddenly, insight dawns: it could have been a locket with a photo of his own 14-year-old daughter, killed in a suicide bombing by Palestinians. It seems that perceiving the meaning of that sight opened Elhanan to a first moment for *mutual validation of pain*. This veiled woman wears, literally, a stereotype of terrorism. Simultaneously, he sees in her—and she in him, apparently—the suffering of bereavement both know in their bones. One side initiates risk and the other side risks in return. Both sides allow themselves to show that they are touched by the sight of the other: she moves toward him, and he toward her. She offers embrace, and he accepts. Then, somehow, all around, enemies are reciprocally offering physical touch, tears, words of opportunity.

Imagine the cognitive dissonance, psychospiritual upheaval, and clash of worldview in their bodies/minds/spirits. Their pain is acknowledged, not rebuffed, by people who represent the enemy. That the expression of pain is mutual seems to draw them into new ways of interacting with their enemies. Palestinian Jalal Khudari, bereaved son, brother, and friend: "The fact of seeing an Israeli feeling pain and loss led me to speak with him, to tell him what had happened to my family."

This is crucial: mutuality is not equality. The touching encounter described above by Elhanan is set in motion because the occupied moved toward their occupiers. This is, sadly, given the human tendency to hoard power, what is required to disrupt asymmetrical power dynamics—the less powerful initiate humane interactions with the more powerful. Whenever we are privileged and protected peoples, we almost never initiate the redistribution of our power. Then again, when we reflected above on invitation, we considered a vignette in which Elhanan had taken the risky first step toward Palestinians, voluntarily relinquished some of the privilege of the occupier, exposed his vulnerability to his enemy. But even so, mutual validation of pain does not override asymmetries in power, pain, and responsibility. A bereaved Palestinian:

> Our suffering is different from theirs. They're the cause of our suffering. Whether or not they suffer, they must deal with the consequences. ... One of them might have lost a son but it doesn't make us equal. It can't! (Ben Mayor et al., 2012)

Also, this is crucial: the enemies continue to be enemies, including the most religious. Israeli Dudu Shilo, twice-bereaved uncle from a family of rabbis and principal of a school for mysticism, says that he cooperates with Palestinians not because they cease to be the enemy but because they continue to be the enemy:

> Because of the way in which they chose to kill citizens, women and children indiscriminately, in my eyes they are terrorists, rather than freedom fighters. So why do I sit with them? Because they are the enemy. Must I forgive them? Not an option.

As noted above, PCFF processes intentionally make space for the conflict to continue in the meetings, not requiring agreement, much less love or forgiveness. As Palestinian Ali Abu Awaad, bereaved brother, says, "we're here to put all our problems on the table and try to reach a mutual understanding." Skepticism abounds about the possibility of experiencing understanding, much less mutuality. Words spoken by bereaved Palestinian Tamer Atrash could have been spoken by an Israeli:

> We're going to sit there and enumerate our rights and they're going to deny them and tell us we have none. Things will get violent, we'll curse each other. Then what? (Ben Mayor et al., 2012)

Indeed, physical non-violence is required, but verbal and psychospiritual conflict rages in the meetings. The diversity strategy of "difficult dialogues" on controversial social issues to promote pluralism is increasingly popular. But this terminology pales when the difficulties are rooted in each person's/people's devastations and core truths, so often rationalized via religion. PCFF processes remind us that even as mutual validation of pain and compassion for one another begin to emerge, in these difficult dialogues the mutual infliction of pain continues. The pain that begs for mutual validation is not past but reoccurring. Participants are deeply touched by mutual recognitions even as they are deeply enraged by mutual elisions and offenses. PCFF processes are a rollercoaster—politically, relationally, psychospiritually.

Arguably most important where the pain is concerned, PCFF processes include visiting physical locations where the pain inflicted, past as well as present, is more viscerally experienced. The two groups travel together to places of Palestinian pain. Israelis experience how Arabs are treated at checkpoints and how the security barrier walls off employees from work, children from schools, families from relatives. They spend unsegregated time in the West Bank, so that the Israelis might experience, alongside the Palestinian participants, mistreatment by Israeli settlers. They travel to ruins of Palestinian villages destroyed in *al-Nakba*, the campaign carried out by Zionists during the 1948 War during which Arabs were massacred and survivors exiled, and at those sites Palestinian participants tell Israelis the stories of how their families suffered. Israelis are taken by Palestinians to the numerous refugee camps established after *al-Nakba*, and see the conditions in which many Palestinian families have lived during the decades that have passed. Bereaved Israeli, Shira Zimmerman:

> Listening to the Palestinians talk today, I feel like this is the first time I've really encountered the conflict. Em … you're always hearing about it, but listening to people tell their painful life story, it feels like I'm encountering it for the first time. And it isn't easy to be on the hurtful side. (Ben Mayor et al., 2012)

The two groups travel together to Yad Vashem, Israel's official memorial to the Holocaust, and Israelis tell how their families continue to suffer because of that genocide. The average Palestinian has little education about the long history of anti-Semitism or even the Holocaust. Imad Amin Abu Nssar, bereaved former soldier:

> We [Palestinians] had heard previously of the Holocaust, but we didn't really know much about it and didn't delve too deeply into the topic. When one hears of the Holocaust from a person whose father or grandfather experienced it firsthand, it is very difficult.

He refers to Holocaust survivors who speak at the meetings, such as Israeli Yaakov Guterman:

> When a Jew or an Israeli talks about security arrangements he's really thinking about his children's gas chamber. He lives in a constant state of anxiety. Is that normal? Of course not. But it's there and you have to understand that. (Ben Mayor et al., 2012)

In the PCFF process, experiencing the present pains and their excruciating histories is exactly what sets in motion not only the mutual validation of pain but also *recognition of the multiplicity of truth*. When the battle is waged not only remotely but also with the people in front of you, the mutuality of anguish and passion in differing histories and truths becomes more perceptible and, for most, undeniably convincing and moving. In PCFF meetings, adversaries grow in understanding of each other as they are moved by the pain and truth in each other's narratives, now unavoidably embodied in persons who have, just a moment ago, mutually embraced.

Again, mutuality is not equality. Asymmetries of power play out especially here. Israelis resist listening to the pain of the Palestinians, or do so reluctantly, knowing it will confront them with the pain their peoples' actions have caused and the inequality of suffering. Palestinian Mazen Faraj, bereaved son, on being a facilitator of a joint meeting: "It was hard to push the Israelis down to hear and receive this information, not just to send information." Israeli Ohad Tal, bereaved friend, demonstrates the dominator's struggle to receive and not just send information to the dominated:

> When you're facing a [Palestinian] victim then you're always on the defensive, you're always trying to explain yourself and prove you aren't some cruel occupier, that the pain they cause you is just as bad as theirs. (Ben Mayor et al., 2012)

Slowly, the recognition of the mutuality of pain and of the multiplicity of truths begin to intertwine. Before a joint meeting, bereaved Israeli Yarden Schwartman is courageous to admit to other Israelis her fear of encountering competing, compelling truth claims: "I'm worried I'll understand them [Palestinians]. I'm worried they'll be right. I live here, this [land] belongs to me, but I'm uncomfortable with it." After many meetings, Israeli Ohad Tal, bereaved friend, sees that enemies' pain and truth can be like mirror images:

> What changed in me is that I understand today more of their pain ... after you understand their point of view, you can understand why, when a mother tells the story of her boy who goes to the street and a soldier points a gun at him or shoots at him, this soldier—from their point of view—has hurt an innocent [Palestinian] person exactly in the same way a suicide bomber kills innocent [Israeli] people. (Ben Mayor et al., 2012)

Finally, Israeli Roni Hirshenson, bereaved father, demonstrates mutual validation of pain and multiple truths, in the midst of inequality:

> I think both sides are demonizing each other, I think, but we have to flip it. We must express sympathy for the sorrow and pain the other side suffers. We need to listen to them and they must listen to us—the Jewish people, who returned after 2000 years of exile, without a homeland and after the experiences of the Holocaust, this is the only place where we can live. [However,] we came to a place that wasn't empty or uninhabited. The people living here are entitled to self-determination, you can't take freedom away, or someone's desire for self-determination and independence ... a person will revolt against you. (Avni et al., 2007)

What can we learn? Caring from a distance is, often, caring amid painful conflict, not expecting, much less requiring, that hostilities end. We do not assume that others enjoy or need, even if we do, the luxury of safe space. In Christian PT&C, we have emphasized forgiveness and reconciliation, as if conflict must end before care can have integrity. But, given that conflict is never-ending, PCFF helpfully reminds us of the reality: difficult dialogues are painful dialogues. Dialogue in our intractable conflicts will mean harsh words rooted in past injustice and conflicting truths, more experience of the power of language and emotion to attack and wound reciprocally. The value of language care (Bueckert and Schipani, 2011a) is not limited to the carefulness of diplomatic words. No, PCFF meetings, like all truth and reconciliation processes, show that we express care for and through language when we facilitate the tough talk necessary for psychospiritually honest expression of our differing convictions and experience of woundedness at the hands of the other. In caring from a distance, enemy love, a notion treasured in many spiritual and religious traditions, is not sentimentalized, not denuded of the very conflict that makes us enemies. Enemies can, indeed, love one another, without first becoming friends.

## Future Steps

We close by enumerating a few further emphases emerging from the case of PCFF that help us chart the future of caring in situations of distance and division. Fundamentally, the profound transformation in which PCFF antagonists come to have benevolent relations is a mystery, religiously and otherwise, as Israeli Rami Elhanan, bereaved father, suggests:

> I am not a religious person—the very opposite—and I have no way to explain the change that came over me in the first meeting with members of the forum.

Thus, first, acknowledge spiritual mysteries like enemy love, conflicting truths, finding a way to go on when what matters most is lost. Theoretical models and lists of competencies for IFSC are valuable but have integrity only if they make space for sacred realities not fully accessible to us. We would all do well to read and imitate Jenny Gaffin's (2009) model and competencies for IFSC: after numerous years of experience, she has come to value "bumbling along with as much goodwill and humility as I can muster" as "the only honest approach possible, and the only stance I can adopt which will free other people up to share their lives with me" (p. 347).

Develop spiritual fortitude to endure the decentering, ambiguity, and confusion inherent to distances and divisions. Equanimity, humility, kindness, remorse, and patience are required. Words spoken at an SIPCC seminar describe well the intense spiritual demands of intercultural and interfaith encounter:

> handle one's own as well as the others' individual and cultural weaknesses, regressive and sometimes aggressive impulses, to bear feelings of impotency, fear of failure, feelings of insufficiency and if possible to turn the crisis into something productive and creative … look at the crisis, the

feeling of lost security and helplessness as a new chance, a different approach and a different way of understanding ... find ways to meet and forms to communicate that endure intimacy and remoteness, touching and defence, understanding and non-understanding. (Rohr, 2006, p. 30)

Approach the unknown in others with reverent curiosity, seeking not to override gaps between us but instead trying to comprehend what is in them and, even more, all that we cannot, will never, comprehend. Practice trust that gaps between our experience and others' have resources for healing and wholeness that we will not immediately recognize. Prioritize understanding and conversation more than agreement.

Acknowledge genocides and the real possibility of annihilation embedded in all injustice. Seek to comprehend how we and our people have harmed others. Prepare to tell and hear, repeatedly, mutually, stories of conflicting pains and truths.

Seek wisdom and spiritual grace to navigate fluctuating asymmetries of power: restrain, relinquish, lend, and assert our power as needed for the sake of caringly just relationality. Study intersectional theory as it develops, including dynamics of religious privilege and bias. In place of the *self*-reflexivity PT&C has prized, develop *relational-analytical-intersectional* reflexivity: identify interconnections of self-with-peoples-and-contexts, question self as well as affirm self, fully examine our power as well as our disempowerment, how our multiplicity of identities leads us, inevitably, to perpetuate and benefit from injustice, not only suffer from it.

Finally, it is commonly asserted that meaning-making distinguishes spirituality and, as well, the kind of care offered by religious and spiritual caregivers. However, PCFF suggests that Martin Walton's claim may be accurate: receptivity of otherness, more than the making of meaning, characterizes lived spirituality (2013). Understandably, caregivers welcome similarities, connections, agreeableness, and other comfortable relations. However, integrity in caregiving amid spiritual and religious plurality may well require that, as a fundamental spiritual desire, we welcome differences, distances, disagreeableness, and other uncomfortable relations. Receiving otherness—religious and otherwise—may be a reliable common ground we experience rarely but, together, can co-create.

## Notes

1 Parents Circle-Families Forum (n.d.). www.theparentscircle.com/Content.aspx?ID=2#. WHeZDbYrLpB (accessed January 11, 2017). Unless otherwise indicated, all information provided relative to PCFF and family narratives is taken from their website at www.theparentscircle.com/Home.aspx.

2 The PCFF website, especially the Reconciliation Center, offers a starting point for readers unfamiliar with the conflict.

# References

Ahituv, Netta. 2014. "The Saddest and Most Optimistic Peace Organization Turns 20." Haaretz, October 17, 2014. Available at: www.haaretz.com/israel-news/. premium-1.620808 (accessed January 30, 2017).

Augsburger, David W. 1986. *Pastoral Counseling across Cultures*. Philadelphia, PA: Westminster.

Augsburger, David. 2014. "Interpathy Re-envisioned: Reflecting on Observed Practice of Mutuality by Counselors Who Muddle Along Cultural Boundaries or Are Thrown into a Wholly Strange Location." *Reflective Practice: Formation and Supervision for Ministry*. Volume 34, 11–22.

Avni, Ronit, Julia Bacha, Joline Makhlouf, Nahanni Rous, Just Vision (Firm), and Typecast Films (Firm). 2007. *Encounter Point/نقطة لقاء*. Widescreen format (16:9). Brooklyn, NY: JustVision.

Ben Mayor, Tor, Ayelet Harel, Yoav Leshem, The Israeli Production Company "2Shot" (Firm), The Parents Circle-Families Forum (Firm), and The Palestinian News Agency "Maan" (Firm). 2012. *Two Sided Story/לסיפור פנים שני/قصة ل ة ذ وجهان*. English version. Israel: Parents Circle-Families Forum.

Bidwell, Duane R. (2018, forthcoming). *Spiritually Fluid: What We Can Learn from Hinjews, BuJus, Buddhist-Christians and Others with Complex Religious Bonds*. Boston, MA: Beacon.

Bueckert, Leah Dawn and Daniel S. Schipani. 2011a. "Interfaith Spiritual Caregiving: The Case for Language Care." In *Spiritual Caregiving in the Hospital: Windows to Chaplaincy Ministry*, rev. edn., edited by Leah Dawn Bueckert and Daniel S. Schipani, 287–308. Kitchener, ON: Pandora.

Bueckert, Leah Dawn and Daniel S. Schipani, Eds. 2011b. *Spiritual Caregiving in the Hospital: Windows to Chaplaincy Ministry*, revised edn. Kitchener, ON: Pandora.

Elsdörfer, Ulrike, Ed. 2013. *Interreligious Encounter on* Cura Animarum. Zürich: Lit Verlag.

Federschmidt, Karl and Daniël Louw, Eds. 2015. *Intercultural and Interreligious Pastoral Caregiving: The SIPCC 1995–2015. 20 Years of International Practice and Reflection*. Norderstedt: Books on Demand.

Gaffin, Jenny. 2009. "The Bumbling Pastoral Worker: Theological Reflections on a Lesbian, Gay, Bisexual, Transgender Interfaith Project." *Practical Theology*. Volume 1, Issue 3, 341–358. DOI:10.1558/prth.vli3.341.

Ganzevoort, Reinder Ruard, Mohamed Ajouaou, André Van der Braak, Erik de Jongh, and Lourens Minnema. 2014. "Teaching Spiritual Care in an Interfaith Context." *Journal for the Academic Study of Religion*. Volume 27, Issue 2, 178–197. DOI:10.1558/jasr.v27i2.178.

Grefe, Dagmar. 2011. *Encounters for Change: Interreligious Cooperation in the Care of Individuals and Communities*. Eugene, OR: Wipf & Stock.

Greider, Kathleen J. 2011. "Religiously Plural Persons: Multiplicity and Care of Souls." In *Pastoralpsychologie und Religionspsychologie im Dialog/Pastoral Psychology and Psychology of Religion in Dialogue*, edited by Isabelle Noth, Christoph Morgenthaler, and Kathleen J. Greider, 119–135. Stuttgart: Kohlhammer.

Greider, Kathleen J. 2015. "Religious Location and Counseling: Engaging Difference and Diversity in Views of Religion." In *Understanding Pastoral Counseling*, edited by Elizabeth A. Maynard and Jill L. Snodgrass, 235–256. New York: Springer.

International Association for Spiritual Care. n.d. "Home Page." Available at:https://ia-sc.org/ (accessed December 28, 2016).

International Council on Pastoral Care and Counselling. n.d. "Home Page." Available at: www.icpcc.net/ (accessed December 28, 2016).

Kang, Bhavdeep. 2015. "Two Mothers Bound by Tragedy Find Purpose after Grief." *NYTLive*, November 20. Available at: http://nytlive.nytimes.com/womenintheworld/2015/11/20/two-mothers-bound-by-tragedy-find-purpose-outside-of-grief/.

Lartey, Emmanuel Yartekwei. 1997. *In Living Colour: An Intercultural Approach to Pastoral Care and Counselling*. London: Cassell.

Lartey, Emmanuel Yartekwei. 2002. "Embracing the Collage." *Journal of Pastoral Theology*. Volume 12, Issue 2, 1–10.

Lartey, Emmanuel Yartekwei. 2013. *Postcolonializing God: An African Practical Theology*. London: SCM.

Lee, Insook. 2011. "Zen and Pastoral Psychotherapy: A Reflection on the Concept of No-I." *Journal of Pastoral Theology*. Volume 21, Issue 1, 3-1-3-13.

Louw, Daniël, Takaaki David Ito, and Ulrike Elsdörfer, Eds. 2012. *Encounter in Pastoral Care and Spiritual Healing: Towards an Integrative and Intercultural Approach*. Zürich: LIT Verlag.

McGarrah Sharp, Melinda A. 2013. *Misunderstanding Stories: Toward a Postcolonial Pastoral Theology*. Eugene, OR: Pickwick.

Miller-McLemore, Bonnie J. and Melinda A. McGarrah Sharp. 2010. "Are There Limits to Multicultural Inclusion?: Difficult Questions for Feminist Pastoral Theology." In *Women Out of Order: Risking Change and Creating Care in a Multicultural World*, edited by Jeanne Stevenson-Moessner and Teresa Snorton, 314–330. Minneapolis, MN: Fortress.

Parents Circle-Families Forum. n.d. "Home Page." Available at:www.theparentscircle.com/Home.aspx (accessed January 11, 2017).

Ramsay, Nancy J. 2014. "Intersectionality: A Model for Addressing the Complexity of Oppression and Privilege." *Pastoral Psychology*. Volume 63, Issue 4, 453–469. DOI:10.1007/s11089-013-0570-4.

Rohr, Elisabeth. 2006. "Intercultural Competence." *Intercultural Pastoral Care and Counseling: The Magazine of SIPCC*. Number 13, 26–31.

Roth, Arnold. 2014. "First Understand the War and the Grief." *The Algemeiner*. June 27, 2014. Available at: www.algemeiner.com/2014/06/27/first-understand-the-war-and-the-grief/ (accessed January 27, 2017).

Schipani, Daniel S., Ed. 2013. *Multifaith Views in Spiritual Care*. Kitchener, ON: Pandora.

Schipani, Daniel S. and Leah Dawn Bueckert, Eds. 2009. *Interfaith Spiritual Care: Understandings and Practices*. Kitchener, ON: Pandora.

Schlosser, Lewis Z. 2003. "Christian Privilege: Breaking a Sacred Taboo." *Journal of Multicultural Counseling and Development*, Volume 31, 44–51. DOI:10.1002/j.2161-1912.2003.tb00530.x.

Society for Intercultural Pastoral Care and Counseling. n.d. "Home Page." Available at:http://sipcc.org/aktuelles&tl=en (accessed December 28, 2016).

Sorajjakool, Siroj. 2001. *Wu Wei, Negativity, and Depression: The Principle of Non-Trying in the Practice of Pastoral Care*. New York: Haworth.

Temme, Klaus. 2011. "Seelsorge and Interreligious Dimensions: Christian-Muslim Cooperation in the German Context, Using a CPE Model." *Revista Pistis and Praxis: Teologia e Pastoral*. Volume 3, Issue 2, 449–465.

Walton, Martin Neal. 2013. "Discerning Lived Spirituality: The Reception of Otherness." *Journal of Pastoral Care and Counseling*. Volume 67, Issue 2, 1–10. DOI:10.1177/154230501306700206.

Weiß, Helmut. 2011. "'I Saw Souls': Remarks on the Theory and Practice of Intercultural and Interfaith Spiritual Care." *Revista Pistis and Praxis: Teologia e Pastoral*. Volume 3, Issue 2, 467–494.

# 6

# Womanist Pastoral Theology and Black Women's Experience of Gender, Religion, and Sexuality
*Phillis Isabella Sheppard*

> *Religion is everywhere. Religion might be an answer as well as, in some cases, a problem*
>
> (Octavia Butler)

On the evening I had given myself to complete this chapter, I was confronted with the news that yet another black teen-aged male, unarmed and not engaged in a criminal act, was shot and killed by a police officer (Fernandez and Haag, 2017). Jordan Edwards was 15 years old. The now fired police offer, used a shot-gun to fire into a car driving away. Jordan was leaving a house party and was shot in the head with a rifle. His two brothers and a friend, also in the car, witnessed his murder. The police initially lied about the circumstances surrounding his murder. His brothers watched him die. Jordan Edwards' mother is lamenting. Her deepest fear, that her son might be murdered in the streets, has materialized. Her fear ripples across time as a fear shared by most black mothers; it is not a new fear. It is a fear written down in memory and re-enlivened across the landscape of black life. The black lesbian feminist poet Audre Lorde captured well the effect of this reality on black and white feminist coalitions.

> But Black women and our children know the fabric of our lives is stitched with violence and with hatred, that there is no rest. … For us, increasingly, violence weaves through the daily tissues of our living— … Some problems we share as women, some we do not. You fear your children will grow up to join the patriarchy and testify against you, we fear our children will be dragged from a car and shot down in the street, and you will turn your backs upon the reasons they are dying. (Lorde, 1984, p. 119)

*Pastoral Theology and Care: Critical Trajectories in Theory and Practice,*
First Edition. Edited by Nancy J. Ramsay.
© 2018 John Wiley & Sons Ltd. Published 2018 by John Wiley & Sons Ltd.

Lorde directs us to grapple with, at the deepest levels, the difference that interlocking features of gender, race, and class make in women's lives. In the case of black women, Lorde argues, the likelihood of violence is an ever-present dread.

From its earliest development, womanist pastoral care and theology has maintained a methodological commitment to an epistemology based in the particularity of black women's lives and an intersectional approach to analysis and practice. This chapter explores that trajectory of intersectionality and particularity in relation to what I propose is its underdeveloped attention to the meaning and function of religion, specifically black church experience, in black women's lives. In so doing, I will propose a womanist psychology of religion that argues for the necessity of placing gender, race, sexuality, and cultural and religious practices in critical dialogue. Such a dialogue encourages us to grapple with the psychology or psychological meaning of religious experience for black women, and the methodological approach necessary to sustain the interlocking features of black women's experience.

In this chapter I contribute to womanist pastoral theology by offering an intersectional perspective on black women's experience of religion. Intersectionality, as articulated by Kimberlé Crenshaw (1989), was in response to the way in which, particularly in law, cases involving discrimination failed to recognize that black women are frequently the target of racial and gender discrimination rather than a single form. A single-issue analysis essentially renders some aspects of black women's experience invisible. In addition to race and gender, sexuality, gender representations, and class are targets of discrimination, micro-aggressions, and violence. Recognizing that black women experience these forms of oppression simultaneously is to see the inseparable intersectional links.

As I take up this intersectional approach, through religious experience, I emphasize that practices of formation shape experience and self-understanding and the places in womanist pastoral theology and care that include the psychological role of religion. I attend to religion for two reasons: religion as a feature of black life is often assumed, and because sexuality *and* religion are treated as separate or discrete experiences. My diagram below is an attempt to demonstrate that practices, explicit and implicit, cultural, religious, and sexual underlay how one comes to be in the world as gendered, racial, and religious. That said, a deep intersectional approach directs our attention to the fact that scant attention has been paid to what I am calling the complicatedness of black women's religious engagement and practices.

Where womanist pastoral theology and care has given attention to religion, we have often assumed the congregational or communal nature of religion and, in my view, have given less attention to the interior, psychological nature of religious engagement at the intersection of broad cultural experience—with rare exceptions. Exceptions include *A Womanist Pastoral Theology against Intimate and Cultural Violence* by Stephanie Crumpton (2014).

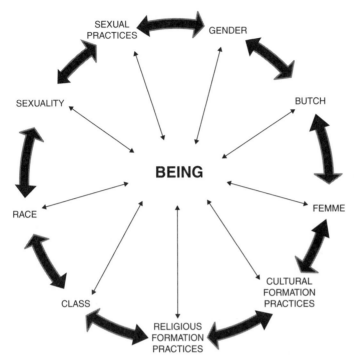

**Figure 6.1** Case example of converging influences on being (created by Arelis Benetez and Phillis Sheppard, 2017).

In a recent article I laid out some groundwork for a womanist-lesbian pastoral ethics, and reiterate the methodological commitments here:

> As a womanist pastoral and practical theologian, I am committed to a methodology that privileges particularity as an epistemological given; thus lived experiences are a running thread through this work. It is also interdisciplinary in its sources and iterative in approach, the process grapples ... with the work of critical reflection on strategic practices. ... I take seriously the womanist commitment to position black experience and sources of knowledge ... to make sense of the world and [black women's] action in it. (Sheppard, 2016, p. 168)

Therefore, at this point I am concerned with black women's simultaneous negotiation of religion along with gender, race, class, and sexuality—that is, formative aspects of self. The simultaneity of experience provides the soil in which religious engagement develops, and shapes the meaning of religion.

This negotiation, a meaning-making process, is not as direct and self-evident a process as one might imagine. Ascertaining meaning in the practices of religion and the psychological processes involved is no small feat, and to do so focused on black women's practices and experiences requires awareness that one is approaching areas demanding both curiosity but great sensitivity and respect, and a posture of receptive introspection.

I am concerned with the everyday religion in the lives of black women as well as the nature, meaning, and varieties of religious experience. When I reference "everyday religion" I mean to signify that religion is embedded in a social and cultural context—a life infused with a multiplicity of values, linguistic communications, and systems of formation—wherever it is occurring, and cannot be limited to buildings or even to previously defined practices. This means that we must recognize that a turn to the interior-social relationship cannot collapse into a black version of the psyche theorized as a psychological structure separate from the influence and shaping of the external world. For instance, I have been writing this chapter in the time of Black Lives Matter, Black Girl Magic, and demands for justice in the policing in black and brown neighborhoods. In fact, in the US the demands for radical substantive change include a call for the transformation of religious ideologies and spiritualities whose theological anthropologies are steeped in language that insults lesbians, gay, bisexual, transgender, and queer (LGBTQ) identified persons, and denies they are, along with the rest of humanity, the mirror of the imago dei. The lack of health care for all has implications not only for those in medical distress today but also for future generations who are unable to receive preventive care. And the inhospitable rhetoric and policies toward immigrants and refugees not only expose these neighbors to prolonged suffering and possible death, but cut the US off from the corporate goods that would benefit our society if we fully embraced the diversity presenting itself at our borders, the mosques and temples in our communities, and varieties of cultures already living as our neighbors. And, I would be remiss if I did not name the divide let loose during the presidential campaigning of 2016. In 1984 Audre Lorde wrote that operative in the cultural and individual psyches is "a mythical norm, which each one of us within our hearts knows that is not me. In America, this norm is usually defined as white, thin, male, young, heterosexual, Christian, and financially secure" (1984, p. 116). And now, in the US, we have a president who espouses sexism, xenophobia, and anti-Muslim policies, and directs unchecked verbal violence to those who counter his depiction of beauty, gender, immigrants, disabilities, and his ideology of wealth and white privilege as the hallmark of normal. That which Lorde believed to be only on the edge of consciousness is now the publically espoused normativity by those in power.

## Pushing Against the Grain of Imposed Normativity: Womanist Pastoral Theologizing

The reign of cultural terror directed at those who do not fit the bill for normativity seems to be the *modus operandi* in this season and has re-enforced for me the need for womanist pastoral theology to *continue* to challenge the broader discipline of pastoral theology for its lack of black and brown voices in our scholarship, our guilds, and our institutions, and furthermore, to strongly urge pastoral theology to ask of its disciplinary self how depictions or representations of black women's lived embodiment of gender-race-sexuality is often ignored in our discourse or given short shrift especially when black women are recognized as having a race, or a gender, or a sexual orientation, and (maybe) a class status. In actuality, we should write class-gender-race-sexuality and in linking these terms signify that for black women these are interlocking facets of experience, and constitutive features of *being*. This notion of *being* captures Kimberlé Crenshaw and others' development of intersectionality (Crenshaw, 1989, 1991), but simultaneously conveys the ways in which we embody and house these realities, and the way in which our psychological orientation to ourselves and the world is shaped by these intersectional and interlocking realities. In other words, in speaking of *being* we recognize that these factors matter inside and out in the world. As such, we also realize that "black people's being often does not register in the normative categories assigned to describe existence."[1]

This not falling within normative categories as black women is a nexus between US black women and black women in the UK. Lorraine Dixon in her article "Reflections on pastoral care from a womanist perspective" appropriates "mothering" as a metaphor for womanist pastoral care and notes that when examining her own life and in ministry with black women, Caribbean women new to Great Britain, she recalled

> arriving in Britain from the Caribbean and being met by discrimination and "colour bars". They, like so many other Black women, found ways to work around and against racism. They did this by encouraging their community to work together, to unite in a common goal of empowerment. ... They established hair salons to cater for Black women's hair but they also provided a safe meeting place to share information and news. (2000, p. 7)

It is this awareness of the potential to experience negative aspects of this *being* as well as life-giving aspects that contributed to the rise to womanist theologies, as well the decision by womanists to take an invested standpoint in their scholarship. Marjorie Lewis, writing from a Jamaican black British standpoint, conducted research on racism within her predominantly white denomination. The women she interviewed lamented that they could not discuss the deep pastoral concerns they carried because the mostly white male pastors "do not understand suffering." This was brought home even more forcefully for Lewis when she realized that the church could not effectively "nurture the spirituality of my adolescent daughter" (2004, p. 86). And Christine Wiley, as late as 1991, complained that her program in pastoral psychotherapy was a reflection of the "Eurocentric approach" and "was heavily oriented toward white males" (1991, p. 355). Thus, in her pastoral counseling with African American women, for whom culture, gender, and race were clinical features of their care, Wiley had to make her own way.

## Womanist Pastoral Theologizing

When I began my clinical and doctoral programs in 1989–1990, womanist pastoral theology was only beginning to create a space within the discipline. The work was focused on creating a perspective specific to black women's pastoral care needs arising out their experiences in church and society, creating a voice distinct from the more prevailing perspectives emerging out of ethics and theology, and correcting the near absence of black women's voices in the discipline. The trajectory included black women's experience of religion and the complicated nature of religious engagement because of sexist theologies and practices in many church contexts and the combined practices of sexism and racism in the broader society. The institutional experience of religion was both balm to fight off the stress of societal mistreatment and struggle in the church to transform sexist practices of exclusion from leadership roles.

At this juncture, several voices were becoming established contributors to defining the contours of womanist pastoral perspectives. Linda Hollies' edited volume, *Womanistcare: How to Tend the Souls of Women*, was published in 1992. This edited collection actually grew out of a quickly called—I would say "emergency"—gathering of black women "from the pastoral care professions" in 1991. This gathering of black women came to the meeting feasting on the published works of ethicist Katie Cannon, theologians Jacqueline Grant and Delores Williams, and the biblical scholar Renita Weems. Marsha Foster Boyd, in her article emerging from this meeting, "Theological Implications of *WomanistCare*" turned to scripture and hymnody to address the subject of care and black women's relationship with and understanding of Jesus. Her theological reflection on the hymn by Frank Graf "My Savior Cares" asks a series of questions related to "Does Jesus Care" during hard times to which there is the answering refrain "Oh, yes, He cares, I know He cares, His heart is touched with my grief; When the days are weary, the long nights dreary, I know my Savior cares" (Graf, 2001 (1901)). This statement of faith made this a crucial aspect of religious experience in her articulation of a womanist pastoral theology. But Foster Boyd also made it clear that a womanist pastoral theology must be situated in black women's social location and must take the social, historical, class, and religious contexts of black women's lives seriously. Turning to Katie Cannon she concurred that black women's social location leaves them vulnerable to exploitation, commodification, and oppression of their bodies and psyches (Cannon, 1988). Carolyn McCrary directed her attention to the need for healing for black women suffering from the results of physical and emotional abuse. She emphasized communal healing and the necessity for a model of health that fostered interdependence. McCrary was early to develop a psychodynamic approach to womanist pastoral care (McCrary, 1990, 2000). Carroll Watkins Ali dismissed psychodynamic theories and utilized an Afrocentric black psychology to focus on communal healing and social transformation (Ali, 1999). In early womanist scholarship, religion was primarily approached at face value, that is, the intersectional realities of black women's lives were engaged without fully integrating a psychology of religion that would see gender, race, and sexuality as part and parcel of religious meaning and engagement. I would argue, however, that the epistemological claims and aims suggest a psychology of religion was nascent in these works.

## Womanist Pastoral Epistemological Claims and Aims

As a result, from its inception, the epistemological claims that womanist pastoral theologians articulated were grounded in the social realities of black women's lived experiences—experiences that had shaped their lives and communities. The analogy "Womanist is to feminist as feminist is to lavender" struck a chord for black women who had a troubled relationship with feminist aims and methods, and increasingly resisted the need to particularize feminist with black feminist. This, combined with Patricia Hill Collins' articulation of "another epistemology ... an experiential, material base underlies a Black feminist epistemology, namely collective experiences and accompanying worldviews that U.S. Black women sustained based on our particular history ..." (Collins, 2000, p. 256), provided the soil on which to begin to build a womanist approach. That said, it must be noted that, at this nascent point in its development, the collective experience represented in womanist pastoral theology was overwhelmingly Christian, heterosexual, cis-gendered, and Southern in context, representation, and cultural aesthetics. Walker's third definition, "Loves the Spirit" seemed to assume the Holy Spirit that black folks experienced in churches, and her fourth definition, "Also: A woman who loves other women, sexually and/or nonsexually" (Walker, 1983) very rarely made it into the scholarship.

Furthermore "black women" most often meant US black women without explicit naming of the context, and even though there is very often synergy between the experiences of black women of the US and black women from across the globe, the nature of race and racism, for instance, is lived out and experienced differently based on history, language, and country. In the UK, Marjorie Lewis in her critical assessment of womanist theology locates two areas of critique when considering the appropriation of the term womanist for use in the UK: first, it must be acknowledged that "womanist" emerged from the experiences of black Southern Christian women and therefore is not a term that captures the global experiences of black women. In the end, she rejects the term but interestingly she rejects it in a "womanist" way: she privileges her social location and particularity as a Jamaican black woman living in the UK. This cultural divide, she determines, is too wide for US womanist theology. While Lewis is accurate in criticism and assessments of womanist perspectives, she does remind US womanists that black experience is diverse in region, sexuality, class, and sexuality, and that the ways in which oppressive systems operate in black women's daily lives are contextually informed. Thus, black women in the US and other parts of the world will share experiences of oppression but not all experiences will manifest in the same way. Second, womanist theology, with rare exception, is generally still very silent on the experience of women's sexuality. The case in this chapter will grapple with this reality.

Even with these brief critiques, it is clear that black women—first generation womanists—who adopted and developed the term womanist did so because "black feminist" as an identity and methodology was no longer evocative, descriptive, or adequate, and they sought to have a term closer to their experiences of being black women. Therefore, in brief, an appreciation of the realities of black women's experiences, in and out of the academy, gave rise to its initial articulation and focus and continues to shape the content of its ongoing development.

## Intersectional Realities in Black Women's Religious Experience

While womanist pastoral theologians have increasingly given deep attention to sexism in church and society, embodiment and trauma, negative cultural representation and abuse of black women, black women's spirituality and religious practices, and psychodynamic pastoral counseling and psychotherapy,, sexuality remains an underdeveloped aspect of womanist pastoral theology. Furthermore, sexuality as a co-constituent of religious experience, if referenced, is often steeped in assumptions about heterosexuality and given a cursory analysis. This created a scholarly picture of black religion as Christian, institutional, and a faith-fueled social activist project, and, while denominationally diverse, it was painted on a primarily Protestant canvas.

Religion and sexuality in womanist pastoral approaches often become a point of concern because they converge in clinical work (Crumpton, 2014; Sheppard, 2014), during pastoral leadership and opportunities for care, as well during personal professional discernment. During this early phase of development the voices most referenced, and who admittedly influenced my own work, were primarily mainline black Protestants (notable exceptions included Catholic theologians M. Shawn Copeland, Diana Hayes, and Jamie Phelps).

Despite the considerable scholarship devoted, in the past several decades, to the study of black religion, very little sustained attention has been given to the psychology of African American religious practices. A womanist pastoral theological engagement with religious experience allows for the creation of conversations between black women's lived religion and womanist methods. A womanist pastoral approach to religion makes black women's everyday lived experience of religion the fulcrum for its work and, in so doing, it also exposes how black women are, by and large, invisible in current psychologies of religion. But it also looks to dismantle the pervasiveness of hegemonic realities of whiteness, heteronormativity, and notions of self. As such, a womanist pastoral perspective work will complicate the ground of black religious experience.

Much of the cultural and psychological discourse concerning black religious expression assumes a cognitive psychology position on why African American women engage in religious practices, such as affiliation, historical significance, mental health, etc. I do not dispute the accuracy of these claims. However, I enter the dialogue through self-psychology, interested in something broader and open to ambiguity and begin with these three questions: first, "What is the relationship between black women's religious experiences in private and cultural spaces and psychological processes?" "What kind of methodology is required for such a project?" "What are the implications of this relationship for a womanist pastoral perspective on religion?"

I maintain that black religion operates in the lives of practitioners as it does because powerful psychodynamic forces are at play. These forces shape how and what we enact, re-enact, and embody in religious practices, and influence the sites where we seek to satisfy the most powerful of needs. For instance, in her book, *Three Eyes for the Journey: African Dimensions of the Jamaican Religious Experience*, Dianne Stewart, reveals her complicated relationship with Christianity:

> The validation that I felt after reading James Cone's works empowered me to pursue an even more steadfast search within Black Christianity for answers to my questions about God and humanity, but a lot of damage had already been done. In the furthest reaches of my spirit, I realized that Cone's books could not erase the ubiquitous Whiteness of Jesus Christ, which was deeply embedded in my consciousness and subconsciousness. My intellect was loyal to the Black Christ but nothing in

> my social reality, including my black Church community, reinforced Cone's Black Christ proclamation. I knew the Black Christ was reinforced, but I did not believe it. (2005, p. xi)

Psychological undercurrents are clearly operative in and out of the religious environ, and these kinds of dynamics require that we dig beneath the surfaces of religion. We need a womanist understanding of religion that allows for the complicated nature of religious experience, and that attends to the demands placed on womanist pastoral theologians and our constructive work.

## Emerging Psychologies of Black Religion

Black religion has historically been, and continues to be, a point of entrance for understanding black life, and recent work in the study of black women continues in this vein. However, womanist and black feminist psychological approaches are limited (Mattis, 2000, 2002), and furthermore, in white feminists' psychologies of religion, black women's experiences are seldom taken up for robust consideration.[2]

> Despite considerable evidence regarding the authoritative roles of religion and spirituality in the lives of women generally, and African American women in particular, explorations of the spiritual lives of women remain limited in research on both the psychology of religion and the psychology of women. (Mattis, 2000, p. 1)

Mattis' empirical research suggests that for black women, religion and spirituality have an important role as a coping mechanism. Specifically, her interests are concerned with the intersection of religion and spirituality and positive social and psychological development for African Americans (Mattis, 2011). Others have also challenged the prevailing singular models of black religion and religious experiences (Taylor et al., 2004). These researchers give consideration to the importance of context, and in so doing, point toward the necessity of examining the interlocking features of religious experience. They argue that a multitude of intersectional issues shape black experience of religion such as class, region, and education, as well as gender and denomination. Their biggest contribution in this work is its empirical evidence to discuss, in particular, the "functions of religion" and the "effects of religion" (Taylor et al., 2003).

Cheryl Townsend Gilkes argues for the need for a culturally situated psychodynamic perspective on religion (Gilkes, 1980). She critiques social science research that focused on social pathology and readily labeled black community social life as deviant without researching distinguishing difference from deviance. In "The black church as a therapeutic community," Gilkes observed some new mental health treatment models seem to "possess overwhelming similarities to the activities of the black church" and elements of religious practices appearing in some black religious contexts "act as a deterrent to ... psychiatric symptoms within the black community" (Gilkes, 1980, p. 31). Gilkes' argues further that black churches provide "a true asylum and a regular setting for group therapy and an objective mediator between perceptions of experience of black people and the messages of the wider social system" (Gilkes, 1980, p. 31). Therefore, there is a culturally specific group psychology of black religious practices and the aim of the group psychology, expressed in unique black religious practices, is therapeutic. The therapeutic action provides four functions: (1) "the articulation of suffering"; (2) location of persecutors; (3) provision of asylum for "acting out"; and (4) validation of experiences. "Also provides for an alternative set of positions which provide self-esteem and role continuity ..." where black religious practices heal mental health suffering (Gilkes, 1980, p. 32).

While Gilkes "redefines black religious experience as therapeutic" (1980), it is important to note that Gilkes does not define black religious experience as psychological. Thus, she is interested in the efficacy of black church practices to contribute to mental health wellness. She is not pursuing the internal processes that contribute to one's experience of religion as therapeutic or not, or the dynamics of black religious culture that, according to her argument, create a therapeutic space. I would add to Gilkes' work that there are a multiplicity of meanings that are possible in the worship context and that these might be explored. Her work stimulates questions such as: What are religious practices doing socially and individually where mental health is stable? And what is the impact of personal meanings of religious practices on the sociality of the practice, and on whether healing is experienced by some and not others? Clearly there are ways in which religion functions, effects, and is engaged for reasons not always explicit or known. I am arguing that religion and religious experience is not as "straightforward" as these primarily positive outcome models suggest, especially in terms of the way religion functions, in the life of the individual and communities, beyond the manifest and obvious. It is this multivalent nature of black religious experience, in its exchange between the personal, the religious cultural, and, ultimately, religious practices, that makes the meaningfulness of black religious experience powerful, deeply psychological, and in many respects, outside our awareness. The combination of the explicitly religious and unclaimed psychological dimensions can thwart critical analysis. A result is that deep inside black religious experience we discover a habitus—of "religious" formational practices—based in, and requiring of individuals and communities, the turning of a blind eye, the mechanism of disavowal. In other words, religious practitioners are both invited to consciously engage certain aspects of their experience and the dynamic forces operative in religious contexts, and to disavow others.

## Religion—It's Complicated

Like many who began graduate school over 25 years ago, my introduction to the study of black religion assumed a fairly one-dimensional read: black religion is Christian, institutionalized, and a faith-fueled social activist project, and, while denominationally diverse, it was painted on a primarily Protestant canvas. Womanist approaches to black religion were in an embryonic phase, and the voices most referenced, and who admittedly influenced my own work were mainline black Protestants (notable exceptions included Catholic theologians M. Shawn Copeland, Diana Hayes, and Jamie Phelps). Consequently, as a graduate student in a Protestant seminary, my black Catholic lesbian experience, and emerging shift in identity from black feminist to womanist, made me something of an oddity. I became interested in the complexity of black women's experience of religion while interviewing black women for a project related to spirituality, sexuality and the lingering effects of abuse. The women I interviewed mostly described themselves as religious and somewhat-to-occasionally involved in institutional religion. By most standards, their narratives of religion were complicated experiences stippled with hope and betrayal. Religion, while described as a needed resource in their day-to-day survival, was also a source of confusion, pain, and longing for acceptance. For most, there existed an uneasy disconnect between what they heard preached about religion and sexuality, and what they practiced in their day-to-day lives. Quite often these women felt that they could not live up to the ideals around sexuality either because of sexual abuse, gender "performance," or lesbian identity.

### Case: Karen[3]

I turn next to a case study of "Karen." In employing a case study approach, a method very common in the discipline of pastoral theology and care and in womanist approaches, I am not unaware of some of the challenges we must face. An obvious one is how to present the material with respect and attention to making the material anonymous enough to afford as much privacy as possible for those who share their stories with us, and simultaneously convey an authentic rendering of the important features of the narrative. The womanist method employed here privileges the "case" and thereby demands that we relinquish the privilege that theory and principles have held in our scholarship as pastoral theologians, and has in fact formed us as pastoral theologians. Very often we treat narrative as a blank canvas waiting to absorb the already established theoretical constructs—thus making the narrative subject to, rather than in dialogue with, the constructive process. Karen's case is included because she represents the complexity of the relationship between self, religion, and sexuality. Her lived experience demands that womanist pastoral theology and care include voices

often under-represented and that the field critically evaluate its conceptualiza-
tions of self, gender expressions, formation, and how religion contributes to, and
undermines, black women's subjectivity. Thus, her experience raises ethical considerations for a womanist pastoral theology and its psychology of religion.

Karen was a self-identified butch lesbian when I interviewed her in 1986. In
addition to early experiences of sexual abuse, Karen had as a teen been married to
a man who was abusive. Concurrent with this relationship, Karen had a long-term
relationship with a woman. After three children, and several more attempts to be
with a man, Karen began dating women exclusively. She was much like Cheryl
Clarke's "Althea," who was "very dark, very butch and very proud … and did not
care who knew she kept company with a woman" (Clarke, 2006). Not that Karen
lived free of secrecy concerning her identity, sexuality, and gender. She grew up in
an abusive home that seemed impervious to her suffering, harsh and often uninterested in her personhood, and in the public eye, the adults in her life were
viewed as respectable caregivers. Secrets festered but were out of awareness.

Karen's development occurred in a context where sexual orientation and gender identity emerged in communities that presented these aspects of identity in
rigid terms. As a teenager she identified as a butch lesbian among her lesbian
friends. Being butch was often seen as a hardwired fact very few could "decide"
her gendered way of being and this included dress, language, and, to some
degree, work and play. In Karen's life, being butch was frequently marked by class
affiliation. She was of a solidly urban working class roots, as were most of her
friends, and her community affiliations reflected this. She worked security in a fac-
tory and partied at a black lesbian bar where the rules of engagement were based
on firm gendered roles—butches generally initiated, and femmes responded.

Karen met a woman with whom she bought a home and began raising the
children as a couple. Karen was quite happy in this relationship and even
described her partner as the love of her life. The area that she experienced a
remaining lack was in terms of her religious life. Karen felt she could not attend
religious services because she believed being a lesbian was sinful, and what she
heard in the black Baptist church concurred with her. She declared herself spiritual, a believer in God but church was not a place she could practice her
Christian faith. She seldom mentioned her longing to be involved in religious
activities, and when she did, it was always with a deep longing. She lived with a
split in that she accepted that she was a lesbian, and experienced this as a pleas-
urable expression of her self, however, could not negotiate and reconcile being
in a relationship with a lesbian with her religiosity.

When I encountered Karen 20 years later, much of this earlier way of being
was, in presentation and identity, in abeyance. I discovered that Karen had married a man. "Bill" was a black preacher and she, suddenly, a "preacher's wife."
Karen did not look like the woman I had previously interviewed. She had
"femmed up" she said, because "now that I'm back in the church, I need to be the

kind of woman God and Bill expect." In my view, Karen's appearance was so radically different that she almost appeared jarring—her heels were higher; her make-up pronounced and her dress was floral and fell just mid-calf. Her talk was punctuated with Christian spiritual sayings (amen, amen; God is in control). She added me to a daily email list where she sent out regular commentary about how a Christian is to live, act and conduct her life.

## Forming a Religious Self, Converting Gender and Sexuality

One way of viewing the transformation in/of Karen is to say she was engaged in performing gender, embodiment, and sexuality congruent with her context and that, in terms of her own psychology of meaning, coherence between her inner values, ideals, and images related to sexuality and gender—a dominant need—was achieved. Regardless of my initial surprise, Karen's current gendered identity representation led her to experience a sense of integration that she had not previously known. There was a "compulsory" aspect to her new sense of black womanhood but one that also allowed her to distance herself from her previously embodied, and similarly compulsory "butch" way of being. The compulsory nature of gender in her context is not unique. In her research on gender representation by black lesbians in New York City, Mignon Moore found that "there are various physical representations of gender in black lesbian communities. They suggest that these portrayals of gender are not arbitrary ... [and that] presentations of self among black lesbians are not mere sexual play. ... Once formed, the gender style women choose tends to remain consistent over time" (Moore, 2006, p. 114). Her research also suggests gender presentation, while generally persistent, develops in terms of an individual's particular style. As one of her interviewees noted: "When you first come out, you're just being gay, you don't realize how the community is" (Moore, 2006, p. 128). It is in the process of trying to figure out how to relate socially that clarity emerges about gender style (Moore, 2006). Furthermore, Moore observed that the gender expectations "imposed by these norms also grants women a certain agency ..." (Moore, 2006, p. 129) in those communities. This might suggest that a very powerful psychocultural experience would have to be operative to disrupt and convert this "gender style" once established.

In both Karen's past and present self-identification, dress, language, and attitude were thought of as static categories as if these are all hardwired, in her self, by the present. The religious context mirrored this gendered and sexuality imago or template, and religion—in her practice of it and her longing for it— was a defining psychocultural force in her life. When in compliance with her own internal expectations, and those represented in the public sphere, related to gendered embodiment, Karen's experience of religion left her feeling affirmed and sustained in terms of gender and sexuality. Religion was the glue. Clearly Karen experienced a deep form of kinship in her church. And this kinship and related activities reinforced her current self. More importantly, Karen's sense of her self seems most strengthened by her capacity to name herself. Unlike the narratives of Christian conversion that emphasize sinfulness of the past life, Karen emphasizes the *fit* of her current identities. She thought living as a lesbian and butch was wrong because they were in conflict with the church teachings as well as her beliefs about her self. Patricia Hill Collins reminds us

> an affirmation of the importance of Black women's self-definition and self-valuation is the first key theme that pervades historical and contemporary statements of Black Feminist thought. Self-definition involves challenging ... the knowledge-validation process that has resulted in externally defined, stereotypical images of Afro-American womanhood. Self-valuation stresses the content of Black women's self-definitions. (Collins, 1986, p. 16)

And, furthermore, allows "Afro-American women to reject internalized, psychological oppression" (Collins, 1986, p. 18). Karen's experience situates her such that she knows the experience of *being*, embodying, her self as an outsider and insider in terms of gender, sexuality, and race—in black religion. As a lesbian who self-identified as butch, she challenged stereotypical images and definitions of black woman operative in the broader social context as well as among lesbians, but this challenge was asymmetrically valued in relation to the internal image she maintained of religious black woman. Therefore Karen's subjective experience of her self was not an individual internal dynamic but rather a set of complex interacting dynamics that included her inner life populated with her fantasies, desires, conflicts, and notions of who she hoped to be and the values inhabiting her sites of cultural affiliation. Of course, cultural experiences, such as religion, "are embodied experiences, and ... culture is inextricably tied to the formation of self and bodily experiences" (Sheppard, 1997). Furthermore, if it is true that the manner in which a person configures her association to her cultural group reflects her state or relationship to her self (Gehrie, 1980, p. 381), then it follows that the ways in which Karen structured her sexuality and gender identity *in* her cultural contexts reflects the state of her sense of self or self state. Kohut's self psychological view would, in addition, hold that "communal experiences of ... religions, the meaningful beauty of integrated symbols of his self (sic) ... are ... motivated by the loss of the secure cohesion, continuity and harmony of ... self" (Kohut, 1978, p. 926). This understanding of religion, its place in the inner life, and the maintenance of the self assumes that cohesion and harmony are the product of engagement with religion through the loss, and that religion, in some respects, is compensatory for this loss.

This perspective is limited in reach, however. A womanist pastoral perspective on religion does not limit religion to a breakdown in self-cohesion, but also holds that the capacity to engage religion is a discrete self-object experience, and a developmental achievement and, thus, contributes to one's engagement in the world (Sheppard, 2011). But religion is only part of what contributes to Karen's identity cohesion, and in particular, it is her religious context's specific symbols related to sexuality and gender that add to the shaping of her identity. Furthermore, Karen experiences, in her self-assessment, not loss in her turn to religion but rather relinquishment of some aspect of her identity, and gain in other aspects.

The exchange between the intrapsychic and the cultural reveals the necessity of a womanist pastoral perspective on religion. Thus, in the case of Karen, for example, Karen's sense of self as a religious person is shaped by her desires and attachment to her sexual and gender orientations as represented in her black communities. McGuire has suggested that the "religious meanings attached to gendered bodies are socially defined, contested and changeable" (McGuire, 2008, p. 159). However, until she changed, Karen did not experience her gender and sexuality as changeable. Gendered bodies are also racial bodies situated and experienced in racial religious contexts, and the racial self, unlike gender and sexuality, is less changeable. The sense of unchangeableness of race and racial embodiment in the social milieus in which Karen lived is represented most by the fact that Karen never indicated that the self-transformation of her understanding of gender expression and sexuality affected her identity in terms of race. Race was treated as a biological given, and therefore, her understanding of her racial self-identity could not change, was not subject to the content of her desires and, therefore, was not included in Karen's self-narrative of transformation. While it seems that the intersectionality of race, religion, gender, and sexuality is transparently powerful on the one hand, this was not so for Karen. This may be because the ideology of gender and race did not change in the various contexts in which Karen's life formed meaning; instead, her relationship to specific gender and sexuality representations were reconfigured internally and externally. In other words, among her butch–femme community and her church community, these categories were similarly defined, understood, and expressed. In her religious context, she was required to be anything but butch. Psychologically, the leap seemed not to be a significant one for her.

Karen's religious context prescribed gender and sexuality by legislating transgressing embodiment. Women primarily seemed to fall under the heading of differing degrees of the "respectable black church lady." Most other forms of gender expression were disavowed or, through the theological discourse of sin, repentance, holiness, and total transformation, were marked as religious violations and subject to strategic religious practices aimed at altering not only sexual behavior but also the psychology that informed behavior. Karen and those around her would soundly reject notions about fluidity of gender and sexuality or queer identity. The sermon was a central site for the "strait-jacket-ing" of gender. In *Katie's Canon: Womanism and the Soul of the Black Community*, Katie Cannon takes note of the woman-focused disciplinary use of the sermon, and challenges womanists to undertake reading and listening practices that work to eradicate negative depictions of black women in black preaching (Cannon, 1995). Along with preaching, other seemingly innocuous practices were also engaged to shape women's, and men's, views of gender and sexuality to bring them in line with particular religious teachings. On one occasion, during a Sunday morning service, Karen's husband began preaching a sermon about love and hospitality, but mid-way through his preaching he began shouting about homosexuals sinning and heading "straight toward hell." Karen did not seem surprised, and while the congregation joined the "amens" with vigor, Karen did not. Karen was subject to these prescriptive and forma-tive practices, on a most intimate level, and was conforming to them, externally and in her psychology of her self. In many respects, her self-transformation narrative was surprisingly void of inner conflict or complexity for her, and, possibly, as a result, she had garnered something that she could not have in her previous expression of her self as a black lesbian butch: Karen was now a reli-gious leader as the preacher's wife. She was asked to pray in services. Congregants turned to her for help. She was respected.

## Converting Sexuality through Religion

When I asked her how this religious experience lined up with her attraction to women, she initially challenged that such an attraction remained, "I don't notice women that way anymore," but upon reflection added:

> well, to be honest, there's a woman I care about. She's married too, and we just vowed not to betray our marriages; her husband is a preacher too. I'm happy with my life this way. I love Bill and I love the church. And I *care* about her; I don't want her that way. Sometimes I miss the lifestyle and the friends; not the sex, but this is my life now. I never lied to Bill about who I was and we just prayed about it, and we've been together fifteen years.

Karen's experience of religion is intricately tied to her understanding and embodiment of gender, sexuality, and aspects of black church culture rhetoric and spirituality specific to her context. We might even think about her new-found life as one of "converting"—her gender and her sexuality. Furthermore, we are left with the question of how her newly structured self-expression might be understood psychologically, in the culture of a conservative black religious context, and what processes and practices keep it intact; that is, how has Karen existed with self-coherence in two distinctive ways? In the theory of self-psychology, the self develops, when in an empathically mirroring milieu, toward coherence and continuity over time. Karen's longing for and experience of religious practice was tied to her desire and longing for a psychologically and socially acceptable gendered and sexuality identity. In other words, her longing was for a context where she could experience the supportive mirroring of her sexual and gendered self, in a particular religious context, and thereby add to the strengthening of self-experience. The turn toward the practice of religion disrupts her sense of self and provokes a dismantling that cannot be sequestered from the rest of her life, and ultimately results in social–sexual identifications she can accept. Karen's experience challenges notions of a psychology of the self where the evidence of a formed sense of self is in her experience of herself as "cohesive, harmonious, firm in unit in time and space, connected with ... the past" (Kohut, 1984) with regard to gender and sexuality. It is religion, and the practices related to her newly formed status, that serve to create a firm and (more) harmonious self, but it is not a self that is contiguous across time and space. Religion, gender identities, and sexualities, as integral to psychological and cultural experience, are, then, tethered in her transformation. Her narrative pushes the boundaries of what we study when we study black women's experience of black religion.

When womanist pastoral theology privileges the role of experience as a primary source for womanist theology, we are speaking of the intersectional reality that is inherent in the convergence of race, gender, sex, classism, and heterosexism, as well as transphobia in black women's lives and culture. Our analyses are informed by the premise that experience is socially constructed, culturally informed, and infused with responses to the oppressive *and* constructive forces that shape black life. This includes oppression in the broader culture, the black community, religious institutions, familial relationships, and the psychological impact of oppressive ideologies. Conversely, we recognize that experience also includes those individual and collective practices, responses, aimed at resisting and eradicating the demoralizing effects of systemic injustices.

## Conclusion: Womanist Pastoral Ethics from the Ground of Emergent Being

There are ethical implications of womanist pastoral practice in this emergent approach to womanist psychology of religion, and Karen's life brings to the foreground several pastoral ethical dimensions for womanist pastoral theology to consider. Fleshing out intersectionality to more fully include lived experiences of religion, gender, and sexuality strengthens womanist pastoral theology's methodological commitment to ground our work in black women's lives.

There a womanist intersectional analysis brings with it an ethical obligation to fully represent the complexity of lived experience and to integrate the capacity of complexity in lived experience to interrogate our previous constructions. Karen's fluidity of gender representation, sexual expression, and identity can challenge fixed notions of self—that is, that the person who has developed a cohesive self looks and identifies in fixed public, religious, and relational mode. Karen's sense of her self is not linear, as in an epigenetic model of development, but she experiences her self as *her self*. In their article "'I am just so glad you are alive': New perspectives on non-traditional, non-conforming, transgressive expressions of gender, sexuality and race among African Americans," Layli Phillips and Marla Stewart rightly argue that "established models of queer identity have taken their form from established and widely accepted stage models of racial and ethnic identity" (Phillips and Stewart, 2008, p. 379), and are not able to account for complexity of identity and affiliation. For instance, they argue that it is problematic that these models are not able to theorize individuals' simultaneous "psychological affiliation with multiple social groups" (Phillips and Stewart, 2008, p. 379). Nor, in my view, do they account for gender, sexuality, and religious identification such as Karen's. In other words, there is not enough of the intersectional in these models. Karen's life interrogates the ideology and theoretical explanation of what constitutes a cohesive self. That is, I am suggesting that a cohesive self is determined by, in this case, Karen's experience of her self, and not an external litmus test of culturally biased privileging of asymmetrical power hierarchies in social relationships. In other words, ideologies of the cohesive self very often ignore system power and its mark on psyches. Nor do they give weight to the idea of a *cohering* self. Furthermore, Karen's coherence is also emerging in the context of her subjective experience of spirituality, which is experienced in and beyond the dogma of her church. The ethical demand here is **that lived experience is always privileged** and has the *efficacy to reform our theories* (of self, embodiment, gender, and sexuality) and *practices of care*. Karen's experience directs us toward the necessity of ethical and intentional practices of *formation*. Formation, then, is an aim of pastoral ethics, and the aim and means must be interrogated to ensure that their effect engenders a vision of black women's being that is not conformity or even static being, but *emergent being*. Emergent being presses the question how do womanist pastoral theologies and ethics contribute to development?

As an interdisciplinary pursuit, I turn to the psychological concept of mirroring. The contexts depicted in the "Karen" case study reveal similarities and differences in the practices of mirroring—that is, practices, habits, and spaces that acknowledge and value self-expressions that represent and mirror the stated views and ideologies undergirding a community's self. As such, in both of these formative contexts discussed from Karen's life, we see that mirroring was a linchpin for identity of individuals and communities.

The ethical demand provoked by lived experiences is that womanist pastoral theology must critically read its implicit views of the self and its formation especially with regard to gender, race, religion, and sexual identities, and requires an analysis that appreciates the reality that black women may hold, with minimal internal conflict, seemingly opposing views. Karen, for instance, experienced deep satisfaction with a sense of kinship and mirroring in her role as a "first lady" as the preacher's wife. She experienced this satisfaction even though he held negative views about lesbians and gays. This did not seem to interfere with her sense of being valued and respected by him even though she did not support his most negative views. The interlocking *lived experience* of gender, race, religion, and sexuality are crucial for womanist pastoral theologies that are relevant and potentially efficacious in black women's resistance to the forces that deny their humanity and restrict their voices in public and religious spaces. The absence of such a commitment is an ethical failure and reveals the underside of theological anthropologies that, implicitly or explicitly, deny all black women full humanity, and theologizes embodiment from a heterosexual normative view.

The ethical or moral vision embedded in prioritizing lived experience suggest that womanist pastoral ethics must be grounded in a non-hierarchal relationality between womanist theologians, the women in our cases narratives, and the various communities that permit us entrance. Furthermore, we are obligated to situate ourselves in the narratives we construct for our research based on case analysis and acknowledge that we do not enter black women's lives as if we are entering "research space" to which we have no investment or obligation. We do not have, as Joyce Ladner wrote in reflecting on her research with black women, some "value-free sanctuary" (Ladner, 1972, p. xxvi) absent of bias or commitment to a side. The side on which I stand is that of black women's fullness of being, unfiltered, unapologetic, and meaningful on their terms and in dialogue "with my original purpose" (Ladner, 1972, p. xxxi) for the research. The shift to privileging lived experience is both a methodological and an ethical claim and emerges out of critically engaged reflection and dialogue with black women. Just as black women's being is emergent, so is womanist pastoral theology.

## Notes

1 Courtney Bryant in conversation, 4 August 2014.
2 Psychology of religion efforts from a psychoanalytic perspective have generally not discussed race, and feminist psychologies of religion have not generally discussed black women's *experience*. Important discussions of psychoanalysis, race, and religion can be found in the work of Celia Brickman (2002, 2008).
3 Karen is also discussed in Sheppard (2006). Referenced with permission.

# References

Ali, Carroll Watkins. 1997. *Survival and Liberation: Pastoral Theology in African American Context*. Atlanta, GA: Chalice Press.

Brickman, Celia. 2008. "The Persistence of the Past: Framing Symbolic Loss and Religious Studies in the Context of Race." In *Mourning Religion: Method, Meaning, and Identity in a Post-Modern World*, edited by Diane Jonte-Pace, William Parsons, and Susan E. Henking, pp. 44–62. Charlottesville, VA: Virginia University Press.

Brickman, Celia. 2002. "Primitivity, Race and Religion in Psychoanalysis," *Journal of Religion*. Volume 81, Issue 1, 53–74.

Cannon, Katie. 1995. *Katie's Cannon: Womanism and the Soul of the Black Community*. New York: Continuum International Publishing.

Cannon, Katie. 1988. *Black Womanist Ethics*. Atlanta, GA: Scholars Press.

Chatters, L.M., R.J. Taylor, K.D. Lincoln, A. Nguyen,, and S. Joe. 2011. "Church-based Social Support and Suicidality among African Americans and Black Caribbeans." *Archives of Suicide Research*. Volume 15, 337–353.

Clarke, Cheryl. 2006. *The Days of Good Looks: The Prose and Poetry of Cheryl Clarke, 1980 to 2005*. Boston, MA: Da Capo Press.

Collins, Patricia Hill. 1986. "Learning from the Insider Within: The Sociological Significance of Black Feminist Thought." *Social Problems*. Volume 33, Issue 6, 14–32.

Collins, Patricia Hill. 2000. *Black Feminist Thought: Knowledge, Consciousness and the Politices of Empowerment*. New York: Routledge.

Crenshaw, Kimberlé. 1989. "Demarginalizing the Intersection of Race and Sex: A Black Feminist Critique of Antidiscrimination Doctrine." *University of Chicago Legal Forum*. Volume 1, Issue 8, 139–167.

Crenshaw, Kimberlé. 1991. "Mapping the Margins: Intersectionality, Identity Politics, and Violence against Women of Color." *Stanford Law Review*. Volume 43, 1241–1299.

Crumpton, Stephanie M. 2014. *A Womanist Pastoral Theology against Intimate and Cultural Violence*. Basingstoke: Palgrave Macmillan.

Dixon, Lorraine. 2000. "Reflections on Pastoral Care from a Womanist Perspective." *Contact* 132 (2000): 3–10.

Fernandez, Manny and Matthew Haag. 2017. "Police Officer Who Fatally Shot 15-Year-Old Texas Boy is Charged With Murder." *The New York Times*. May 5.

Gehrie, Mark, J. 1980. "The Self and the Group: A Tenative Exploration in Applied Self Psychology." In *Advances in Self Psychology*, edited by Arnold Goldberg. New York: International Universities Press.

Gilkes, Cheryl Townsend. 1980. "The Black Church as a Therapeutic Community: Suggested Areas for Research into Black Religious Experience." *Journal of the Indenominational Theological Center*. Volume 8, 29–44.

Graf, Frank E. 2001 (1901). "My Savior Cares." 478. Chicago, IL: GIA Publications, African American Heritage Hymnal.

Hollies, Linda, Ed. 1992. *Womanistcare: How to Tend the Souls of Women*. Joliet, IL: Woman to Woman Ministries, Inc. Publications.

Kohut, Heinz. 1978. *The Search for the Self: Selected Writings of Heinz Kohut*, Volume 2. Edited by Paul H. Ornstein. Madison, WI: International University Press.

Kohut, Heinz. 1984. *How Does Analysis Cure*. Edited by Arnold Goldberg and Paul E. Stepansky, Chicago, IL: University of Chicago Press.

Ladner, Joyce. 1972. "Introduction to Tomorrow's Woman: The Black Woman." In *Feminism and Methodology*, edited by Sandra Harding, p. 78. Bloomington, IN: Indiana University Press.

Lewis, Majorie. 2004. "Diaspora Dialogue: Womanist Theology in Engagement with Aspects of the Black British and Jamaican Experience." *Black Theology*. Volume 2, Issue 1, 85–109.

Lorde, Audre. 1984. "Age, Race, Class, and Sex." In *Sister Outsider: Essays and Speeches*. New York: The Crossing Press.

Mattis, Jacqueline. 2000. "African American Women's Definitions of Spirituality and Religiosity." *Journal of Black Psychology*. Volume 26, Issue 1, 101–122.

Mattis, Jacqueline. 2002. "Religion and Spirituality in the Meaning Making and Coping Experiences of African American Women: A Qualitative Analysis." *Psychology of Women Quarterly*. Volume 26, 309–321.

Mattis, Jacqueline. 2011. "Jacqueline Mattis, Applied Psychology Chair, Awarded NYU's MLK Faculty Award." Available at: http://steinhardt.nyu.edu/site/ataglance/2011/01/jacqueline_mattis_applied_psyc.html (accessed May 17 2017).

McCrary, Carolyn. 1990. "Interdependence as a Normative Value in Pastoral Counseling with African Americans," *Journal of Interdenominational Theological Center*. Volume 18, 1–2, 119–147.

McCrary, Carolyn. 2000. "Intimate Violence against Black Women and Internalized Shame: A Womanist Pastoral Counseling Perspective," *Journal of Interdenominational Theological Center*. Volume 28, 1–2, 3–37.

McGuire, Meridith B. 2008. *Lived Religion: Faith and Practice in Everyday Life*. Oxford: Oxford University Press.

Moore, Mignon. 2006. "Lipstick or Timberlands? Meanings of Gender Presentation in Black Lesbian Communities." *Signs: Journal of Women in Culture and Society*. Volume 32, Issue 1, 113–139.

Phillips, Layli and Marla Stewart. 2008. "'I Am Just So Glad You Are Alive': New Perspectives on Non-Traditional, Non-Conforming, Transgressive Expressions of Gender, Sexuality and Race among African Americans." *Journal of African American Studies*. Volume 12, Issue 4, 378–400.

Sheppard, Phillis. 1997. "Fleshing the Theory: A Critical Analysis of Theories of the Body in Light of Black Women's Experience." PhD Dissertation, Chicsgo Theological Seminary, Chicago, p. 220.

Sheppard, Phillis. 2006. "No Rose Colored Glasses: Womanist Practical Theology and Response to Sexual Violence." In *In Spirit and Truth: Essays in Theology,*

*Spirituality and Embodiment*, edited by Phillip J. Anderson and Michelle Clifton-Soderstrom, pp. 241–256. Chicago, IL: Covenant Press.

Sheppard, Phillis. 2011. *Self, Culture and Others in Womanist Practical Theology*. New York: Palgrave Macmillan.

Sheppard, Phillis. 2014. "Religion—It's Complicated! The Convergence of Race, Class, and Sexuality in Clinicians' Reflection on Religious Experience." In *The Skillful Soul of the Psychotherapist: The Link between Spirituality and Clinical Excellence*, edited by George S. Stavros and Steven J. Sandage, pp. 45–67. New York: Rowman & Littlefield.

Sheppard, Phillis. 2016. "Womanist-Lesbian Pastoral Ethics: A Post Election Perspective." *Journal of Pastoral Theology*. Volume 26, Issue 3, 152–170.

Stewart, Dianne M. 2005. *Three Eyes for the Journey: African Dimensions of the Jamaican Religious Experience*. New York: Oxford University Press.

Taylor, R.J., L.M. Chatters, and J. Levin. 2004. *Religion in the Lives of African Americans: Social, Psychological, and Health Perspectives*. Thousand Oaks, CA: Sage.

Walker, Alice. 1983. *In Search of Our Mothers' Gardens: Womanist Prose*. San Diego, CA: Harcourt Brace Jovanovich.

Wiley, Christine. 1991. A Ministry of Empowerment: A Holistic Model for Pastoral Counseling in the African American Community." *Journal of Pastoral Care*. Volume 45, Issue 4, 355.

7

# Analyzing and Engaging Asymmetries of Power

Intersectionality as a Resource for Practices of Care

*Nancy J. Ramsay*

> *You shall be called the repairer of the breach, the restorer of streets to live in.*
> (Isaiah 58:12 b)

## Introduction and Literature Review

In this chapter we explore intersectionality as a methodological resource for the critical trajectory of public pastoral theology that emerged in the US in the late 20th century to address abuses of power that create asymmetries of opportunity especially related to forms of difference treated oppressively such as gender, race, nationality, and class. The arc of literature in this trajectory points to the need for methodological strategies that will enhance analysis and strategic engagement of such asymmetries of power. These asymmetries quietly shape the normative assumptions and practices of powerful cultural institutions, which in turn organize our social identities to reproduce patterns of privilege and marginalization in persons' self-understanding that are often held unreflectively. We will also explore possible generative reciprocities between intersectionality and public pastoral theology and practices of care. We will begin with close attention to the literature in public pastoral and practical theology emerging in multiple contexts in the last five years. Then we will explore the metatheory known as intersectionality and assess its adequacy for addressing the needs of this critical trajectory.

As a preface, I note this chapter is shaped by my own personal, professional, and religious identity as a Protestant pastoral theologian whose social identities are largely formed by privilege. My Scots ancestry includes complicity in colonial practices. Ancestors who migrated to the US indirectly benefited from the wealth that slavery and Jim Crow laws inequitably brought to white

*Pastoral Theology and Care: Critical Trajectories in Theory and Practice,*
First Edition. Edited by Nancy J. Ramsay.

Americans. They farmed the fertile Midwestern land that Native Americans were earlier forced to abandon in a process of oppression and genocide. My family benefited from the economic privileges that the GI Bill inequitably offered my father and other white veterans after World War II. While I know the marginalization and violence of sexism that continues to shape my culture, I also am more protected than women of different racial identities. I experience the privileges of heterosexism. As a Christian in the US, I am also protected from the religious oppression that is increasing here. I receive the socio-economic benefits of a professional education. As a pastoral theologian, I seek to be, to teach, and to develop scholarship in solidarity with those whose experiences are dominated by oppression. The goal of relational justice that first named this trajectory in the field of pastoral theology in the US is also my own.

## Review of Literature

By the 1980s, pastoral theologians in the US began to recognize that practices of care focused on individuals were inadequate for addressing the structural and systemic distortions of injustice such as racism. It became clear that the field would require methods that explored care in relational and systemic contexts that presumed the interconnection of love and justice (Smith, 1983). By 1993, the metaphor of a "living human web" (Miller-McLemore, 2012) further clarified that this new trajectory was actively engaging issues of difference and power in individual, relational, and ecclesial contexts as well as in public structural and systemic contexts. Larry Graham captured the guiding vision of this trajectory in his phrase "relational justice" (1995). In the brief review that follows, we will see how pastoral and practical theologians in the US and around the world continue moving toward strategies for addressing issues of power and difference. Across 30 years these two intersecting issues became prominent themes in public pastoral and practical theology as well as practices of care. The complexity of accounting for the multiplicity of differences organized by asymmetrical power (Collins and Bilge, 2016) and efforts to assess the scope of inequities insinuated in normative systems and structures are recurring themes.

A fuller description of the emergence of this trajectory is detailed in *Pastoral Care and Counseling: Redefining the Paradigms* (Ramsay, 2004), a supplement to the *Dictionary for Pastoral Care and Counseling* (Hunter, 1990). The contributors' essays name the reciprocal ways theory and practice fund each other and include resources to foster contextual transformation such as critical theories and liberation theologies. The essays point to two concurrent paradigms operative in the field: communal contextual and intercultural. Both reflect similar commitments for care shaped by love and justice but focused differently. The communal contextual paradigm addresses ministries of care within local faith communities and through such communities attending to their social contexts including attention to inequities in power and difference such as homophobia, racism, ethnocentrism, and economic injustice. The intercultural paradigm is also funded by critical theories and gives particular attention to cultural differences including religious differences and their political and hermeneutical importance for revising practices of care locally and internationally. Both paradigms continue to include public theology as a prominent aspect of theory and practice. The intercultural paradigm, for example, now draws on decolonial and postcolonial theory to inform practices of care and the self-awareness of those practicing care (Andraos, 2012; McGarrah Sharp, 2012, 2013, 2016; Lartey, 2013, 2016).

Issues of power and difference in pastoral and practical theology now, of necessity, also include recognition of religious plurality, which poses ontological and epistemological challenges for those who teach and practice pastoral care. As Kujawa-Holbrook asks, how does the field itself decolonize the Christianity that shaped it (2016, p. 154)? In this context pastoral and practical theologians such as Kathleen Greider (2012, 2015) have noted the importance of encouraging a highly reflexive literacy among Christians regarding not only other religious traditions but Christianity as well. Religious plurality, alterity, and multiple religious belonging are international in scope and fraught with asymmetries of power that reflect not only colonialism's association with 18th- and 19th-century Christian mission, but concurrent precolonial, colonial, and neocolonial realities (Lartey, 2016).

The horizon of public pastoral theology largely coincides with public practical theology (Graham and Rowlands, 2005; Miller-McLemore, 2012). In *The Wiley-Blackwell Companion to Practical Theology* (Miller-McLemore, 2012), scholars in a wide range of international contexts shaped by colonialism describe practices of care in the public pastoral theology trajectory giving clear attention to matters of economic inequities whether addressed within postcolonial themes or showing the influence of decolonial critiques in contexts such as Brazil (Streck, 2012, pp. 525–533).

In the US, attention to economic policies that shape experiences of socioeconomic class is prominent in both the communal contextual and intercultural paradigms. In particular, pastoral theologians are tracing the personal and cultural indicators of the destructive influence of neoliberal economics, which takes capitalism—so central to coloniality—to new extremes (LaMothe, 2012, 2014, 2016a, 2016b; Rogers-Vaughn, 2015, 2016). Cedric Johnson probes the intersections of neoliberal capitalism with race in *Race, Religion, and Resilience in the Neoliberal Age* (2016).

South African practical theologians voice parallel concerns for economic stratification intertwined with racism (Dames, 2010; Mouton, 2014; Du Toit, 2017a, 2017b). Each describes the persisting, divisive legacy of apartheid and forms of white resistance to assuring economic justice that reflect neocolonial practices. Their protests that real justice remains unfulfilled, resonate with important changes in ecumenical conversation at the World Council of Churches that signal a reversal from a more colonial model of *diakonia* as service to those on the margins to interpreting *diakonia* through the mission of those marginalized congregations as they initiate "acts of public witness against the structures of evil and injustice in the world" (Gill et al., 2014, pp. 249–251).

Attention to economic and political justice and the legacy of coloniality joins the practices of care in and by congregations and the urgency for intercultural awareness and reflexivity. Lebanese practical theologian, Michel Andraos (2012), teaching in Chicago, links economics with colonialism and epistemology. Citing Mignolo (2007, p. 451) and Quijano (2000), Andraos points to the important intercultural claim of decolonial theory that decenters the presumed universality of European rationality and reclaims the multiplicity of epistemologies that colonialism ignored. Reflexivity thus becomes a quandary. Jaco Dreyer, a South African practical theologian, deepened this challenge to reflexivity as he recognized it included Eurocentric ontological assumptions as well as Western epistemology (2016, pp. 90–109). McGarrah Sharp (2016) and Lartey (2016) use postcolonial theory to explore the challenge coloniality creates for reflexivity and the capacity to trust and learn from one another. Lartey (2016) names the challenge of "reading" the multiple layers of social context that reflect the simultaneous complexity of precolonial, colonial, modern, and postmodern dynamics in international contexts such as sub-Saharan Africa, where he notes there is an "eruption of subjugated indigenous knowledge" (p. 23).

The arc of literature seeking relational justice now names coloniality as powerfully contributing to foundational asymmetries of power through epistemology and ontology as well as contextual asymmetries such as sexism, racism, Christianity, and neoliberal capitalism. LaMothe (2014, pp. 375–391) recently proposed a "pastoral political theology" that anticipates how this arc in the literature points toward congregational and more public practices of care via broad-based community organizing arising in the US as well as internationally (Day et al., 2013, p. 10; Day, 2014, pp. 375–391).

## Methodological Implications

Clearly, no simple or formulaic methodology will be useful for the complexity public pastoral and practical theologians are engaging. Further, such complexity calls for a wide range of approaches. As Lartey cautions (2016, p. 31), those in countries previously colonized especially need to devise methodologies that "fit" their experience rather than using those shaped by Western imaginations. Methodological choices are also not simple for those whose heritage is shaped ontologically and epistemologically by the legacy of the colonizers, and who want to deconstruct the power of that colonial gaze for their understanding of themselves and others.

Contemporary pastoral theology requires resources that help us read and resist asymmetries of power and privilege that at once organize individuals' sense of identity such as sexism, racism, and heterosexism, as well as structural asymmetries insinuated in key cultural institutions that articulate and reproduce norms in ideology, governance, and economics. Attention to asymmetries of power also points to prioritizing methodological resources that help ensure we hear and learn directly from the experience of those oppressed by asymmetries such as colonialism, racism, sexism, and neoliberal capitalism.

## Intersectionality as a Valuable Resource for Pastoral and Practical Theology

The metatheory known as intersectionality aligns well with methodological needs posed by the current goals of pastoral and practical public theology. Intersectionality's guiding principles echo the theoretical, methodological, and ethical values and goals of practical and pastoral theology and related practices of care. In this review we will note ample opportunities for practical and pastoral theologians to contribute to this metatheory.

As a metatheory, intersectionality includes a dynamic range of methodological approaches that share common philosophical, hermeneutical, political, and practical commitments to critical analysis and critical praxis that challenge hegemonic power through coalitions forged across diverse groups seeking social justice. It promotes a resistant, interrogative knowledge that presumes an "architecture of structural inequalities and asymmetrical life opportunities" (May, 2015, xi and 6).

Intersectionality began to emerge beginning in the mid-20th century through the voiced experience of women "of color" whose wisdom is shaped by the hegemonic legacies of coloniality via chattel slavery and colonial conquest with concurrent erasure of locally shaped identities and imposition of a European ontology and epistemology. African American women led the way. Frances Beal's essay, "To Be Black and Female," published in 1969 (Beal, 1970, 1995, pp. 146–155) examines the intersections of race, gender, and the foundational role of capitalism (as cited in Collins and Bilge, 2016, p. 66). Better known is the 1977 Combahee River Collective "Black Feminist Statement." It adds heterosexism to the hegemonic forces of racism and patriarchy, and names the underlying influence of capitalism. It offers a politically informed analysis of oppressive, interlocking, systemic power that functioned hegemonically (Collins and Bilge, 2016, pp. 69–71). Publications followed by indigenous women in North America, Chicanas (Moraga and Anzaldúa, 1983), and Asian women (Anzaldúa, 1987).

Toward the end of the 20th century two African American scholars proved especially helpful in articulating intersectionality as a metatheory—Kimberlé Crenshaw, a legal scholar who is credited with coining the term (1989, 1991) and Patricia Hill Collins, a professor of sociology. Given the historical and continuing experience of women whose lives are shaped by marginalizing forces, intersectionality is deeply informed by attention to asymmetries of power as it organizes individual and group identity (Weber, 2010; May, 2015; Collins and Bilge, 2016) and as it misshapes social institutions such as media, education, politics, and economics to reproduce and extend patterns of subordination and privilege (Collins, 2000; Weber, 2010). However, this is a methodology that is useful for all persons who seek relational justice. Marginalization and privilege are intimately related, and those seeking to resist hegemonic power whose heritage is shaped by the inheritance of privilege are equally served by intersectional methodologies.

Methods identified as authentically intersectional reflect a shared cluster of core principles. Even these principles may vary slightly among interpreters. However, the following six principles summarized by Collins and Bilge (2016, pp. 25–30) and May (2015) reliably identify intersectional methodologies. These principles demonstrate a remarkable alignment with methodological goals that shape public pastoral and practical theology reflected in the literature review earlier in this essay.

1) Social inequality is the precipitating challenge calling for an intersectional response. The theory presumes a complex, multi-axis cause for inequalities such as racism, patriarchy, and classism (Collins and Bilge, 2016, pp. 25–26).

2) Power relations are organized at the level of individual and group identity through the intersections of aspects of social identity such as sexuality, race, and gender. Power relations are also experienced in cultural contexts through the normative influence of interactive "domains of power" such as ideology, politics, and economics which are constituted by various institutions whose influences are interdependent (Weber, 2010, pp. 34–38; Holvino, 2012, pp. 161–191; Collins and Bilge, 2016, pp. 26–27).

3) Relationality or solidarity across differences (May, 2015, p. 34) is the context for developing a dynamic understanding of power through the lens of shared experiences at the intersections of social identities among those who comprise the coalitions that construct rich analyses and critical praxis (Collins and Bilge, 2016, pp. 27–28). May notes that honoring relationality may call for strategies such as "bracketing" the hegemonic influence of Western rationality and "bias" to support the value of coalitional analyses that honor a fuller range of ontological experiences and epistemological practices (Lugones, 2010 and Babbit, 2001 as cited in May, 2015, 186ff).

4) Social context shaped historically and geographically is critical for deeply understanding the particularity of intersecting power relations; domains of power that structure such relations; and the particular knowledges and hermeneutical standpoints that inform the intersectional analyses and emerging critical praxis. Further, allowing history to inform a study of context helps ensure that coalitions account for the diverse hermeneutical and even ontological knowledges present and important for any analysis and response (May, 2015; Collins and Bilge, 2016, pp. 28–29).

5) Complexity is the presumed character of any intersectional analysis because, as the prior four principles demonstrate, social inequality arises from multiple, simultaneous dynamics of intersecting power relations and structures of power. Many intersectional theorists use the term "matrix thinking" to help capture the overlay of interpretive frames that may be used.

6) Social justice is the telos of any intersectional approach. As May puts it, intersectionality is not "neutral": it seeks to develop a resistant imaginary (2015, pp. 28, 34). The complexity of social justice is foregrounded by the dynamic, historical, and political character of power that organizes identity and informs intersectional analyses and strategies. Collins and Bilge (2016, p. 30) concede that this telos may sometimes be limited to shaping the critical analysis.

The following graphic illustrates the way the core principles of intersectionality that function as guiding commitments for its practice give shape to the complex, dynamic character of matrix thinking and shape analyses of the asymmetries of power that organize and structure experiences of persons and groups. This schematic is informed by theorists such as Lynn Weber (2010), Evangelina Holvino (2012), and Patricia Hill Collins and Sirma Bilge (2016). The holographic image that portrays the simultaneous co-construction of identities and interdependence of domains of power is used with the permission of Evangelina Holvino (2012, p. 173). The vertical arrows in the graphic that join aspects of social identity to the formative influence of domains of power and all to the foundational influence of a geographic and historical location visualize the reciprocity of influence for each aspect of the context. This reciprocity points to ways in which Charles Taylor's discussion of social imaginaries (2004) informs intersectional analysis. Cultures' normative ideas may emerge from a smaller often elite group and then take on a life of their own in the ebb and flow of the culture. Such cultural conversations help both explain the ways asymmetries of power form and reinforce ideological norms via media, education, and cultural symbols that enter the domains of power. But those conversations also help explain how the initiation of "resistant" or "interrogative" knowing can alter normative assumptions and initiate a recursive process into all levels of context, domains of power, and social identity (May, 2015, pp. xi and 6).

# Exploring the "Fit" for Intersectionality as a Methodological Resource for Pastoral and Practical Theology

Intersectionality has much to commend it as a methodological resource for pastoral theologians. It engages the complexity of power and difference especially through the frames of postcolonial and decolonial critiques, and it offers resources for shaping effective critical analysis and strategic resistance

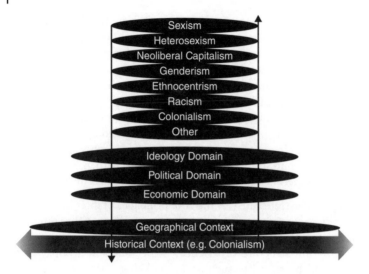

**Figure 7.1** Intersectional model (from Holvino, 2012).

informed by practices of solidarity. We will explore points of correlation across the six core principles and note those locations where pastoral theologians themselves can contribute to expanding the constructive resources for this metatheory such as: the individual and relational consequences of neoliberal economics, embodiment shaped by historical effects of oppression, and religious identity as an important aspect of personal and social identity also shaped by asymmetries of power. Further, it is important to begin by recognizing the deep alignment in a core methodological principle for pastoral and practical theology: the synergy of critical analysis and critical praxis as reciprocally informative (Collins and Bilge, 2016, p. 33).

## Social Inequality

Social inequality as the difficulty that prompts engagement and social justice as the telos of effective intersectional analysis and praxis demonstrate a deep ethical alignment between intersectionality and pastoral and practical theology. Of course, for theologians shaped by Christian tradition, the resonance of equality and justice is not limited to any particular concept of universal human rights. However, intersectionality's priority for assuring the worth and protection of each life signals a good fit in ethical values. Further, the ways intersectional methods prioritize deep and wide listening for what equality will entail among those differently oppressed prompts pastoral theologians toward more careful listening for the historical legacy of inequality and the particularity and scope of justice identified by those who are oppressed. For example, Collins and Bilge remind us, "Intersectional frameworks reveal how race, gender, sexuality, age, ability, and citizenship relate in complex and intersecting ways to produce economic inequality" (2016, p. 16).

## Power Relations

Intersectionality is especially helpful for understanding how asymmetries of power organize the co-construction of social identities such as racism, sexism, heterosexism, and classism at both individual psychosocial and social identity group levels. Intersectional theorists help clarify that social identities are not additive and separable but co-construct one another so that we experience complex identities in a simultaneous fashion. Different aspects of identity become more salient as our attention is turned from one situation to another (Holvino, 2012). This concept of simultaneous co-construction clarifies the problem with relying on single axis analyses such as distortions of racism or sexism, since these aspects of identity do not arise in isolation from each other. The lens of intersectionality's concept of power domains is especially helpful for theological analysis and strategic interventions. This lens helps public, pastoral, and practical theologians recognize the veiled ways privilege and stigma are normalized and continue outside of awareness such as through the media in the case of ideology, public policy enforcement via bureaucratic processes in the political domain, or credit policies in the economic domain. Through its attention to ways asymmetries of power organize persons' experiences of identity (racism, sexism, etc.), intersectionality assists pastors and pastoral theologians in the work of helping persons recognize how forces of dominance and oppression shape their experience personally and via social groups with whom they identify (Wijeyesinghe and Jones, 2014, p. 16). Helping persons individually and corporately develop this reflexivity is especially important for enhancing capacities for pursuing transformative change individually and corporately, as Collins asserts (2010, pp. 274–275).

Pastoral and practical theologians also can make constructive contributions to this intersection of power and identity in part because of our familiarity with psychological dimensions of identity as experienced emotionally. Womanist pastoral theologian, Phillis Sheppard, for example, describes ways experiences of embodiment demonstrate the enduring legacy of oppressive practices such as rape and lynching that were common for Africans forced into chattel slavery. Her work offers to intersectional theorists a deeper window into the complex ways asymmetries of power penetrate emotional levels of experiences of identity with lasting consequences for engaging asymmetries of power (2016, pp. 219–249). Pastoral theologians such as Greider (2011, 2012, 2015), Kujawa-Holbrook (2016), and Bidwell (2015) demonstrate ways in which religious affiliation and religious experience participate in the asymmetrical complexity of social identity. Intersectional methodological attention to multiple axes of identity and asymmetries of power may inform pastoral theological responses to this urgent dilemma.

## Relationality Through Solidarity Across Difference

Intersectionality's preference for analyzing and challenging asymmetries of power through coalitions that prioritize solidarity rather than sameness is methodologically important for public pastoral and practical theology seeking to understand the experience of those whose lives are shaped by marginalization. Intersectional analysis presumes that knowledge of the complexity of oppressions cannot rely on a single point of view. Collaborative or coalitional knowing ensures a fuller analysis and more effective strategic response. Further, as May and others note, since the voices of those with a colonial heritage are more dominant in the field now, pastoral and practical theologians do well to practice strategies of listening that deliberately invite a wider range of experience that does not draw on the hermeneutical or ontological assumptions of the Eurocentric rationality that coloniality claimed as normative. Public pastoral/practical theologian, Pamela Couture demonstrates this practice exceptionally well in *We Are Not All Victims* (2016). Pastoral and practical theologians particularly may be able to contribute to such analyses our own efforts to deconstruct the ways Western Christianity, as developed in the West, is itself deeply insinuated by the assumptions of coloniality.

## Social Context

There is a helpful convergence between pastoral theology and intersectionality in prioritizing the need for close readings of social contexts and the formative power of their historical and geographical particularity. Two aspects of historical and geographical context are especially evident in contemporary, public pastoral and practical theology and offer constructive possibilities to intersectional analyses: the historical legacies of colonialism through the frames of decolonial and postcolonial critiques, and neoliberal economics in its expanding forms and influence.

Intersectionality's preference for amplifying the voices of those whose experience is shaped by the consequences of colonialism and now neocolonialism is a resource for pastoral theologians who are beginning to expand our reliance on postcolonial critiques to draw on decolonial theory as well. As Walter Mignolo advises, postcolonial and decolonial theories, "both walk in the same direction, following different paths"; however, the latter allows us to hear the voices of those who know first-hand the reality of the extraordinary violence of colonialism rather than through a more Eurocentric critique (2011, p. 55). Andraos, McGarrah Sharp, and Lartey's use of decolonial and postcolonial theories, as noted earlier, demonstrate that current scholarship by pastoral and practical theologians can expand intersectional analyses and praxis in areas of pedagogy, hermeneutics, and the complexity of recovering identity distorted by coloniality.

Because of pastoral theologians' close attention to interior experience, we are able to add to the initial ways neoliberal policies are emerging in intersectional cultural analysis. Through his clinical practice, Rogers-Vaughn (2016) describes ways the self-understanding of many individual Americans is changing by virtue of a gradual and thoroughly radical individualism shaped by neoliberal economics. Having dismissed obligations for the most vulnerable, neoliberal economics presumes hierarchical economic stratifications that justify "losers" as an inevitable side effect of creating economic winners. Over time, "neighbors" become competitors in each other's eyes. Similarly, Cedric Johnson (2016) offers resources largely absent in intersectional theory through critical engagement with the intersections of racism, neoliberal economics, spiritual resources, and ritual practices that help sustain resilience in the practice of resistance.

## Complexity

Attention to the complexity of lived experience is an important convergence in pastoral and practical theological analysis and praxis in intersectionality. Both approaches insist that the method be apt for the context and forego forcing a "fit" between the two. Presently, intersectionality contributes a richer analysis of the ways power misshapes social identities and domains of power. As noted earlier, pastoral and practical theologians offer resources for deeper understanding of the embodied, emotional experience of persons shaped by asymmetries of power.

## Social Justice

Social justice and social inequality reciprocally inform each other. Pastoral and practical theologians offer important contributions from the wealth of reflection in Jewish and Christian traditions regarding the character of justice and love and their conceptual linkage. As Daniel Day Williams wrote, "*Justice is the order God's love requires*" (Williams, 1968, p. 250, italics in original). While any conversation about love, love defined by particular religious traditions, as well as the relation of love and justice, must be developed non-normatively in public contexts, such explorations bring considerable, complex richness to intersectional resources. It will also prompt interpretive richness through the reflections of those whose lives and spiritualities were distorted by colonial versions of Christianity. Public pastoral and practical theologians are only beginning to engage the ways religious plurality will expand understanding of both love and justice and shape collaborative endeavors toward justice in the public sphere with those whose interest in justice are not shaped religiously (Ramsay, 2014, pp. 117–139). This intersectional learning will be relevant for effective community-wide organizing efforts.

## Intersectional Implications for Pastoral Practice

The following fictionalized, composite case is informed by qualitative research I conducted with several congregations. It illustrates the experience of hundreds of moderate to progressive congregations in the US whose members largely reflect racial and economic privilege. They are initiating caring ministries with those often marginalized by such aspects of identity as race, ethnicity, and socio-economic class. These ministries create opportunities for more privileged persons to see and talk about the implications of faith as they encounter inequities of power shaping social identity and domains of power that shape systems and structures that were previously invisible to them.

I developed this case to feature ways intersectionality pierces the veil of privilege to disclose asymmetries of power operative culturally and through social identities because I believe this is a compelling need currently in contemporary pastoral and practical theology. In the case that follows we see the sorts of change and possibilities for solidarity with marginalized populations that can arise through intersectional strategies. Currently, descriptions of intersectional strategies more often reflect coalitions of marginalized populations, and readers are able to find recent descriptions of such engagements in Collins and Bilge (2016).

## A Case

Paula is one of three Euro-American clergy who serve a thriving 1500-member Episcopal congregation, St. Stephen, in a southern metropolitan area of the US. A 34-year-old woman, Paula grew up in a middle class family where both parents worked. The membership at St. Stephen is overwhelmingly Euro-American and middle to upper middle class. Recently a core group of laity succeeded in strengthening the vision of the vestry and the congregation for stronger missional outreach. The new clergy team is guided by this missional vision. During seminary, Paula worked in a faith-based urban community ministry that served individuals and families, including new immigrants, who were economically vulnerable. Paula is drawn to the congregation's clear decision to engage the needs of the working poor who live in a nearby area of the city and whose children attend an elementary school near the church.

Currently, St. Stephen has an international outreach program in Antigua that includes a yearly trip to support an Anglican congregation in a rural area that the denomination helped them identify. The church has also just responded positively to a Diocesan request to host a Muslim refugee family from Syria. The vestry led a discussion process with the congregation and acted positively after a good congregational response to the opportunity. A team of parishioners, staffed by Paula, is preparing to receive the family.

A year ago, the congregation launched a ministry to serve the needs of the working poor and some homeless who live in a nearby area, though their living conditions reflect a markedly different situation than the relative affluence of many members at St. Stephen. The ministry, titled, "Good Samaritan," distributes food weekly for those whose food stamps run out before the end of the month and food for those without homes who also come weekly. A clothes closet is also on site. Every Wednesday volunteers from St. Stephen cook and serve an evening meal followed by a Eucharistic worship service with adult Bible study and church school classes for children. Paula's responsibilities at Good Samaritan include recruiting and supporting volunteers and supervising a staff person who leads the complex work of managing the services offered. There is some overlap among the volunteers at Good Samaritan across the other two outreach programs.

Near the close of the first year of operation, Paula convenes a representative group of lay volunteers at Good Samaritan to invite them to talk about their experience. All in the group are Euro-American and most are economically privileged. She asks what is working well, and what is proving meaningful for them.

All say they find sharing the meal with persons from the community and sharing the Eucharistic service are powerful experiences. Receiving the bread and wine standing beside those with so little reminds Bill, "We are all God's children." Diane chokes up when she says, as a mother, she carries in her heart images of the children coming up for second and third helpings each week. She did not know there were hungry children in the city. Joyce talks about the Bible study with adults after the meal. They are helping her see biblical texts in new ways. Raul, for example, observed recently that probably the workers hired last in the story in Matthew 20 had been waiting all day hoping for work. He knew what that was like. That interpretation makes such a difference. Dave will always remember Patricia's comment at dinner that she and Hector bring their children to the evening program so they will know the homeless man they see in the neighborhood is a person God loves just as God loves them. Betsy enjoys working with Gladys as her co-teacher of the early elementary class. The class worked a lot better after Gladys, a community participant, asked to co-lead it with her. Gladys has great ideas, and the children are responding better.

Then Paula invites the group to share any concerns they have. Bill grumbles about the nice cars he sees in the parking lot as persons come for a bag of groceries. After visiting a family last week, Diane wonders about seeing last week's groceries from Good Samaritan were unopened, but take out containers from fast food places were on the counter. A widescreen TV was in the small living room. How could they afford the TV and still be on food stamps? Is the congregation really helping people in need? Or are we are providing food they don't like? Dave voices his disillusionment that despite months of helping Frank to get back on his feet from a health crisis and find a job, last week Frank said he lost the job and was about to lose the room he rented. The work was too hard to reach by bus due to the limited bus schedule and the recent fare hike. The foreman didn't care about the bus schedule and fired him. Dave wonders,

"Why can't Frank 'man up' and find a job and stick with it?" Diane is puzzled by how many children come on Wednesdays without parents because their parents work two or even three jobs. How do these parents manage to carry such loads, and why are they still barely able to cover expenses? Joyce finds such stories hard to hear after coming back from Antigua last month. She was glad the church bought materials needed to repair and paint the school, but why isn't St. Stephen helping feed the children in that parish who are hungry every day? Such poverty haunts her. "Why aren't we focused on changing that? And why are children hungry in our own city?" Dave wants to know what to say when some of the Euro-American and African American participants complain that the Hispanics are taking their jobs. He thinks that might be true. But how should he respond to such comments? They all need assistance, but he says there are differences and tensions among the participants. Paul mentioned that the reading and discussion he was doing for the refugee reception team made him wonder if poor persons who aren't Christian feel welcome at Good Samaritan. He hoped so, but he doubted it.

They all agree that Good Samaritan is a powerful spiritual and emotional experience and very complicated for them as well. They are startled to find they are learning as much about themselves as they are about the participants. All of them also say they had no idea how big the gaps are in services between the poor and middle class citizens in the city. Their ministry matters, but it is not enough. But they doubt anyone could change realities that are so complex.

As she listened, Paula was remembering some of her experiences in her seminary field work in the city. She, too, had many of these unsettling experiences as she encountered differences she hadn't needed to notice before. She is pleased many congregants are beginning to notice systemic issues and wonder about change. Maybe now they are ready to think about how their faith can engage the seemingly invisible systems and structures at work in their city shaping their lives and the lives of those they serve in their outreach ministries. What, she wondered, would she hear if she convened a group of the participants who've been coming for the past year? If the participants felt free to talk honestly about their experience with the volunteers, she knows a whole new range of possibilities will emerge for this ministry.

## Intersectionality as it Informs Our Pastoral Response

As we use the lens of intersectionality to reflect on this case, we will see that in practice, the six core principles of intersectionality function integratively rather than in a linear fashion to inform a critical analysis and praxis. In particular we also see how formative the social context becomes for each of the other five principles. For the purposes of this chapter, we will seek to distinguish the function of each principle.

There is much to commend in the motivation and commitment of St. Stephen Parish and these parishioners who have volunteered for a year in a ministry that is more challenging than they expected. The congregation and these volunteers apparently imagined that their ministry at Good Samaritan was an opportunity to offer a "hand up" to those who were like themselves but were simply "down on their luck." With a hand up, they imagined these persons and their families could be "back on their feet."

## Social Inequality

With Paula we hear that the opportunity for sustained interaction and sustained relationships for some volunteers is crumbling their earlier assumptions about the situation of those they serve at Good Samaritan. They imagined that their experience of their city and its services was common to all and equitably available, but they have now encountered evidence that creates fault lines in those assumptions. Without experiences that challenge such normative versions of life in their city and country, these congregants would have no reason to question their assumptions. Instead of persons who are just down on their luck or have made poor decisions, they now experience a more complicated scenario. The working poor they meet at Good Samaritan are very hard working parents as dedicated to their children's education and religious values as they are. They think deeply about their faith. They try hard to meet the needs of their children and to find work. Close conversations with them reveal a socio-cultural, political, and economic context that creates a maze of challenges these parishioners could not have imagined. Somehow the playing field seems not so level as they had always imagined. How to explain this social inequality?

## Power Relations

Power relations are especially salient in this case and point to two intersecting levels in which asymmetries of power shape public and personal experience. The first and more encompassing are the three domains of power shaped via intersecting institutions in each: *ideology* (cultural symbols, media, education, religion, etc.), *political* (bureaucracies of governance through which policies are implemented that shape personal and communal access to services and resources), and *economic* (local financial policies, mortgage and housing policies, national regulations, international trade practices, etc.). The second and equally powerful lies in the way asymmetries of power that function normatively organize individual and group social identities such as racism, heterosexism, neoliberal capitalism, etc.). These politicized aspects of identity cannot be understood in isolation as if additive. They co-construct each other and function simultaneously.

In this case we see how the intersections of the domains of ideology, politics, and economics construe a picture of the social context in ways that allowed these otherwise thoughtful and well-meaning congregants to be remarkably unreflective about the socio-economic realities of the persons they meet at Good Samaritan. This absence of critical reflectivity is in fact understandable. These are persons whose view of their country and world is shaped by institutions that comprise the domains of power through which normative understandings are promulgated. For example, the volunteers rely on national and local media and their own experience to interpret their context. They find the city council attends to services that they need in their neighborhoods and to the schools their children attend. The recent small hike in bus fares announced in the media that complicated Frank's employment seemed reasonable. They grew up shaped by the assumptions of neoliberal economic policies that government should limit services especially to those who seem to make repeatedly poor choices about education and employment. They regret the historical realities of chattel slavery and genocide of indigenous peoples and believe now every American begins on a "level playing field." After all, the country recently twice elected a black president. They aren't aware that the GI Bill benefits that their fathers received after World War II were not available to African American veterans. They had no idea that the absence of those benefits coupled with government-sanctioned segregated housing practices meant their parents accumulated equity in their homes while African Americans could not. Nor do they understand that these housing decisions and subsequent employment, banking, and educational practices shaped their very racially segregated experience. They do not know how the credit practices of the International Monetary Fund (IMF) contribute to the levels of poverty they see in Antigua.

This partial litany of social and historical injustices characterizes the gap between the world as the volunteers at Good Samaritan imagine it and the world in which those they serve live. The litany discloses what Christian theologians describe as sin, the "negation" of the obligations of compassion and justice toward all persons (Matsuoka, 1998) that creation in God's image prescribes. This litany describes two aspects of this "negation of relation." Social or original sin reflects the ways sin posits itself in historical life by creating deep inequalities in access to resources and freedoms that ensure human dignity and protection under the law. "Sin as lie" describes how those who are privileged by interlocking systems of advantage posited by social sin learn rationalizations to explain and to avoid acknowledging complicity in the consequences of inequitable access to resources and protection for those whom God also loves (Farley, 1990; Suchocki, 1995). Sin as lie then also co-opts such persons into participating in social sin with various rationalizations rather than choosing to resist it. The seeming naiveté that domains of power intend to create and the ways they disguise current practices that reproduce such inequalities align closely with this central claim about power and sin in Christian theology (Ramsay, 2010, pp. 344–346).

Dave's comments about Frank demonstrate how asymmetries of power organize his unreflective sense of his social identities and those of others. In suggesting that Frank showed no initiative in getting a job and should "man up" and get to work, we see how privilege weaves through the interstices of Dave's racial, socio-economic, and gender identity to create his assumptions about how any "responsible" man will support himself and his family. Dave has no idea how this view reflects ways racial and economic privilege shape his normative assumptions about masculinity and agency. He is unreflective about how racism, sexism, and neoliberal capitalism differentially shape his access to employment options and success in his field; education to prepare for employment; and structural supports for access to employment. Dave's unreflective experience leads him to imagine that every person is able and responsible for making his or her own way in a country where those who try hard enough will succeed. Dave and the other volunteers in this conversation have no close friends who identify by another race or nationality, who vary significantly from their socio-economic level, or who are not Christian. It is no surprise that they came to this ministry assuming that they and those they want to help live in the same "world."

Power relations also point to another important implication for the practice of critical reflexivity. For those of us with European ancestry, the challenge of critical reflexivity is profound because it is ontological as well as hermeneutical. Euro-Americans have learned to imagine ourselves through a deeply flawed understanding of a uniquely privileged and hierarchical location within the human community and to marginalize others. For those whose heritage is colonial oppression, critical subjectivity calls for deconstructing the colonizers' attempted erasure of identity and revaluing their own worth and experience. The depth of this challenge for Paula and the volunteers affirms the practice of coalitional solidarity central to intersectional practice to which we turn now.

## Solidarity

Identities and perspectives organized by privilege "protected" these volunteers from relationships and conversation that could have challenged their assumptions prior to this experience. Their praxis and sustained experience in an environment of real difference are in fact precisely what now prompts their critical analysis. As pastoral and practical theologians affirm, reflective engagement with lived experience is the source of new constructive theological wisdom. That is what has begun to happen here. It would not be accurate to describe their experience to date as solidarity, but their sustained relationships, and for some, deepening friendships are what may prompt the reciprocity in learning that change through coalitional action requires.

Paula, the priest serving this missional effort, is already also thinking about ways the congregation's efforts could be more effective if they join in a community-based group whose common goals include changing political/

bureaucratic and economic/banking and housing practices to ensure such services are equitably offered and protect the most vulnerable. Such coalitional work will require that she and the volunteers become more skilled in articulating the faith-based commitments of St. Stephen's outreach to those whose motivations are not shaped religiously. In this regard, St. Stephen's situation illustrates the public practical theology strategy that Elaine Graham describes as an "apologetics of presence"—a resistant knowing that speaks truth to power as it seeks the "welfare of the city" (Jer. 29:7) (Graham, 2013, pp. 212–213). Graham's point echoes a commitment clearly present in the field to demonstrate a religious/spiritual sensibility that prioritizes constructive, politically informed engagement to promote the wellbeing of all God's people, regardless of religious status simply because through the lens of faith, they are our neighbors. Ammerman's recent research on rationale supporting practices of spirituality and religious affiliation in the US also reveals that the most widely held definition of spiritual commitment in the US is an "ethical spirituality" that expresses a humanistically based obligation of compassion and functions as a political and strategic commitment to neighbor love regardless of any other aspect of social identity (Ammerman, 2013, p. 272).

Intersectionality would also affirm Paula's afterthought following the conversation with volunteers, that she could learn important information by talking with participants. Coalitional praxis resides in the authenticity and particularity of the wisdom of those closest to the gaps in justice and compassion. It is the shared learning that prioritizes experience unfamiliar to the volunteers' experience that has prompted their dawning realization that the work before them is not what they first imagined but is indeed authorized by the faith that prompted their choice to serve their neighbors.

## Historical and Geographical Social Context

Two factors loom large in describing the formative consequences of historical and geographical context for the experience of these volunteers: colonialism and the related subsequent rise of neoliberal capitalism. In each exploration of the prior five intersectional principles we have recognized the ways colonialism inflects this method. The colonialism that arose in the 15th century is like a three-legged stool including the emerging patriarchal capitalism that prompted its hunger for bigger profits, the fiction of race, and practice of racism to authorize the commodification or subjugation of other people. The mid-20th-century rise of neoliberal economics extends the consequences of colonialism anew. No aspects of social identity or of the norms that circulate through the three domains of power are untouched by these realities.

The volunteers at Good Samaritan, who initiated and now help staff this outreach ministry, unwittingly understand the situation and experience of the people they seek to serve through the historical and economic consequences of the past 500 years. The literature review of the past 30 years in pastoral and practical theology confirms that only now are the fields becoming alert to the distortions created by the historical and geographical realities of coloniality. These fields' experience is not unlike the "cracks" in the self-understanding of the volunteers, who begin to wonder what else they don't understand. For pastoral and practical theologians, this prompts a readiness to draw on decolonial, liberatory, and resistant hermeneutics that shape intersectional methodologies. Doing so would also enrich wider intersectional resources.

## Complexity

Presuming the complexity of lived experience is a shared principle of both intersectional and pastoral and practical theology. Analysis of this case illustrates how intersectionality can "thicken" pastoral and practical capacities to assess the dynamics of power as it organizes identity, normative cultural understanding, and practices of care in ways that are typically out of awareness for those whose identity is more privileged. Intersectional approaches can guide our exploration of how religious difference may be complicated further at the interstices of race, tribe, gender, and sexual identity, or otherwise problematized in many cultures. The current research by pastoral and practical theologians who are exploring the rich complexity that religious difference brings to social identities will be an asset for future intersectional resources.

## Social Justice

Intersectional theorists and public pastoral and practical theologians share Iris Marion Young's apt description of social justice that it "requires not the melting away of differences, but institutions that promote reproduction of and respect for group differences without oppression" (1990, p. 47). She was countering the prominence of distributive justice, which presumes the possibility of justice distributed equally regardless of inequalities such as those our case illustrates. As she then demonstrated, achieving social justice requires carefully accounting for and resisting asymmetries of power that exploit, marginalize, disempower, culturally subsume, and or violently harm others (pp. 47–65). As we recognize in this case, ideological norms can certainly limit well-intentioned persons' capacities to discern how destructive forces of power obscure what social justice would require.

Certainly, intersectional theorists are right to assert how critical coalitional conversation is for identifying harm and discerning shared assumptions of what social justice would look like in any given situation. Many world religions such as the Abrahamic traditions would also affirm that justice is shaped by the obligation to care for the needs of those who are most vulnerable. As Larry Graham's phrase, "relational justice" anticipated, pastoral and practical theologians have constructive resources to contribute to intersectional conversations about justice as an obligation that enacts care or love. Many theologians recognize that love has everything to do with power. Public pastoral and practical theologians affirm that sharing insights from religious traditions in public processes of discernment presume that such wisdom is offered as useful without normative status. Certainly love is not a simple or generic term nor easily translated from the normative context of religious traditions to a larger public context where it is one value among others. However, religious reflection across millennia and diverse contexts is also an asset for the complex ethical, emotional, and political realities that lie ahead for congregations and community-based organizations, especially in a culture where love is often reduced to sentimental and apolitical emotion. For example, theologian Daniel D. Williams described justice as ordered by love that is particular rather than general, freely offered, open to the possibility of suffering for others, responsive to the freedom and individuality of another in ways that inevitably affect those who love, and reflective in assessing the situations that shape the needs of others (1968, pp. 114–122). Such ideas may well be useful for the intersectional discernment of coalitions in public contexts.

## Practices of Care for Intersectional Engagement

While this brief review illustrates ways intersectional methodologies and pastoral and practical theology implicitly inform each other in situations such as the Good Samaritan outreach program, it is also clear that the complexity of practicing care invites explicit attention to ways to draw on the resources of intersectionality. As the volunteers suggested to their priest, the complexity of the situation can be overwhelming. Pastors such as Paula who help prepare parishioners to join in an intersectional coalitional process need pedagogical resources to help parishioners learn effective skills for practicing care that will promote relational justice in the midst of the complex inequalities they have come to realize are operating quietly out of view and in their own identities.

The volunteers' growing recognition of gaps between their experience and that of those they seek to help provides a good opening for Paula to draw on the conceptual and experiential resources of social justice education (SJE) to support a journey that is necessarily as personal as it is intellectual (Wijeyesinghe and Jackson, 2012; Adams et al., 2016). Of course Paula and the parishioners will recognize in this pedagogy resources for a deeply spiritual journey of confession and repentance. SJE opens for them a journey that resonates with theological themes of justice and neighbor that challenge and reject the inequalities they have learned to see. SJE is an interdisciplinary, conceptual, and pedagogical resource that is easily adapted for faith-based contexts. Well aligned with intersectionality's core principles, SJE helps persons of faith such as these parishioners and those who come to Good Samaritan for assistance to become reflective together about how the complexity of power as oppression and privilege organizes their own multiple and simultaneous social identities through larger systems of oppression and privilege such as racism, classism, and heterosexism. They also explore how institutional and cultural dynamics are likely to impact their social identities (Adams et al., 2016, p. 40).

The conceptual and experiential resources available through SJE presume and support the value of coalitional efforts. They support revising learned, relational power dynamics shaped by privilege and marginalization to help ensure the possibilities of power shared by groups of diverse persons who join in resisting aspects of oppression. Such shared work enriches the pool of experience of gaps in justice as well as widening the vision for what restoring justice will require. Intersectional coalitions are shaped by mutuality in decision making that finds common ground in shared goals. As the case suggested at its close, Paula already imagines that the educational work she will initiate with those involved in outreach at St. Stephen will likely also point to joining a coalition of others in the city. However, SJE affirms her sense that this sort of coalitional work will best begin with an educational process that encourages more mutuality in the dynamics between volunteers from St. Stephen and those who seek assistance at Good Samaritan. After all, for St. Stephen volunteers, the best teachers about the real situation in their city are those who know firsthand the gaps that have been invisible to the membership at St. Stephen.

## Conclusion

Together we have explored the feasibility of intersectionality as a methodological resource for public pastoral and practical theology as it is practiced internationally in efforts to engage and promote justice ordered by practices of care or love. Initial indicators affirm the close alignment between the core principles of intersectional methodologies and those of public pastoral and practical theologians. There is an especially timely reciprocity between the wisdom voiced in the particular socio-historical, embodied experience of formative contributors to this metatheory and the needs for theologians addressing the consequences of coloniality and neoliberal economics for practices of care. We also find significant, constructive possibilities that lie in future explorations between intersectional methodologies and public pastoral and practical theology.

## References

Adams, Maurianne, Lee Anne Bell, with Dianne J. Goodman and Khyati, Y. Joshi. 2016. *Teaching for Diversity and Social Justice*, 3rd edn. New York: Routledge.
Ammerman, Nancy. 2013. "'Spiritual But Not Religious?' Beyond Binary Choices in the Study of Religion." *Journal for the Scientific Study of Religion*. Volume 52, 258–278. https://doi.org/10.1111/jssr.12024.

Andraos, Michel Elias. 2012. "Engaging Diversity in Teaching Religion and Theology: An Intercultural, De-colonial Epistemic Perspective." *Teaching Theology and Religion.* Volume 15, Issue 1, 3–15. https://doi.org/10.1111/j.1467-9647.2011.00755.x.

Anzaldúa, Gloria. 1987. *Borderlands/La Frontera.* San Francisco, CA: Spinsters/Aunt Lute Press Foundation Press.

Babbit, Susan E. 2001. "Objectivity and the Role of Bias." In *Engendering Rationalities,* edited by Nancy Tuana and Sandra Morgen, pp. 297–314. Albany, NY: SUNY Press.

Beal, Frances. 1995 [1970] "Double Jeopardy: To be Black and Female." In *Words of Fire: An Anthology of African-American Feminist Thought,* edited by B. Guy-Sheftall, pp. 146–155. New York: New York Press.

Bidwell, Duane. 2008. "Practicing the Religious Self: Buddhist-Christian Identity as Social Artifact." *Buddhist-Christian Studies.* Volume 28, 3–12. https://doi.org/10.1353/bcs.0.0017.

Bidwell, Duane R. 2015. "Religious Diversity and Public Pastoral Theology: Is it Time for a Comparative Theological Paradigm?" *Journal of Pastoral Theology.* Volume 25, Issue 3, 135–150. https://doi.org/10.1080/10649867.2015.1122427.

Collective, Combahee River. 1995 [1977] "A Black Feminist Statement." In *Words of Fire: An Anthology of African-American Feminist Thought,* edited by B. Guy-Sheftall, pp. 232–240. New York: New York Press.

Collins, Patricia Hill. 2000. *Black Feminist Thought: Knowledge, Consciousness, and the Politics of Empowerment,* 2nd edn. New York: Routledge.

Collins, Patricia Hill and Sirma Bilge. 2016. *Intersectionality.* Malden, MA: Polity Press.

Couture, Pamela. 2016. *We Are Not All Victims: Local Peacebuilding in the Democratic Republic of Congo.* Zurich: Lit Verlag.

Crenshaw, Kimberlé Williams. 1989. "Demarginalizing the Intersection of Race and Sex: A Black Feminist Critique of Anti-Racist Politics." *The University of Chicago Legal Forum.* Volume 140, 139–167.

Crenshaw, Kimberlé Williams. 1991. "Mapping the Margins: Intersectionality, Identity Politics, and Violence Against Women of Color." *Stanford Law Review.* Volume 43, 1241–1299. https://doi.org/10.2307/1229039.

Dames, Gordon E. 2010. "The Dilemma of Traditional and 21st Century Pastoral Ministry: Ministering to Families and Communities Faced with Socio-Economic Pathologies." *HTS Theological Studies.* Volume 66, Issue 2, 1–7. https://doi.org/10.4102/hts.v66i2.817.

Day, Katie. 2014. *Faith on the Avenue: Religion on a City Street.* New York: Oxford University Press. https://doi.org/10.1093/acprof:oso/9780199860029.001.0001.

Day, Katie, Esther McIntosh, and William Storrar. 2013. *Yours the Power: Faith-Based Organizing in the USA.* Boston, MA: Brill. https://doi.org/10.1163/9789004246010_002.

Dreyer, Jaco. 2016. "Knowledge, Subjectivity, (De)Coloniality, and the Conundrum of Reflexivity." In *Conundrums in Practical Theology*, edited by Joyce Ann Mercer and Bonnie J. Miller-McLemore, pp. 90–109. Boston, MA: Brill. https://doi.org/10.1163/9789004324244_006.

Du Toit, Nadine Bowers. 2017a. "'Ma se kind': Rediscovering Personhood in Addressing Socio-economic Challenges in the Cape Flats." In *Practicing Ubuntu: Practical Theological Perspectiveson Injustice, Personhood and Human Dignity*, edited by Jaco Dreyer, Yolanda Dreyer, Edward Foley, and Malan Nel, pp. 55–66. Zurich: Lit Verlag.

Du Toit, Nadine Bowers. 2017b. "Poverty and Inequality in South Africa: What's Compassion Got to Do With It?" in process.

Farley, Wendy. 1990. *Tragic Vision and Divine Compassion*. Louisville, KY: Westminster John Knox Press.

Gill, Theodore, Kim Dongsung, and Isabel Apawo Phiri. 2014. "Editorial: New Perspectives on Diakonia." *The Ecumenical Review*. Volume 66, Issue 3, 249–251. https://doi.org/10.1111/erev.12114.

Graham, Elaine. 2013. *Between a Rock and a Hard Place: Public Theology in a Post-Secular Age*. London: SCM Press.

Graham, Elaine and Anna Rowlands. 2005. *Pathways to the Public Square: Practical Theology in an Age of Pluralism International Academy of Practical Theology, Manchester, 2003*. Munster: Lit Verlag.

Graham, Larry Kent. 1995. "From Relational Humaness to Relational Justice: Reconceiving Pastoral Care and Counseling." In *Pastoral Care and Social Conflict*, edited by Pamela Couture and Rodney Hunter, pp. 220–234. Nashville, TN: Abingdon.

Greider, Kathleen. 2011. "Religious Multiplicity and Care of Souls." In *Pastoral Psychology and Psychology of Religion in Dialogue: Implications for Pastoral Care*, edited by Isabelle Noth, Christoph Morgenthaler, and Kathleen Greider, pp. 119–135. Stuttgart: Kohlhammer.

Greider, Kathleen. 2012. "Religious Pluralism and Christian-Centrism." In *The Wiley-Blackwell Companion to Practical Theology*, edited by Bonnie Miller-McLemore, pp. 452–462. Malden, MA: Wiley-Blackwell.

Grieder, Kathleen. 2015. "Religious Location and Counseling: Engaging Diversity and Difference in Views of Religion." In *Understanding Pastoral Counseling*, edited by Elizabeth Maynard and Jill Snodgrass, pp. 235–256. New York: Springer.

Holvino, Evangelina. 2012. "The 'Simultaneity' of Identities: Models and Skills for the Twenty-First Century." In *New Perspectives on Racial Identity Development*, edited by Charmaine Wiyeyesinghe and Bailey W. Jackson III, pp. 161–191. New York: NYU Press.

Hunter, Rodney, Ed. 1990. *Dictionary of Pastoral Care and Counseling*. Nashville, TN: Abingdon.

Johnson, Cedric C. 2016. *Race, Religion, and Resilience in the Neoliberal Age.* New York: Palgrave Macmillan. https://doi.org/10.1057/9781137526144.

Kujawa-Holbrook, Cheryl. 2016. "Postcolonial Interreligious Learning: A Reflection from a North American Christian Perspective." In *Postcolonial Practice of Ministry: Leadership, Liturgy, and Interfaith Engagement,* edited by Kwok Pui-Lan and Peter Burns, pp. 153–166. New York: Lexington Books.

LaMothe, Ryan. 2012. "Broken and Empty: Pastoral Leadership as Embodying Radical Courage, Humility, Compassion, and Hope." *Pastoral Psychology.* Volume 61, 451–466. https://doi.org/10.1007/s11089-011-0417-9.

LaMothe, Ryan. 2014. "A Modest Proposal: A Pastoral Political Theology." *Pastoral Psychology.* Volume 63, Issue 4, 375–391. https://doi.org/10.1007/s11089-013-0557-1. https://doi.org/10.1007/s11089-011-0417-9

LaMothe, Ryan. 2016a. "Neoliberal Capitalism and the Corruption of Society: A Pastoral Political Analysis." *Pastoral Psychology.* Issue 65, pp. 5–21. https://doi.org/10.1007/s11089-013-0577-x.

LaMothe, Ryan. 2016b. "Colonizing Realities of Neoliberal Capitalism." *Pastoral Psychology.* Issue 65, 23–40.

Lartey, Emmanuel Y. 2013. *Postcolonializing God: An African Practical Theology.* London: SCM Press.

Lartey, Emmanuel Y. 2016. "'Borrowed Clothes Will Never Keep You Warm': Postcolonializing Pastoral Leadership." In *Postcolonial Practice of Ministry: Leadership, Liturgy, and Interfaith Engagement,* edited by Kwok Pui-Lan and Stephen Burns, pp. 21–32. New York: Lexington Books.

Lugones, Maria. 2010. "Toward a Decolonial Feminism." *Hypatia.* Volume 25, Issue 4, 742–759. https://doi.org/10.1111/j.1527-2001.2010.01137.x.

Matsuoka, Fumitaka. 1998. *The Color of Faith.* Cleveland, OH: United Church Press.

May, Vivian. 2015. *Pursuing Intersectionality, Unsettling Dominant Imaginaries.* New York: Routledge.

McGarrah Sharp, Melinda. 2012. "Globalization, Colonialism, and Postcolonialism." In *The Wiley-Blackwell Companion to Practical Theology,* edited by Bonnie Miller-McLemore, pp. 422–432. Malden, MA: Wiley-Blackwell.

McGarrah Sharp, Melinda. 2013. *Misunderstanding Stories: Toward a Postcolonial Pastoral Theology.* Eugene, OR: Pickwick.

McGarrah Sharp, Melinda. 2016. "Literacies of Listening: Postcolonial Pastoral Leadership in Practice." In *Postcolonial Practice of Ministry: Leadership, Liturgy, and Interfaith Engagement,* edited by Kwok Pui-Lan and Stephen Burns, pp. 33–48. New York: Lexington Books.

Mignolo, Walter. 2007. "Delinking: the Rhetoric of Modernity, the Logic of Coloniality and the Grammar of De-Coloniality." *Cultural Studies.* Volume 21, Issue 2–3, 449–513. https://doi.org/10.1080/09502380601162647.

Mignolo, Walter D. 2011. *The Darker Side of Western Modernity: Global Futures, Decolonial Options.* Durham, NC: Duke University Press. https://doi. org/10.1215/9780822394501.

Miller-McLemore, Bonnie. 1993. "The Human Web: Reflections on the State of Pastoral Theology." *Christian Century.* April 7, 366–369.

Miller-McLemore, Bonnie J., Ed. 2012. *The Wiley-Blackwell Companion to Practical Theology.* Malden, MA: Wiley-Blackwell.

Moraga, Cherrie and Gloria Anzaldúa. 1983. *This Bridge Called My Back: Writings by Radical Women of Color.* Albany, NY: SUNY Press.

Mouton, Dawid P. 2014. "Communities Facing Disruption: The Need to Shift from Individual to Community Paradigms of Pastoral Care." *Acta Theologica.* Volume 34, Issue 1, 91–107. https://doi.org/10.4314/actat.v34i1.6.

Quijano, Anibal. 2000. "Coloniality of Power and Eurocentrism in Latin America." *International Sociology.* Volume 15, Issue 2, 215–232. https://doi.org/10.1177/0268580900015002005.

Ramsay, Nancy, Ed. 2004. *Pastoral Care and Counseling Redefining the Paradigms.* Nashville, TN: Abingdon.

Ramsay, Nancy. 2010. "Where Race and Gender Collide." In *Women out of Order,* edited by Jeanne Stevenson-Moessner and Teresa Snorton, pp. 331–348. Minneapolis, MN: Fortress.

Ramsay, Nancy. 2014. "Theological Education in a Secular Age: Challenges and Possibilities." In *The Theologically Formed Heart,* edited by Warner Bailey, Lee Barrett III, and James O. Duke, pp. 117–139. Eugene, OR: Wipf & Stock.

Rogers-Vaughn, Bruce. 2015. "Powers and Principalities: Initial Reflections Toward a Post-Capitalist Pastoral Theology." *Journal of Pastoral Theology.* Volume 25, Issue 2, 71–92. https://doi.org/10.1179/1064986715Z.00000000010.

Rogers-Vaughn, Bruce. 2016. *Caring for Souls in a Neo-Liberal Age.* New York: Palgrave Macmillan. https://doi.org/10.1057/978-1-137-55339-3.

Sheppard, Phillis Isabella. 2016. "Raced Bodies: Portraying Bodies, Reifying Racism." In *Conundrums in Practical Theology,* edited by Joyce Ann Mercer and Bonnie J. Miller-McLemore, pp. 219–249. Boston, MA: Brill. https://doi.org/10.1163/9789004324244_011.

Smith, Archie. 1983. *The Relational Self: Ethics and Therapy from a Black Church Perspective.* Nashville, TN: Abingdon.

Streck, Valburga Schmiedt. 2012. "Brazil." In *The Wiley-Blackwell Companion to Practical Theology,* edited by Bonnie J. Miller-McLemore, pp. 525–534. Malden, MA: Wiley-Blackwell.

Suchocki, Marjorie. 1995. *The Fall to Violence.* London: Bloomsbury.

Taylor, Charles. 2004. *Modern Social Imaginaries.* Durham, NC: Duke University Press.

Weber, Lynn. 2010. *Understanding Race, Class, Gender, and Sexuality,* 2nd edn. New York: Routledge.

Wijeyesinghe, Charmaine and Bailey W Jackson III. 2012. *New Perspectives on Racial Identity Development*. New York: NYU Press.

Williams, Daniel Day. 1968. *The Spirit and the Forms of Love*. New York: Harper and Row.

Wiyeyesinghe, Charmaine and Susan R. Jones. 2014. "Intersectionality, Identity and Systems of Power and Inequality." In *Intersectionality and Higher Education: Theory, Research, and Practice*, edited by D. Mitchell, C. Simmons, and L. Greyerbiehl, pp. 9–20. New York: Peter Lang.

Young, Iris Marion. 1990. *Justice and the Politics of Difference*. Princeton, NJ: Princeton University Press.

# Index

Page references to Figures are followed by the letter 'f' in italics, while references to Tables are followed by the letter 't'. References to Notes contain the letter 'n', followed by the number of the note.

*Pastoral Theology and Care: Critical Trajectories in Theory and Practice*,
First Edition. Edited by Nancy J. Ramsay.
© 2018 John Wiley & Sons Ltd. Published 2018 by John Wiley & Sons Ltd.